Pro PowerShell for Amazon Web Services

DevOps for the AWS Cloud

Brian Beach

Apress®

Pro Powershell for Amazon Web Services: DevOps for the AWS Cloud

ISBN-13 (pbk): 978-1-4302-6451-4

ISBN-13 (electronic): 978-1-4302-6452-1

President and Publisher: Paul Manning
Lead Editor: Jonathan Hassell
Technical Reviewers: Nicholas Beaugeard, Steve Roberts
Editorial Board: Steve Anglin, Mark Beckner, Ewan Buckingham, Gary Cornell, Louise Corrigan, James T. DeWolf, Jonathan Gennick, Jonathan Hassell, Robert Hutchinson, Michelle Lowman, James Markham, Matthew Moodie, Jeff Olson, Jeffrey Pepper, Douglas Pundick, Ben Renow-Clarke, Dominic Shakeshaft, Gwenan Spearing, Matt Wade, Steve Weiss
Coordinating Editor: Anamika Panchoo
Copy Editor: Karen Jameson
Compositor: SPi Global
Indexer: SPi Global
Artist: SPi Global
Cover Designer: Anna Ishchenko

Distributed to the book trade worldwide by Springer Science+Business Media New York, 233 Spring Street, 6th Floor, New York, NY 10013. Phone 1-800-SPRINGER, fax (201) 348-4505, e-mail orders-ny@springer-sbm.com, or visit www.springeronline.com. Apress Media, LLC is a California LLC and the sole member (owner) is Springer Science + Business Media Finance Inc (SSBM Finance Inc). SSBM Finance Inc is a Delaware corporation.

For information on translations, please e-mail rights@apress.com, or visit www.apress.com.

Apress and friends of ED books may be purchased in bulk for academic, corporate, or promotional use. eBook versions and licenses are also available for most titles. For more information, reference our Special Bulk Sales–eBook Licensing web page at www.apress.com/bulk-sales.

Any source code or other supplementary materials referenced by the author in this text is available to readers at www.apress.com. For detailed information about how to locate your book's source code, go to www.apress.com/source-code.

Contents at a Glance

Contents

About the Author

Brian Beach is an enterprise architect with more than 15 years of experience in software engineering and information technology management. Brian is an Amazon Certified Solution Architect, Microsoft Certified Solution Developer (MCSD), and Certified Information Systems Security Professional (CISSP). He holds a BS in Computer Engineering from NYU Poly, an MBA from Rutgers Business School, and is a member of American Mensa. Brian is an advocate for Cloud Computing on the AWS platform and currently manages a team of cloud engineers at a Big Four accounting firm. Brian can be contacted through his blog at http://blog.brianbeach.com or LinkedIn at http://www.linkedin.com/in/brianjbeach.

About the Technical Reviewers

Nick Beaugeard is the Chief Technology Officer and founder of HubOne, Australia's first cloud integrator and Amazon Web Services Advanced Consulting Partner. Nick's been in and around Microsoft Systems Management since 1998, working on all versions of System Center and was a Program Manager at Microsoft working alongside the first developers of PowerShell. Nick lives in Australia with his wife and four kids, and apart from technology, he enjoys cooking, public speaking, and generally thinking up crazy new ideas.

Steve Roberts is a Software Development Engineer at Amazon Web Services with more than 20 years of experience in producing developer tools. He is currently a member of the team responsible for the AWS SDK for .NET, AWS Toolkit for Visual Studio, and AWS Tools for Windows PowerShell.

Acknowledgments

I would like to thank my wife, Karin, for supporting me through the many months of writing this book. I know it has been hard on you and the family. Thank you for your encouragement. I love you.

I would also like to thank the .Net team at Amazon Web Services – specifically Steven Roberts who was an invaluable resource for this book. You guys are doing a great job. Keep up the good work.

Introduction

According to a survey by Forbes Magazine in July 2013, 59% of the CIOs surveyed say that enabling cloud infrastructure is their number one priority (`http://www.forbes.com/sites/louiscolumbus/2013/07/01/cios-on-cloud-adoption-conquer-complexity-and-help-us-grow/`). While cloud has been popular in the open source community for years, enterprises are only just begining to make the transition. This book will prepare you for the transition using the tools you are already familiar with.

Amazon Web Services (AWS) has been the leader in Infrastructure as a Service (IaaS) for years. According to Gartner's 2013 Magic Quadrant, which evaluated the top 15 IaaS vendors, AWS is 5 times the size of the next 14 cloud vendors combined (`https://www.gartner.com/doc/2575815`). If you are going to take the time to learn about cloud, there is no better place to start.

Who Should Read This Book?

Pro PowerShell for Amazon Web Services is for the Windows professional who is ready to make the leap to the cloud. While Cloud Computing has been around for a while now, enterprise adoption is just beginning. This book is written specifically for Windows professionals who already know PowerShell, and want to learn to host Windows workloads in the Amazon Cloud.

Windows professionals find themselves under pressure to move workloads to the cloud, but few books have been written for Windows users, and none include examples in PowerShell. While there are many books on AWS, most are written for the open source community. *Pro PowerShell for Amazon Web Services* will introduce you to Amazon Web Services using a language you already know: Microsoft PowerShell.

This book assumes you have experience with Microsoft PowerShell. It will not teach you how to write PowerShell scripts. There are numerous excellent books on the market already. As an example, Apress offers a book titled *Pro Windows PowerShell* by Hristo Deshev.

On the other hand, I do not expect you to have any experience with AWS. We will start with the basics and build on that foundation. By the time you get to the end of the book you will know everything you need to run Windows workloads.

What Does This Book Cover?

Amazon offers a wide selection of cloud services, enough to fill many books. This book focuses on running Windows workloads on Elastic Compute Cloud (EC2), which is Amazon's virtual machine offering. In addition, we will discuss Virtual Private Cloud (VPC), Simple Storage Service (S3), Identity and Access Management (IAM), Simple Notification Services (SNS), Cloud Watch, Auto Scaling, and Elastic Load Balancing (ELB).

In general, each chapter will introduce a specific topic (e.g., compute, storage, networking, etc.) and provide an overview of the capabilities. Then, we discuss the PowerShell commands available and how to use each. Each chapter ends with one or two exercises that bring together all of the commands introduced in the chapter.

In the early chapters I begin by showing you how to use the Web Console, and then introduce the various commands available in the PowerShell API. As the chapters progress and you get more comfortable with AWS, I will focus less on the Web Console and more on PowerShell. By the end of the book you will be using PowerShell exclusively.

How Much Will This Cost?

How much is this going to cost? In short, not much. AWS offers the "free tier," which allows you to use some resources for free each month. The free tier covers 30GB of storage and 750 hours of micro instance usage each month for the first year of your account. Micro instances are small, single core servers, with 650MB of memory. These are too small to run a production workload, but more than enough to launch a few servers and get comfortable with the platform.

The free tier does not cover everything, but if you use micro instances and are diligent about cleaning up after each exercise, your bill should be very small. Over the roughly six months I was writing this book, I spent a grand total of about $25. You should be able to complete the examples for much less.

A Note on the Code Examples

PowerShell is a complicated language with many tricks and shortcuts. Many developers, myself included, pride themselves on being able to accomplish as much as possible with a single line of code. I have done my best to focus on readability and avoid complicated syntax. For example, the following code:

```
$VPCFilter = New-Object Amazon.EC2.Model.Filter
$VPCFilter.Name = 'vpc-id'
$VPCFilter.Value = 'vpc-12345678'
Get-EC2SecurityGroup -Filter $VPCFilter
```

could have been written in one line like this:

```
Get-EC2SecurityGroup -Filter @{ Name='vpc'; Value='vpc-12345678' }
```

While I think the first version is easier to understand, don't assume that the AWS toolkit does not support advanced syntax features. You are free to use pipelining, splatting, etc.

In addition, I want to point out that the examples in this book are riddled with resource IDs. For instance, in the example above, 'vpc-12345678' is the ID of a Virtual Private Cloud (VPC). Your VPC would have a different ID. Every time you create a resource it is assigned a new ID. As you are reading the book be sure to replace the IDs with IDs specific to your resources.

PowerShell and AWS Tools for Windows

The examples in this book require PowerShell 3.0 or greater and the AWS Tools for Windows 2.0. Cloud Computing is cutting edge technology and the things are changing fast. The examples in this book were tested using PowerShell 3.0 and AWS Tools for Windows 2.0. All the examples have also been tested in PowerShell 4.0, but as of this writing, AWS does not officially support PowerShell 4.0.

Also, as we were finalizing this book in late 2013, Amazon released version 2.0 of the AWS Toolkit for Windows PowerShell. This book was originally written for version 1.0, and while all of the code has been tested in version 2.0, I did not have time to change everything. As a result, you may notice a few discrepancies between the PowerShell documentation and this book.

For example, this book often uses the `RunningInstances` attribute of the `EC2 Reservation` object. In version 2.0 the PowerShell team changed the `RunningInstances` attribute to simply `Instance`. Thankfully, they maintained backward compatibility and most code written for version 1.0 continues to work. While you may see some discrepancies with the latest documentation, rest assured that all examples in the book have been tested with version 2.0.

Using the Accompanying Source Code

The complete source code for the book is available for download at the book's companion web site. Visit `http://www.apress.com` and go to the book's information page at `http://www.apress.com/9781430264514`. You can then download the source code from the Source Code/Downloads section.

■ ■ ■

CHAPTER 1

AWS Architecture Overview

Introduction

If you are anything like me, you cannot wait to get started and launch an application in the cloud. But, before we dive in and start launching servers, let's take a step back and look at the big picture. Amazon Web Services (AWS) is a global platform with data centers around the globe. A little time spent on the architecture will help you understand why, and not just what, we are doing with AWS.

In this chapter, we will discuss the AWS global infrastructure, including regions and availability zones, and how to use them to design a robust application in the cloud. We will also introduce all of the services we are going to discuss throughout the book. Before we do, let's begin by defining Cloud Computing.

What Is Cloud Computing?

It seems that every company has a different definition of Cloud Computing. Amazon describes cloud computing as "the on-demand delivery of IT resources via the Internet with pay-as-you-go pricing" (http://aws.amazon.com/what-is-cloud-computing/).

Cloud computing is about leasing servers and storage from a provider like Amazon. But, it's also about so much more. The cloud offers information technology workers significant cost savings and unimaginable agility. Tasks that traditionally took weeks of work, costing thousands of dollars, can be completed in minutes for fractions of a penny.

In addition, cloud computing offers inconceivable scalability. With a single line of code, you can provision thousands of servers. Most important, you pay only for what you need and give the equipment back when you're done. Furthermore, because you are paying by the hour, running one server for a thousand hours costs the same amount as running a thousand servers for one hour. This is unthinkable in a traditional data center.

Finally, cloud computing is often used in concert with automation. When we combine scalability with automation, we have the ability to build an application that responds to load. In Chapter 8, we will build a self-healing web application that automatically reconfigures itself in response to changes in load. That's what cloud computing is all about.

Regions

AWS is organized into multiple regions around the globe. Each region is designed to be independent of the others. This isolation allows us to design highly available applications that span the globe and ensure low-latency response times to our users.

As you can see in Figure 1-1, there are currently nine regions around the world. With a few exceptions, most of this book will focus on building an application in a single region. We will talk about copying snapshots (or backup files) between regions in Chapter 4, and multiregion hosting in Chapter 8.

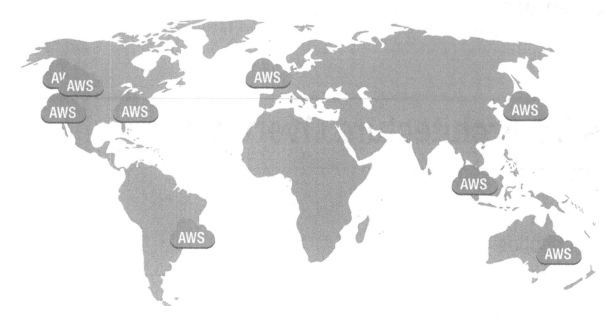

Figure 1-1. *Amazon Global Infrastructure*

All of the examples in this book were completed in Northern Virginia (us-east-1), but you can use the region closest to you. In fact this is the whole idea. By selecting a region closest to your users, you can deliver the best experience by minimizing latency.

Imagine you run an e-commerce site for a U.S.-based clothing company. Most of your users are also in the United States, but recently you have had a small following in Australia. These users are complaining about the web site. They say it is slow and transactions often time out. Before the cloud, you would have to build another data center in Australia.

But using AWS, you can launch a few servers in Amazon's data center. Remember that you are only paying for what you use, so if you only need three or four servers in Australia, that's all you pay for. And it might cost just $1-2 an hour. This is one of the advantages of cloud computing.

Even more important, it may turn out that we are wrong. Maybe the users in Australia were just an anomaly. Within a month, all of the Australian users have moved on. We simply shut done the site in Australia and immediately stop paying. Cloud computing allows us to "fail fast," which lets the company try new things that would have been too expensive in the past.

Another reason you may want to use multiple regions is data privacy. Many companies are required to store data in a specific region. The European Union requires that data about its citizens be stored in Europe. In this case, the Ireland region (eu-west-1) would be a great choice. The specific regions and locations are listed in Table 1-1.

Table 1-1. *List of Regions and Locations*

Region	Location
ap-northeast-1	Asia Pacific (Tokyo)
ap-southeast-1	Asia Pacific (Singapore)
ap-southeast-2	Asia Pacific (Sydney)
eu-west-1	EU (Ireland)
sa-east-1	South America (Sao Paulo)
us-east-1	U.S. East (Northern Virginia)
us-west-1	U.S. West (Northern California)
us-west-2	U.S. West (Oregon)

Notice that there are only eight regions listed in Table 1-1. Earlier, I mentioned there were nine. The ninth region is called GovCloud and is a region specifically designed to store data for the U.S. government. It is located in the Northwestern United States. If you are doing work for the U.S. government, GovCloud may be an option for you.

Regions allow you to deliver your application from the location closest to your users and build redundant applications served from multiple regions. While this is great, Amazon also offers another layer of redundancy called availability zones.

Availability Zones

Each region is further organized into two or more availability zones (AZs). You can think of each AZ as a separate data center. The AZs within a region are isolated from failures but connected with high-speed, low-latency links.

Each AZ has separate power, cooling, and Internet access. In addition, their locations are chosen so they are never in the same flood plain, etc. This allows you to architect highly available applications that span multiple data centers.

Imagine we are deploying an application in a region with two availability zones (see Figure 1-2). We could deploy two servers, one in each AZ, and use an elastic load balancer (ELB) to balance traffic between them. If one of the AZs suffered an outage, the ELB would automatically send all of the traffic to the other AZ. If we are using a relational database service (RDS), we could also enable the multi-AZ option, and AWS will automatically replicate data between availability zones. (We will discuss ELB in Chapter 8 and RDS in Chapter 9.)

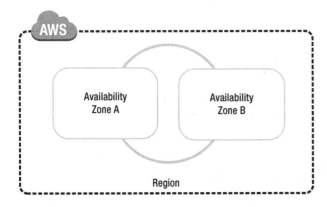

Figure 1-2. *Availability Zones*

Regions and availability zones allow you to build a highly available, low-latency application that you could never dream of building in your own data center. Only a handful of companies around the globe have the resources to match this functionality in their own data centers. Before we wrap up, let's look quickly at the services available.

Services

AWS offers a lot of services and they are adding new services every day. This book is focused on Microsoft Windows, and I discuss only those services that are relevant to building Microsoft applications. Figure 1-3 provides an overview of the services we are going to use in this book.

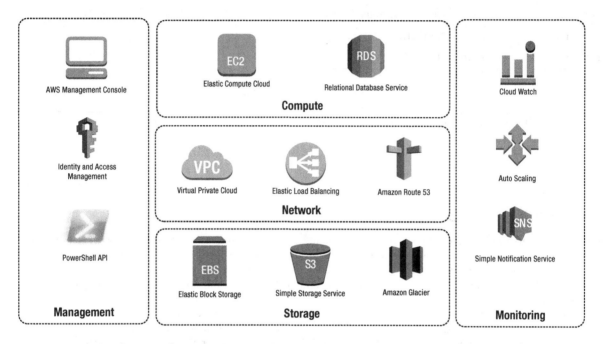

Figure 1-3. *AWS Reference Architecture*

Let's spend a minute discussing these options:

Management

The services in the management category are used to access and configure AWS.

- **AWS Management Console** - The console is the web GUI for configuring AWS. You can configure almost anything using the console, but this is a book on PowerShell. In the early chapters I will show you how to get started using the console, but once we get comfortable we will be using PowerShell almost exclusively.

- **Identity and Access Management (IAM)** - IAM allows you to control access to your account. You can create users and groups and write policies to control access to resources. (We will discuss IAM briefly in Chapter 2 and in detail in Chapter 11.)

- **PowerShell API** - PowerShell gives you full control over all services. You can do things in PowerShell that you cannot do in the AWS Management Console. AWS supports many scripting languages, but with the exception of a single exercise in Chapter 7, this book will focus on PowerShell.

Storage

Starting at the bottom of Figure 1-3 and working up, we have multiple storage options.

- **Elastic Block Storage (EBS)** - EBS is a storage area network we use to create disks for our instances. EBS is a network-based solution similar to iSCSI. You can create volumes from 1GB to 1TB. You can also manage IO operations per second (IOPS). We will use EBS throughout the book, and focus on it in Chapter 4.

- **Simple Storage Service (S3)** - S3 is highly durable object storage in the cloud. You can use S3 to store an unlimited number of files up to 5GB each. S3 uses HTTP/S to read and write objects. Most important, you get 99.999999999% durability. (We will focus on S3 in Chapter 10.)

- **Amazon Glacier** - Glacier is a low cost, cold storage solution. Glacier offers the same high durability as S3 for about 1/10 the cost, but stores data offline and requires advanced notice to access your data. This is a great alternative to tape backup. (We will discuss Glacier in Chapter 10.)

Network

Moving up the stack in Figure 1-3, we have multiple network services that work together.

- **Virtual Private Cloud (VPC)** - VPC allows us to create a private network to isolate your instances from those of other AWS tenants. You can create a custom network topology and control network security. (We will use VPC throughout the book, but focus on it in Chapters 4 and 5.)

- **Elastic Load Balancers (ELB)** - ELB is a managed load balancing solution. You can balance traffic between multiple servers across availability zones. You can create public ELBs on the Internet or use a private ELB to balance traffic between layers of a multitier application. (We will discuss ELB in Chapter 8.)

- **Route 53** - Route 53 is Amazon's managed DNS solution. If you use Route 53 you can balance traffic between multiple regions, and AWS will determine which region is closest to the user and route them automatically. (We will discuss Route 53 briefly in Chapter 8.)

Compute

At the top of the stack there are two compute services we will discuss.

- **Elastic Compute Cloud (EC2)** - EC2 is Amazon's virtual server service. This is how we launch servers, called instances, in the cloud. EC2 offers thousands of images and hardware configurations for every imaginable use case. This is the focus of the book, and we will use EC2 throughout.

- **Relational Database Service (RDS)** - RDS is Amazon's managed database service. RDS supports MySQL, Oracle, PostgreSQL, and Microsoft SQL Server. You can install any of these on an EC2 instance, but with RDS, Amazon manages the administration for you. (We will do a deep dive on RDS in Chapter 9.)

Monitoring

Finally, we have a collection of monitoring services.

- **CloudWatch** - CloudWatch is used to monitor the environment. CloudWatch allows you to create custom alarms and defines what actions to take when an issue arises. For example, you might raise an alarm when CPU utilization is above 80% for an extended period of time. (We will use CloudWatch to monitor instances in Chapter 8.)

- **Auto Scaling** - Auto Scaling, combined with CloudWatch, allows you to automatically respond to changing conditions. In Chapter 8 we will create an application that automatically launches new instances when the application is under high load.

- **Simple Notification Service (SNS)** - SNS is Amazon's notification system. CloudWatch can publish messages to SNS whenever an alarm occurs. You can use SNS to subscribe to events using e-mail, SMS text messages, and many other options. (We will use SNS in Chapters 8 and 9.)

Summary

As you can see, Amazon offers everything you need to create a world-class application in the cloud. Regions and availability zones give you access to resources across the globe and allow you to build a highly available, low-latency application. In addition, Amazon offers numerous services that can be used in concert to create a robust application.

In the next chapter, we will create an account and configure our PowerShell environment. With this in place we can begin using all the services we just discussed. What are we waiting for? Let's get going.

CHAPTER 2

■ ■ ■

Getting Started

In the previous chapter, we described cloud computing and then discussed the benefits of scripting your AWS configuration. Before we get started writing these scripts, we need to create an AWS account and prepare our PowerShell environment.

We will begin by creating a new AWS account and credentials for PowerShell. Then we will install the AWS Toolkit and configure a few default values. Although this might not be the most exciting chapter, it is an important one because the examples in the rest of the book assume that you have followed the steps in this chapter.

Creating an AWS Account

If you don't already have an Amazon Web Services (AWS) account, go to http://aws.amazon.com and click Sign Up to get started. If you already have one, skip ahead to the next section.

To create an AWS account, you will have to sign in using an Amazon.com account (see Figure 2-1). This can be the same account you use to shop on Amazon.com. If you are creating an AWS account for work, you might want to create a separate Amazon account using your work e-mail rather than using your personal account. If you want to create a new account, or have been living under a rock and don't have an Amazon account already, you can create one now.

Sign In or Create an AWS Account

You may sign in using your existing Amazon.com account or you can create a new account by selecting "I am a new user."

My e-mail address is: `aws@brianbeach.com`

⦿ I am a new user.

○ I am a returning user
and my password is:

Sign in using our secure server ▶

Forgot your password?

Has your e-mail address changed?

Learn more about AWS Identity and Access Management and AWS Multi-Factor Authentication, features that provide additional security for your AWS Account.

Figure 2-1. *Creating an AWS account*

If this is the first time you are using AWS, Amazon will ask you to confirm your phone number. Then an automated system will call your phone and ask you to enter a verification code.

Next, you will have to pick a support plan (see Figure 2-2). I am using the free plan. Basically, this means that there is no support. With the free plan, you will have access to the user forums, but there are no guarantees.

Select your AWS Support Plan

All customers receive free support. Choosing a paid support plan will allow you to receive one-on-one technical assistance from experienced engineers and access many other support features. Click here to compare all Support plans.

◉ Basic (Free)
Contact Customer Service for account and billing questions, receive help for resources that don't pass system health checks, and access the AWS Community Forums.

◎ Developer ($49/month)
Get started on AWS – ask technical questions and get a response to your web case within 12 hours during local business hours.

◎ **Business (Starting at $100/month** - Pricing example ☑**) - Recommended**
24/7/365 real-time assistance by phone and chat, a 1 hour response to web cases, and help with 3rd party software. Access Trusted Advisor to increase performance, fault tolerance, security, and potentially save money. (What's this ☑)

◎ Enterprise (Starting at $15,000/month - Pricing example ☑)
15 minute response to web cases, an assigned technical account manager (TAM) who is an expert in your use case, and white-glove case handling that notifies your TAM and the service engineering team of a critical issue.

Figure 2-2. *Choosing a support plan*

After you choose your support plan, you will need to confirm your selections to complete the wizard. Then it's time to create a user account, which is discussed next.

Creating a User Account

Now that you have an AWS account, you will need to create a new IAM user. (IAM stands for identity and access management.) AWS has two types of users: Account Credentials and IAM Users. The e-mail address you used to create the AWS account is called an "AWS Account Credential." You should not use your account credentials for day-to-day activities on AWS. Save your AWS account credentials to change account options and access your bills. Create an IAM user for day-to-day activities instead.

IAM allows you to create multiple user accounts and configure the permissions of each user. If you already have an IAM User with administrator privileges, you can skip to the next section.

Open http://console.aws.amazon.com. If you are not already signed in, use your AWS Account Credential (i.e., the e-mail address used to create the account) to sign in. You will be taken to the AWS Management Console. Click the IAM link at the bottom of the second column (see Figure 2-3).

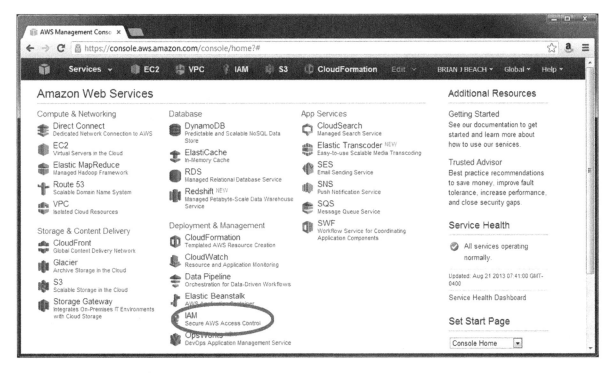

Figure 2-3. *AWS Web Console dashboard*

From the IAM dashboard, click the Create a New Group of Users button (see Figure 2-4).

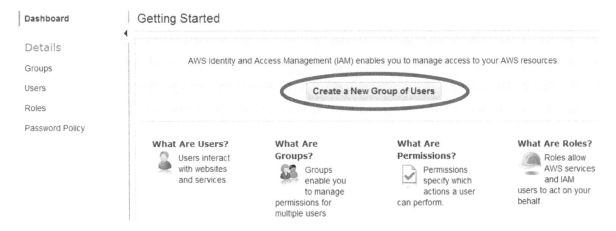

Figure 2-4. *Identity and access management dashboard*

Create a new group called Admins (see Figure 2-5) and then click Continue. Members of the group will have full control over AWS.

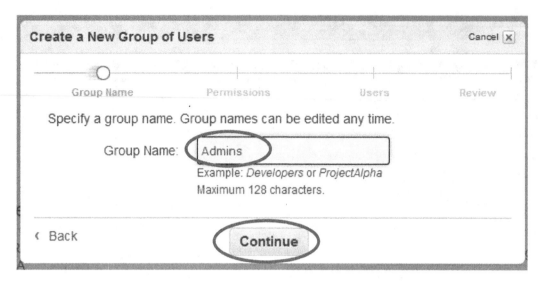

Figure 2-5. *Creating a new IAM group*

Next, choose the Administrator Access Policy Template (see Figure 2-6). A policy template is a set of common permissions. You can also create custom policies, which we will do in a later chapter. For now, use the template.

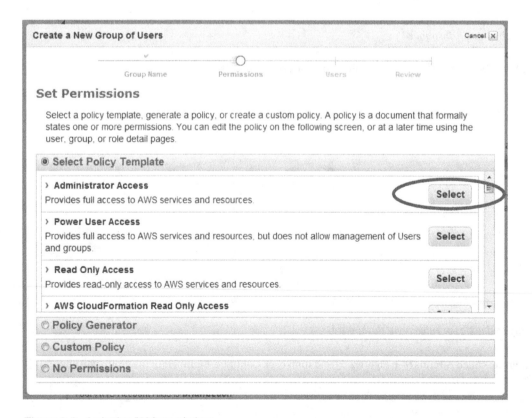

Figure 2-6. *Assigning IAM permissions*

You now have a chance to edit the policy. For now, just leave the default settings and click Continue (see Figure 2-7).

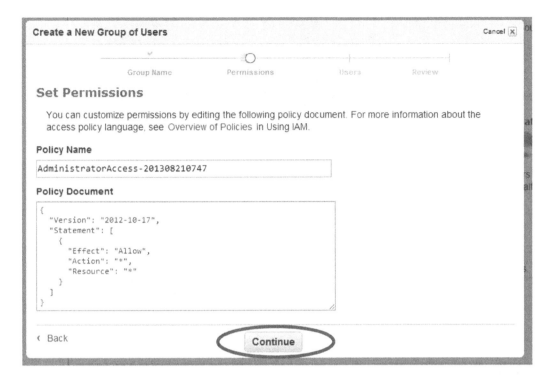

Figure 2-7. *Reviewing the IAM policy*

Now add a new user named admin to the Admins group (see Figure 2-8). Make sure that the Generate an access key for each User check box is selected. Click Continue.

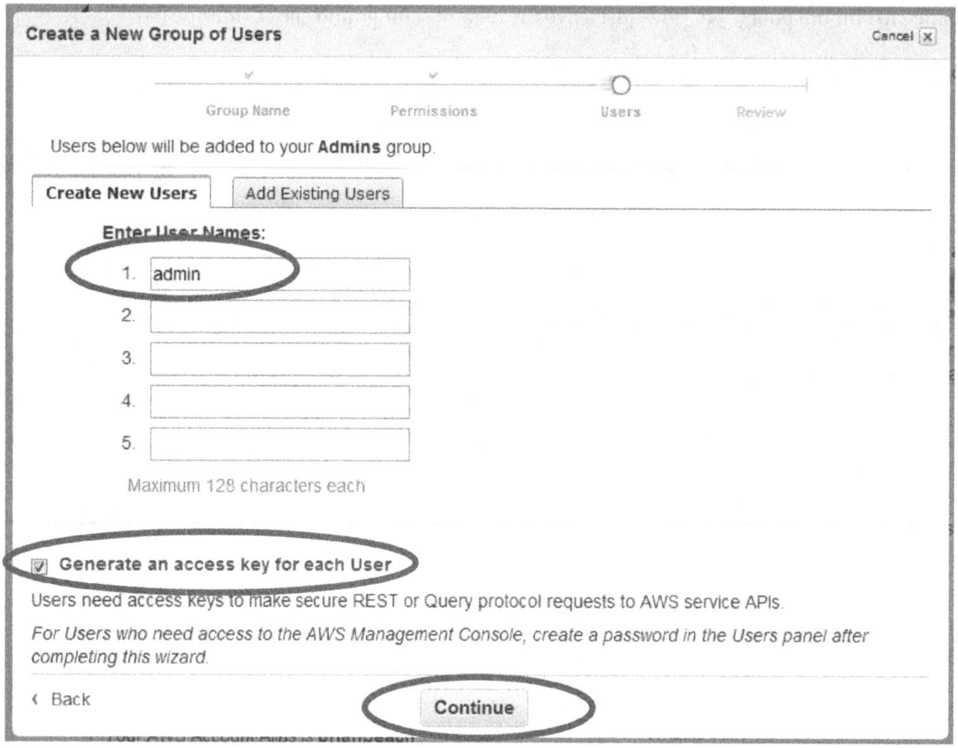

Figure 2-8. *Creating a new IAM user*

Review the options and click Continue to confirm (see Figure 2-9).

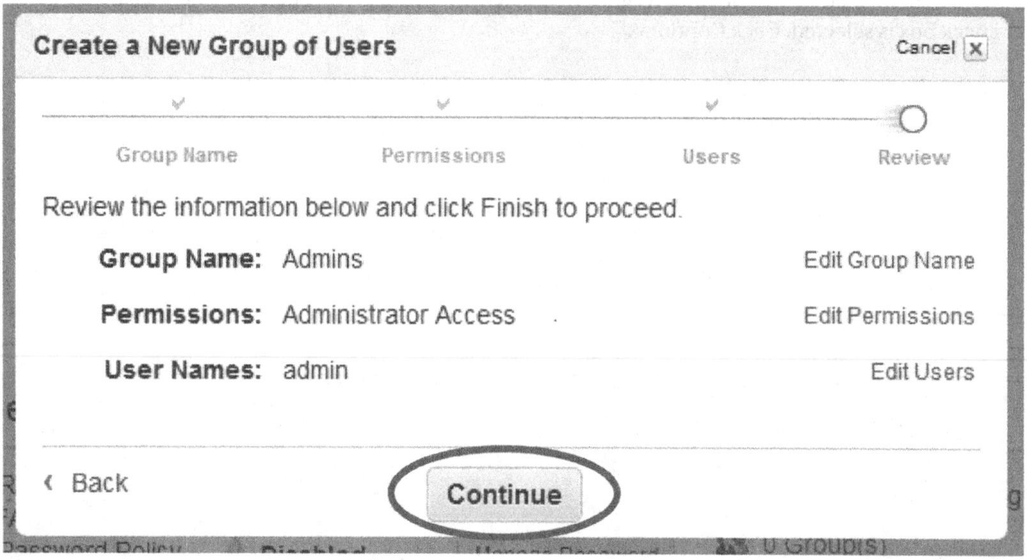

Figure 2-9. *Completing the IAM wizard*

On the next screen, make sure you download the admin credentials and remember where you saved them (see Figure 2-10). You will use these keys to run PowerShell scripts. You will also need to enter your keys again in Chapter 7.

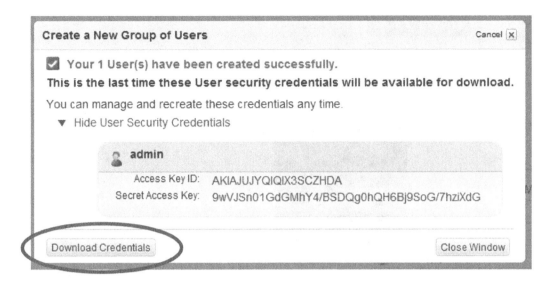

Figure 2-10. *Downloading credentials*

■ **Caution**   Note that AWS does not store your secret key. If you lose your credentials, you will not be able to get another copy and will have to generate a new set.

Note that you have not yet chosen a password. In fact, not all users have a password. See the "Types of Credentials" sidebar for a description of the various credential types and when to use each.

TYPES OF CREDENTIALS

IAM users have three types of credentials, and each one is used for a different purpose:

Username and Password: The username and password are used to access the web console. In addition to the password, you can also opt for Multi Factor Authentication (MFA). MFA uses an authentication code for extra security. MFA requires an authentication device or smartphone application like Google Authenticator.

Access Key ID and Secret Key: The Access Key ID and Secret Key are used to access the REST API. Both PowerShell and the AWS Command Line Interface (CLI) use the REST API. Therefore, you need to download keys to use PowerShell.

Signing Certificates: Signing Certificates are used for the SOAP web services. The SOAP service is being deprecated, so I will not discuss it in this book.

Note that not all users will have all types of credentials. An administrator that does not use the API may only have a username and password, for example, while a developer that does not have access to the web console may only have an Access Key ID and Secret Key.

From the IAM dashboard, click on Users to display the IAM users in your account. Right-click the admin user and choose Manage Password (see Figure 2-11).

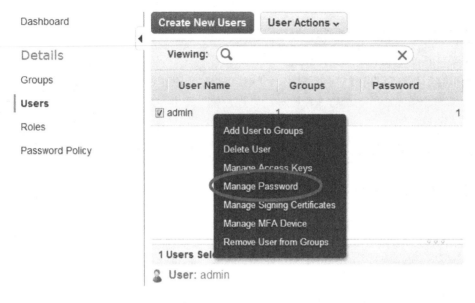

Figure 2-11. *Assigning a password*

Choose the Assign a custom password option, enter the password twice, and click Apply (see Figure 2-12).

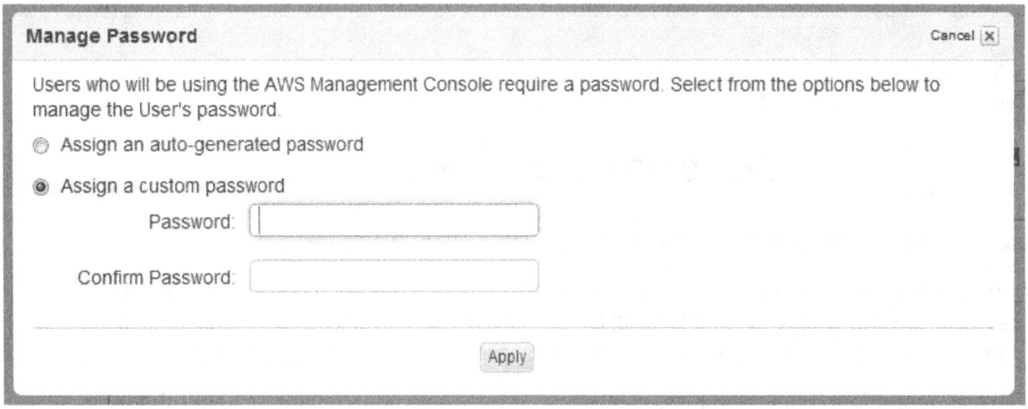

Figure 2-12. *Creating a password*

The last thing we need to do is get the custom sign-in URL for your new account. In order to sign in using your IAM username and password, you must visit the account sign-in URL. Each account has a unique sign-in URL, but the default URL is very difficult to remember; let's change it to something we can remember.

To change the sign-in URL, return to the IAM dashboard and scroll down to the bottom to the AWS Account Alias section (see Figure 2-13). Click the button to specify a friendly account alias.

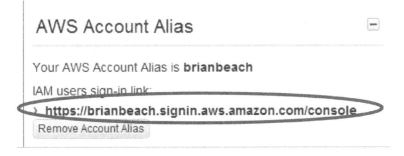

AWS Account Alias

Your AWS Account Alias is **brianbeach**

IAM users sign-in link:

https://brianbeach.signin.aws.amazon.com/console

Remove Account Alias

Figure 2-13. *Setting an account alias*

At this point you should sign out using the menu at the top right of the screen (see Figure 2-14).

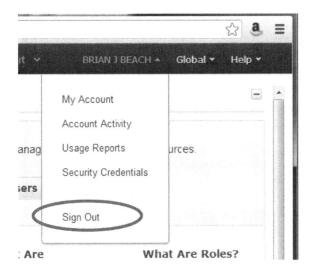

Figure 2-14. *Signing out*

Finally, navigate to the custom sign-in link and sign on as admin (see Figure 2-15).

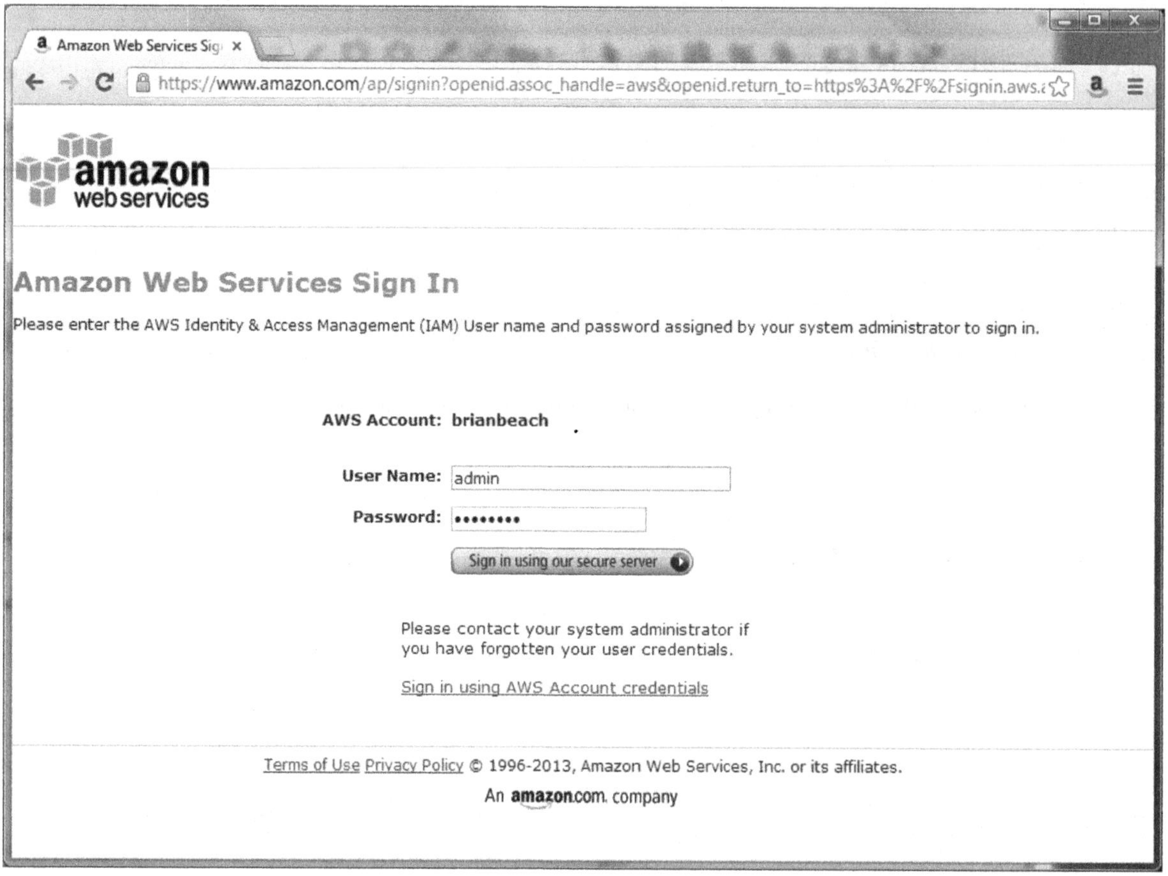

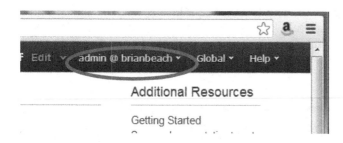

Figure 2-15. *Signing in with IAM credentials*

Note that you are now logged in as an IAM User. Compare the IAM user listed in the top right corner (see Figure 2-16) to the Account Credential in Figure 2.14. Note the IAM user includes the "@ alias."

Figure 2-16. *Signed In as an IAM User*

At this point you have an AWS account and an IAM user with administrative privileges. Next, we are going to install the AWS Tools for PowerShell and configure a few default values.

Configuring PowerShell

AWS Tools for Windows PowerShell requires Windows XP or later and PowerShell 3.0 or later. PowerShell 3.0 is the default for Windows 8 and Server 2012. You can also install PowerShell 3.0 on Server 2008R2 SP1 with the .Net framework 4.0.

You can download the AWS tools from http://aws.amazon.com/powershell/. If you are running your script on an AWS instance (e.g., a server running in the AWS Cloud), the tools are already installed. If you want to run the tools on your own machine, download the installer from the site above. Note that the examples in this book were tested using version 2.0 of AWS tools.

I usually write scripts using the PowerShell Integrated Script Environment (ISE) because it supports IntelliSense and debugging. The PowerShell ISE is a Windows Feature. If it is not already enabled, you may need to enable the feature from Windows Server Explorer. This feature is enabled by default on AWS instances.

Once you have the AWS tools installed, you need to import the AWS PowerShell Module. This Module includes all of the PowerShell commands to manage AWS. Simply type Import-Module and include the path where you installed the AWS Tools.

On a 32-bit OS, type:

```
Import-Module "C:\Program Files\AWS Tools\PowerShell\AWSPowerShell\AWSPowerShell.psd1"
```

On a 64-bit OS, type:

```
Import-Module "C:\Program Files (x86)\AWS Tools\PowerShell\AWSPowerShell\AWSPowerShell.psd1"
```

You will need to import this module each time you start a new PowerShell session.

■ **Tip**   If you are going to be working with AWS often, you may prefer to add the AWS Module to your profile. Your profile is simply a script that runs each time PowerShell starts. Just open it in Notepad and add the Import-Module line.

The profile invoked when you start a PowerShell command prompt can be found at:

```
Documents\WindowsPowerShell\Profile.ps1
```

The profile invoked when you start the PowerShell ISE can be found at:

```
Documents\WindowsPowerShell\Microsoft.PowerShellISE_profile.ps1
```

■ **Note**   If you have never customized your profile, the file may not exist. Just create the folder and file as needed.

Let's check if the AWS tools are working. Type Get-AWSRegion at the PowerShell command prompt and press Enter, as shown here.

```
PS> Get-AWSRegion
```

Get-AWSRegion will list all of the AWS regions (described in Chapter 1) around the globe, as shown in the following code output:

```
Region                      Name
------                      ----
us-east-1                   US East (Virginia)              ...
us-west-1                   US West (N. California)         ...
us-west-2                   US West (Oregon)                ...
eu-west-1                   EU West (Ireland)               ...
ap-northeast-1              Asia Pacific (Tokyo)            ...
ap-southeast-1              Asia Pacific (Singapore)        ...
ap-southeast-2              Asia Pacific (Sydney)           ...
sa-east-1                   South America (Sao Paulo)       ...
```

If the command succeeds, your PowerShell environment is set up correctly. Notice that we did not use the credentials we downloaded earlier. The Get-AWSRegion method does not require authentication. Before you can do anything exciting, you are going to have to supply your credentials. Let's see how to do this in the next section.

Specifying Credentials and Region

Now that we have the AWS tools installed and PowerShell configured, let's try something more complicated. Type the Get-EC2Instance command to list all of the instances deployed in the Cloud. Remember that an instance is Amazon's term for a server.

```
PS> Get-EC2Instance
```

Note that you have not deployed any instances yet, so this command is not expected to return anything. But when we run the command we get the following error:

```
Get-EC2Instance : No credentials specified or obtained ...
```

Before you can use AWS, you need to log in. Remember that PowerShell uses the REST API. Therefore, you will need an access key and secret key in order to use PowerShell.

All of the AWS commands support the AccessKey and SecretKey parameters. You must include the keys you downloaded in the last section. For example, type:

```
PS> Get-EC2Instance -AccessKey AKIA...ZHDA -SecretKey 9wVJ...iXdG
```

Note, however, that we still get an error:

```
Get-EC2Instance : No region specified or obtained ...
```

The credential error is gone, but now we have a new error—we also need to specify a region. Each AWS region is independent. You need to tell AWS which region you want to list the instances in. Note that you cannot list the instances in all regions in a single command. Let's list your instances in the Northern Virginia region. Type the following:

```
PS> Get-EC2Instance -AccessKey AKIA...ZHDA -SecretKey 9wVJ...iXdG -Region us-east-1
```

This code produces the following results:

```
ReservationId  : r-12345678
OwnerId        : 123456789012
RequesterId    :
GroupId        : {}
GroupName      : {}
RunningInstance : {ip-10-1-1-5.brianbeach.com}
```

At this point, you should receive a list of your instances deployed in the specified region. If you just created a new account, you probably don't have any instances yet. As long as you don't get an error, it's working correctly. This is everything you need to execute the scripts in this book, but there are still a few things we can do make life easier. For example, it would be nice to save the default credentials and region so we don't have to add them to every command.

Setting Defaults

It can get cumbersome including the keys on every line of every script. Life would be easier if you had to specify the keys only once. Luckily, Amazon thought of this and included the `Set-AWSCredentials` and `Set-DefaultAWSRegion` commands.

■ **Note** I am no longer including the command prompt (PS>) in my examples. From here on, most examples will be multiline scripts. I am using the PowerShell ISE to edit and run my scripts as a batch.

Just type the script into the top window and click the play button (or press the F5 key). If you prefer, you can enter these commands, one at time, at the command prompt. Personally, I prefer the IDE.

```
Set-DefaultAWSRegion us-east-1
Set-AWSCredentials -AccessKey ACCESS_KEY -SecretKey SECRET_KEY
Get-EC2Instance
```

This script results in the following:

```
ReservationId  : r-12345678
...
```

Notice that once I set a default region and credentials, I can run the `Get-EC2Instance` command without any parameters. This is so much easier. I can simply include these two lines at the top of the script, and I don't have to worry about it again.

If you want to clear the defaults, you can use the `Clear-AWSCredentials` and `Clear-DefaultAWSRegion` commands. For example:

```
Clear-AWSCredentials
Clear-DefaultAWSRegion
```

Setting defaults is great, but we have to remember to set them each time we start PowerShell. We can take it one step further and persist the defaults between PowerShell sessions.

Persisting Defaults

The Initialize-AWSDefaults command will persist the credentials and region between sessions. PowerShell will remember your defaults when you restart PowerShell or reboot your computer. Once you persist the credentials, you no longer need to specify them in your script. This makes the script portable between developers and AWS accounts. Note that unlike the PowerShell profiles, persisted defaults set in the ISE also affect the command line. Type the following:

```
Set-DefaultAWSRegion us-east-1
Set-AWSCredentials -AccessKey ACCESS_KEY -SecretKey SECRET_KEY
Initialize-AWSDefaults
```

Notice the results:

```
Credentials retrieved from Session
Region retrieved from Session
Credentials and region will be saved in this session
```

When you start a new PowerShell session, the default values will be loaded automatically. For example:

```
Get-EC2Instance
```

Now, if the defaults were not already loaded, they will be loaded as needed. This command now produces the following results:

```
Default credentials for this shell initialized from stored default profile
Default region for this shell initialized from stored default profile
ReservationId   : r-12345678...
```

If you want to clear the defaults, you can use the Clear-AWSDefaults command:

```
Clear-AWSDefaults
```

We are almost done discussing defaults, but there is one more option I want to mention: stored credentials. Stored credentials allow you to store multiple credentials and switch between them quickly.

Using Stored Credentials

You may find that you have more than one set of credentials to manage. Maybe you have separate AWS accounts for development and production servers; in my opinion, this is a really good idea. (And I hope you're not running these examples in the same account that you use to host production workloads.)

You can use the Set-AWSCredentials command we discussed earlier to create named profiles and quickly switch between them. To create a named profile, use the StoreAs attribute. For example:

```
Set-AWSCredentials -AccessKey ACCESS_KEY -SecretKey SECRET_KEY -StoreAs "Production"
Set-AWSCredentials -AccessKey ACCESS_KEY -SecretKey SECRET_KEY -StoreAs "Development"
```

Now we can use the stored credentials as an attribute to any command. For example, if you want to list the servers in the production environment, type:

```
Get-EC2Instance -StoredCredentials Production
```

Here is the result:

```
ReservationId   : r-12345678...
```

And, if you want to list the servers in the development environment, type:

```
Get-EC2Instance -StoredCredentials Development
```

The preceding script produces this result:

```
ReservationId   : r-87654321...
```

If you want to swap the default credentials between the development and production profiles, you can use the Set-AWSCredentials command with the StoredCredentials attribute. All subsequent commands will use the production credentials.

```
Set-AWSCredentials -StoredCredentials Production
```

You can list the various credentials you have stored using Get-AWSCredentials. For example, type:

```
Get-AWSCredentials -ListStoredCredentials
```

To get this result:

```
Development
Production
```

Finally, you can remove credentials using the Clear-AWSCredentials command:

```
Clear-AWSCredentials -StoredCredentials Development
```

At this point your PowerShell environment is ready. In the next chapter, we are going to launch a few instances. Before you do that, however, you are going to need an EC2 key pair.

Using Key Pairs

Before we move on to creating instances, you will need a key pair. This key pair is used to encrypt the Windows Password for a new instance. AWS keeps the public key, and you keep the private key. When you create a Windows instance, AWS creates a local administrator account and generates a random password. It then encrypts the random password with the public key and stores the encrypted copy.

You can retrieve the password any time and decrypt it with your private key. Note that AWS does not keep the plain-text password. Therefore, only you can decrypt the password.

■ **Caution**   If you lose your private key, you will not be able to decrypt the password. Be careful with your keys!

To create a key pair, log in using your IAM admin user and choose a region. I will be using Northern Virginia (see Figure 2-17), but you can select the location nearest you.

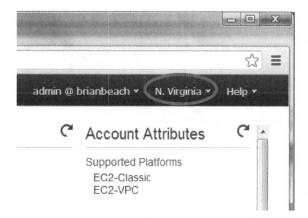

Figure 2-17. *Choosing an AWS region*

From the AWS home page, select EC2. Then choose Key Pairs from the menu and click Create Key Pair (see Figure 2-18).

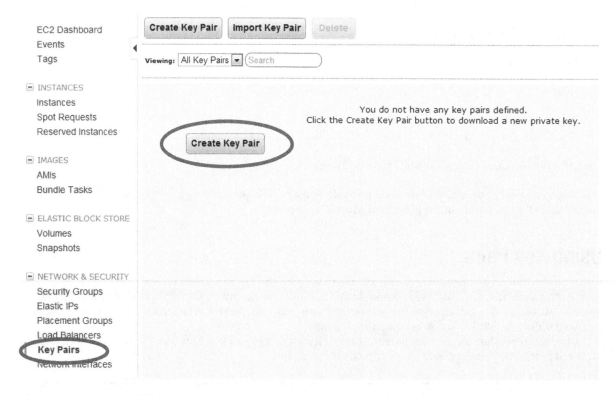

Figure 2-18. *Creating a key pair*

Name the key pair and click Create (see Figure 2-19). Your browser will download the private key. Make sure you save it. Note that the examples in this book assume your key is stored in c:\aws\mykey.pem.

Figure 2-19. *Naming your key pair*

You can also create a new key pair using the New-EC2KeyPair command. This command generates a new key pair and returns the private key. You can save the private key to a file using the Out-File command. Note that you must specify the encoding as ASCII. For example:

```
$KeyPair = New-EC2KeyPair -KeyName MyKey
$KeyPair.KeyMaterial | Out-File -FilePath 'c:\aws\MyKey.pem' -Encoding ASCII
```

That's everything you need to complete the exercises in this book. If you cannot wait any longer to launch an instance, feel free to move on to Chapter 3. But, if you have the patience, I would like to tell you about one more feature: IAM roles.

Using IAM Roles

We have covered a lot of material already in this chapter, but there is one more feature I want to discuss. It is a bad idea to have your production scripts running as an individual user. What happens if that user leaves the company? If you delete her account, all of your scripts will stop working.

You could create an additional IAM user just for running production scripts. But, how do you keep those keys secret? How do you keep a disgruntled administrator you fired from using the keys to terminate all your servers? Luckily, AWS provides a solution for this, too: IAM roles.

An IAM role allows you to grant permission to an EC2 instance. This way, you don't need keys to run PowerShell scripts. In other words, if you assign an IAM role to an instance, the instance has permission to run scripts rather than a user. Any scripts that are run on that instance are implicitly granted the permissions defined to the IAM role. Therefore, you don't have to bother with keys at all. Although you don't have to set credentials, you still need to set the region.

Of course this only works for instances running in AWS. You cannot use IAM roles for machines running in your data center. In addition, you have to assign the role when you create the instance; you cannot assign it later.

To create an IAM role, open the AWS Management Console and navigate to the IAM console. (I assume you know how to do this by now. If not, go back to the "Creating a User Account" section at the beginning of this chapter.) Choose Roles from the left navigation. Then, click the New Role button and name your new role (see Figure 2-20). I will use the name AdminRole for the scripts in this book.

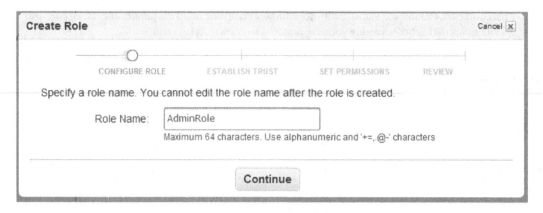

Figure 2-20. *Creating an IAM role*

There are many types of roles available. We want to create an "Amazon EC2" role. Click the Select button next to Amazon EC2 (see Figure 2-21).

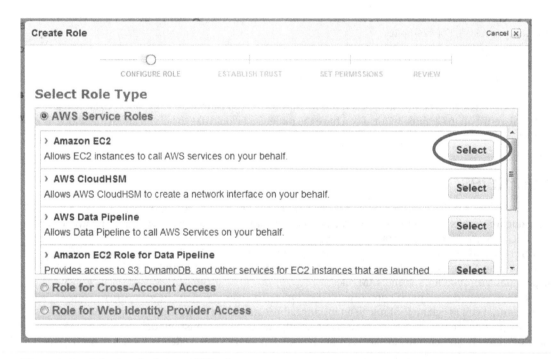

Figure 2-21. *Selecting the Amazon EC2 role*

Let's grant this role administrator permission (see Figure 2-22), even though in a real-life scenario you would want to restrict the role. With administrator permissions assigned to an EC2 instance, anyone who runs a script on that instance will have full control over your account. For the purposes of this book, this is fine, but please be more restrictive in real life.

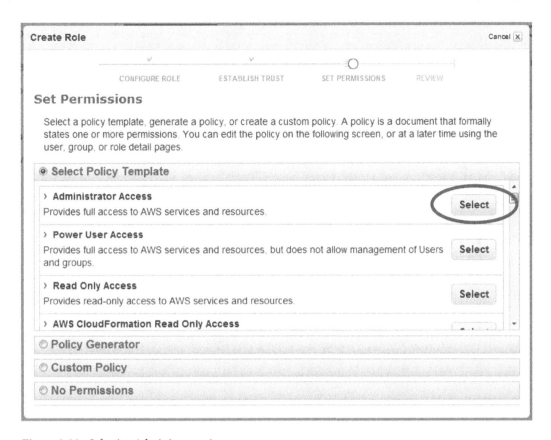

Figure 2-22. *Selecting Administrator Access*

On the next screen, leave the default policy and click the Continue button. Then, on the Review screen, click the Create Role button.

We will use this role in the second exercise of Chapter 3.

Summary

In this chapter we created an AWS account and IAM user. Then we installed the AWS Tools for PowerShell and configured our PowerShell scripting environment with a default region and credentials. Finally, we created an EC2 key pair and an IAM role. We now have everything in place to begin using the cloud. In the next chapter, we will launch a few basic instances.

■ ■ ■

Basic Instance Management

Great! You're done configuring your environment. I know the last chapter was a bit dull, but this chapter is where it gets exciting. You'll jump right in and get started by creating an instance. An EC2 instance is, simply, a server running in the cloud. With a few quick clicks, you will have your first server up and running.

In this chapter we will focus on EC2 Classic instances. These are the instances that have been around since the beginning. Amazon recently, however, introduced Virtual Private Cloud (VPC). VPC adds a lot of new and exciting capabilities, which we will discuss in Chapter 6.

It's important to note that Amazon is beginning to phase out EC2 Classic in favor of VPC—eventually, EC2 Classic will no longer exist. This is an exciting time to be working with cloud technologies. The industry is moving very fast, and while this can be fun, it also causes some inevitable headaches.

As of this writing, for example, AWS has deprecated EC2 Classic in the Oregon region. Lucky for us, they have created a default VPC, which acts very much like EC2 Classic. Other than a few very minor UI changes, all of the examples in this chapter will run in regions where EC2 Classic has been deprecated.

In this chapter you will learn to create new instances and connect them. Then we will discuss how to start, stop, and terminate instances. We will learn various ways to access metadata and add custom metadata tags. In the exercises at the end of the chapter, we will build a PowerShell script to automate the launch process and customize the configuration of an instance.

Creating Instances

Let's get started by creating a new instance. In this section we'll launch a Windows Server 2012 instance. I'll begin by using AWS Management Console. The Console will give you a good overview of all the options available. Then, I'll show you how to do the same thing with a single line using PowerShell.

Launching an Instance with the Web Console

For this first exercise—launching an instance with the Web Console—I am going to include step-by-step instructions with figures. I want to note that the Web Console changes often. Don't be surprised if your console screens look a bit different from my figures.

If you are not already signed in to the Web Console, sign in using the URL and IAM account you created in Chapter 2. Do not use the e-mail address you used to create the account.

When you sign in, you will be taken to the AWS Management Console home page. The home page lists all of the AWS services available. Click the EC2 link (see Figure 3-1). Elastic Compute Cloud (EC2) is Amazon's service for creating servers in the cloud.

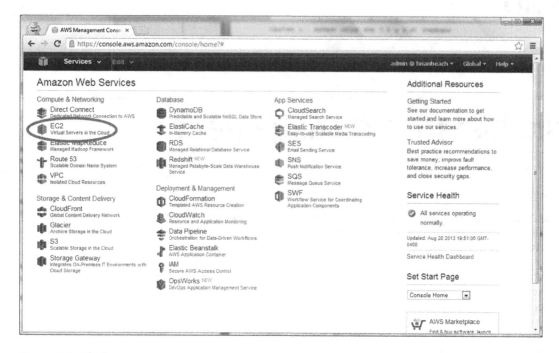

Figure 3-1. *The home page*

On the EC2 dashboard, make sure the region in the top right corner is the same one you used to create your key pair in the last chapter (e.g., Northern Virginia), as shown in Figure 3-2. Then click the Launch Instance button to start the wizard.

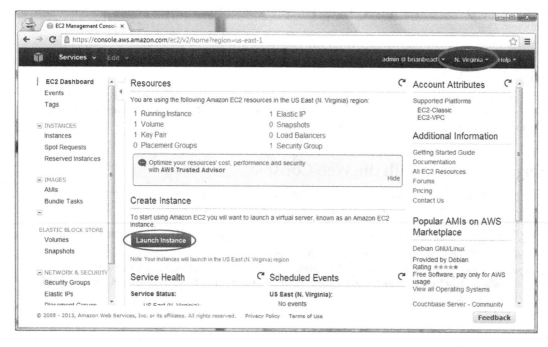

Figure 3-2. *EC2 dashboard*

The first page of the wizard lists the Amazon Machine Images (AMI). An AMI is a template used to create a new instance. The quick start tab includes the most common images. There are additional images available from the other tabs, currently more than 20,000. For now, we just need a basic version of Windows to get our feet wet. Find "Microsoft Windows Server 2012 Base" and click the Select button (see Figure 3-3).

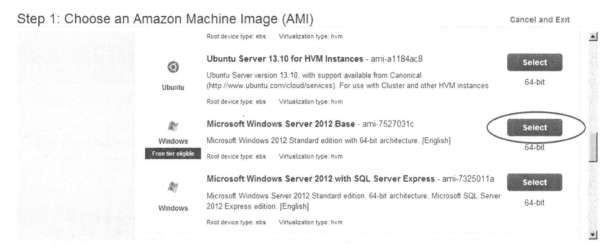

Figure 3-3. *Choosing an AMI*

On the instance details page, ensure that the Instance Type is set to T1 Micro and click the button that says "Next: Configure Instance Details" (see Figure 3-4). The Instance Type is the virtual hardware we want to use. There are numerous combinations of processors, memory, etc. Only the micro instance is eligible for the free tier. You can read more about the free tier on the AWS web site. (An up-to-date description of the Instance types is available here: http://docs.aws.amazon.com/AWSEC2/latest/UserGuide/instance-types.html.)

Step 2: Choose an Instance Type

Amazon EC2 provides a wide selection of instance types optimized to fit different use cases. Instances are virtual servers that can run applications. They have varying combinations of CPU, memory, storage, and networking capacity, and give you the flexibility to choose the appropriate mix of resources for your applications. Learn more about instance types and how they can meet your computing needs.

Currently selected: t1.micro (up to 2 ECUs, 1 vCPUs, 0.613 GiB memory, EBS only)

	Micro instances
All instance types	Micro instances are a low-cost instance option, providing a small amount of CPU resources. They are suited for lower
Micro instances Free tier eligible	throughput applications, and websites that require additional compute cycles periodically, but are not appropriate for applications that require sustained CPU performance. Popular uses for micro instances include low traffic websites or blogs, small administrative applications, bastion hosts, and free trials to explore EC2 functionality.
General purpose	

Size	ECUs ⓘ	vCPUs ⓘ	Memory (GiB)	Instance Storage (GiB) ⓘ	EBS-Optimized Available ⓘ	Network Performance ⓘ
t1.micro	up to 2	1	0.613	EBS only	-	Very Low

> Micro instances are eligible for the AWS free usage tier. For the first 12 months following your AWS sign-up date, you get up to 750 hours of micro instances each month. When your free usage tier expires or if your usage exceeds the free tier restrictions, you pay standard, pay-as-you-go service rates.
>
> Learn more about free usage tier eligibility and restrictions

Cancel | Previous | Review and Launch | **Next: Configure Instance Details**

Figure 3-4. *Choosing an Instance Type*

Skip the next two pages by clicking the button that says "Next:....". We will review all of these advanced options in future chapters. On the Tag Instance page, assign a name to the instance and click the button that says "Next: Configure Security Group" (see Figure 3-5).

Step 5: Tag Instance

A tag consists of a case-sensitive key-value pair. For example, you could define a tag with key = Name and value = Webserver. Learn more about tagging your Amazon EC2 resources.

Key (127 characters maximum)	Value (255 characters maximum)	
Name	MyServer	⊗

Create Tag   (Up to 10 tags maximum)

Cancel   Previous   Review and Launch   Next: Configure Security Group

***Figure 3-5.** Tagging the Instance*

On the Configure Security Group screen, select the default group from the list of existing security groups (see Figure 3-6) and click the button that says "Review and Launch." Security groups act like a firewall within AWS. You can use security groups to control what traffic is allowed to flow to and from the instance. (We will spend time looking at security groups in Chapter 6.)

Step 6: Configure Security Group

A security group is a set of firewall rules that control the traffic for your instance. On this page, you can add rules to allow specific traffic to reach your instance. For example, if you want to set up a web server and allow Internet traffic to reach your instance, add rules that allow unrestricted access to the HTTP and HTTPS ports. You can create a new security group or select from an existing one below. Learn more about Amazon EC2 security groups.

Assign a security group: ○ Create a **new** security group
⦿ Select an **existing** security group

	Security Group ID	Name	Description	Actions
☑	sg-033e6b6b	default	default group	Copy to new

Inbound rules for sg-033e6b6b

Cancel   Previous   Review and Launch

***Figure 3-6.** Configure Security Group*

Take a minute to review the options we selected on the next page and click Launch. This will load the key pair dialog box. Select the key pair you created in the previous chapter (see Figure 3-7). Remember that AWS uses this this key to encrypt the Windows administrator password. Select the confirmation box and then click "Launch Instances".

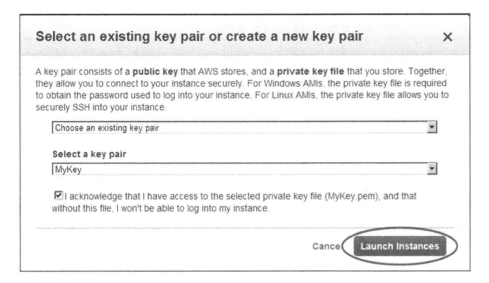

Figure 3-7. *Choosing your key pair*

You just launched your first server in the cloud. Click the "View Instances" button, and you wil be taken to the EC2 Instances page. You should see your new instance in the list with a state of "pending."

It will take about 10 minutes for the instance to launch. While we are waiting, let's discuss how we can do the same thing in PowerShell using a single line of code.

Launching an Instance with PowerShell

In PowerShell, we use the New-EC2Instance command to create instances. This is a really rich command that can do everything the wizard can do. For now we will focus on the basics of the New-EC2Instance command.

In the following example, I have specified only the required parameters.

```
$AMI = Get-EC2ImageByName -Name 'WINDOWS_2012_BASE'
New-EC2Instance -ImageId $AMI[0].ImageId -KeyName 'MyKey' -InstanceType 't1.micro'
    -MinCount 1 -MaxCount 1
```

Let's look at each parameter in turn, most of which are the same ones we saw when using the wizard in the preceding section:

- ImageId specifies which AMI to use. An AMI is the image you want to launch. The image IDs are different in each region; therefore, my examples will use Get-EC2ImageByName to look up the correct ID in the current region. (We will discuss the Get-EC2ImageByName command in Chapter 7.)

- MinCount and MaxCount specify how many instances to launch. See the sidebar on reservations for details.

- KeyName is the name of the key pair we created in the last chapter. It is used to encrypt the administrator password. Technically, this parameter is optional, but without it you will not be able to retrieve the admin password.

- InstanceType describes the hardware we wish to use. This parameter is also optional. But, remember that only the "t1.micro" instance is eligible for the free tier. If you don't specify the InstanceType, Amazon will launch a "small" instance.

RESERVATIONS

Let's spend a minute talking about the MinCount and MaxCount parameters. New-EC2Instance always creates instances in batches called *reservations*. We are going to be using the reservation object in many of the scripts later in this chapter.

A reservation is a batch of instances launched at the same time. Even if you only want a single instance, you create a batch of size one. That's what I did.

Even Amazon has a finite number of instances available. AWS will try to launch the number of instances specified in MaxCount. If it cannot, Amazon will launch the largest possible number above MinCount. If MinCount is more than Amazon EC2 can launch, no instances are launched.

Despite the name, New-EC2Instance actually returns a reservation object rather than an instance. If you want to check the individual instances, the reservation includes a list called RunningInstance. You can use a zero-based array syntax to read the individual instances. For example:

```
$AMI = Get-EC2ImageByName -Name 'WINDOWS_2012_BASE'
$Reservation = New-EC2Instance -ImageId $AMI[0].ImageId -KeyName 'MyKey'
 -InstanceType 't1.micro' -MinCount 2 -MaxCount 2
$Reservation.RunningInstance[0].InstanceId
$Reservation.RunningInstance[1].InstanceId
```

Produces the following output:

```
i-36d1455c
i-38d14552
```

By the way, I should mention that although the attribute is called RunningInstance, it also contains instances that are in a stopped state.

You may have noticed that I did not specify the security group (i.e., Firewall.) Unlike the Web Console wizard, the API will use the "Default" group if you don't specify one.

There are numerous additional parameters to the New-EC2Instance command. These correspond to the options we skipped in the wizard. Don't worry. We will talk about them all in later chapters.

Windows instances take about 10 minutes to launch regardless of how we create them. The instance(s) you launched with PowerShell are probably still launching, but the one we launched with the AWS Management Console is probably ready; let's go check it now.

Connecting to an Instance

Returning to the Web Console, let's check on that instance we launched earlier.

Remember, from the last chapter, that AWS will generate a new administrator password and encrypt it using your key pair. On the Instances page, select the instance, and click the Connect button at the top of the screen. Then click the "Get Password" button (see Figure 3-8).

Figure 3-8. *Connect to Your Instance*

Now, click the "Choose File" button (see Figure 3-9) and locate the private key you created in Chapter 2. Then click the "Decrypt Password" button.

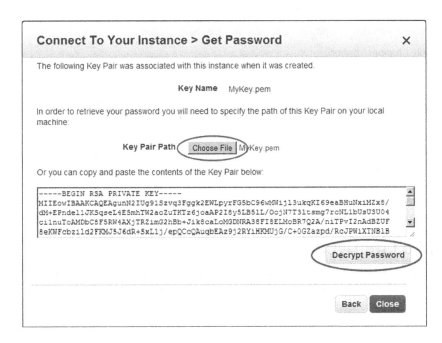

Figure 3-9. *Decrypting the password*

The dialog will now show the temporary password. Click the Download shortcut file link (see Figure 3-10). This will launch a Remote Desktop session and prompt you for the password you just decrypted. Type it in and click the Connect button.

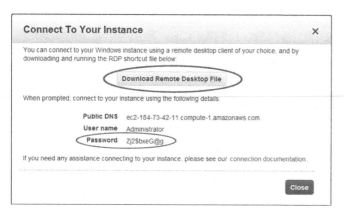

Figure 3-10. Downloading the shortcut file

Great! Now you know how to create and connect to an instance using the web console.

_____

■ **Note**   Depending on which region you are running in, you may need to add a rule to the security group to allow Remote Desktop Protocol (RDP). Follow the instructions below. We will discuss Security Groups in detail in Chapter 6.

- From the EC2 Web Console, choose Security Groups.

- Select the group named "default" and choose the Inbound tab.

- Choose RDP from the "create a new rule" dropdown, and click the "Add Rule" button.

- Finally, click the "Apply Rule Changes" button.

_____

You can, of course, retrieve the password using PowerShell. The PowerShell command is Get-EC2PasswordData command. Get-EC2PasswordData takes an instance ID and the path to the private key and returns the password. Note that your instance ID will be different from mine. Each instance has a different ID. You can get the ID from the instances page of the AWS Management Console.

```
Get-EC2PasswordData -InstanceId 'i-2143eb59' -PemFile 'c:\aws\MyKey.pem'
```

The preceding code will return an error if the password is not available yet. Remember, it takes about 10 minutes to launch a new instance. We will discuss how to test for password availability in the first exercise at the end of this chapter.

Now that you know how to launch and connect to an instance, let's talk about starting, stopping, rebooting, and terminating instances.

Managing the Instance Life Cycle

Now that you have a few instances created, you will want to be able to manage them. You can Start, Stop, Reboot, and Terminate (i.e., Delete) an instance by right-clicking it in the AWS Management Console. Figure 3-11 shows the relevant portion of the context menu.

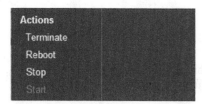

Figure 3-11. Instance life cycle menu options

The equivalent PowerShell commands are all pretty simple. They each have a parameter called `Instance`, which is the id of the instance you want to start, stop, etc.

To start an instance, you use `Start-EC2Instance`:

```
Start-Ec2Instance -Instance i-38d14552
```

To reboot an instance, you use `Restart-EC2Instance`:

```
Restart-Ec2Instance -Instance i-38d14552
```

To stop an instance, you use `Stop-EC2Instance`:

```
Stop-Ec2Instance -Instance i-38d14552
```

To terminate an instance, you use `Stop-EC2Instance` command with an additional attribute, `Terminate`. You will be asked to confirm the terminate command. You can add the force attribute to suppress the prompt.

```
Stop-Ec2Instance -Instance i-38d14552 -Terminate -Force
```

Listing Instances and Metadata

You have already seen the list of instances in the Web Console. You can use the `Get-EC2Instance` to list instances in PowerShell. The primary purpose of `Get-EC2Instance` is to return a list of all the instances in your account. In addition, you will use the `Get-EC2Instance` command to get metadata about the instance. Metadata includes information such as the IP address, drive configuration, and type of instance.

```
Get-EC2Instance
```

The preceding command returns the following results:

```
ReservationId  : r-2143eb59
OwnerId        : 123456789012
RequesterId    :
GroupId        : {}
GroupName      : {}
RunningInstance : {ec2-54-226-246-207.compute-1.amazonaws.com}
...
```

Of course, you can use any of the standard PowerShell commands with the AWS commands. For example, we can format our list of instances as a table.

```
Get-EC2Instance | Format-Table
```

The preceding command returns the following results:

```
ReservationId         OwnerId          ...     RunningInstance
r-12345678            123456789012     ...     {ec2-54-226  ....
r-2345678a            123456789012     ...     {ip-10-1-1-5 ....
r-345678ab            123456789012     ...     {ip-10-1-1-6 ....
...                                    ...                  ...
```

If you want a specific instance, use the Instance parameter. For example:

```
Get-EC2Instance -Instance i-2143eb59
```

This command returns the following results:

```
ReservationId  : r-12345678
OwnerId        : 123456789012
RequesterId    :
GroupId        : {}
GroupName      : {}
RunningInstance : {ec2-54-226-246-207.compute-1.amazonaws.com}
```

If you have been paying attention, you probably noticed that Get-EC2Instance returns a reservation object. Remember that New-EC2Instance always creates a batch called a *reservation*. When you call Get-EC2Instance, AWS returns the reservation that includes that instance. The RunningInstance attribute includes the specific instance you requested.

To access the instance metadata, you need to read the first instance in the RunningInstance list. For example:

```
(Get-EC2Instance -Instance i-2143eb59).RunningInstance[0]
```

This command returns the following results:

```
InstanceId           : i-2143eb59
ImageId              : ami-12121212
InstanceState        : Amazon.EC2.Model.InstanceState
PrivateDnsName       :
PublicDnsName        : ec2-54-226-246-207.compute-1.amazonaws.com
StateTransitionReason :
KeyName              : MyKey
AmiLaunchIndex       : 0
ProductCode          : {}
ProductCodes         : {}
InstanceType         : t1.micro
LaunchTime           : 2013-01-01T00:00:00.000Z
Placement            : Amazon.EC2.Model.Placement
KernelId             :
RamdiskId            :
Platform             : windows
Monitoring           : Amazon.EC2.Model.Monitoring
SubnetId             :
VpcId                :
PrivateIpAddress     : 10.1.1.6
IpAddress            :
SourceDestCheck      : True
GroupId              : {sg-3ac5aa55}
GroupName            : {default}
StateReason          :
Architecture         : x86_64
RootDeviceType       : ebs
RootDeviceName       : /dev/sda1
BlockDeviceMapping   : {/dev/sda1}
```

```
InstanceLifecycle     :
SpotInstanceRequestId :
License               :
VirtualizationType    : hvm
ClientToken           :
Tag                   : {}
NetworkInterfaceSet   : {}
EbsOptimized          : False
InstanceProfile       :
```

This will give you a great deal of information about the instance including storage, network, and other details. We will use this information throughout the rest of the book. But before we get into that, let's look at one other way to access the metadata: the metadata URL.

Using the Metadata URL

Get-EC2Instance is a great way to get information about an instance, but there is another way: the metadata URL. The metadata URL returns much of the same information as Get-EC2Instance, but always returns information about the current instance.

The metadata URL is a web service that returns metadata about the *current* instance. The URL is http://169.254.169.254/latest/meta-data. Note the metadata service is only available from a script running on the EC2 instance. You cannot use the API from a machine outside the AWS data center. Nor can you use the metadata service to get information about another instance.

Opening the metadata URL in Internet Explorer lists all of the options available (see Figure 3-12).

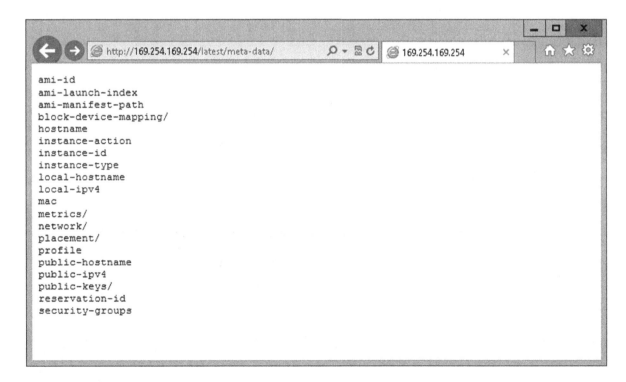

Figure 3-12. Metadata URL example

Navigating to any of the sub-URLs will return useful information about the instance. For example, navigating to http://169.254.169.254/latest/meta-data/instance-type will return the type of hardware you are running on (see Figure 3-13).

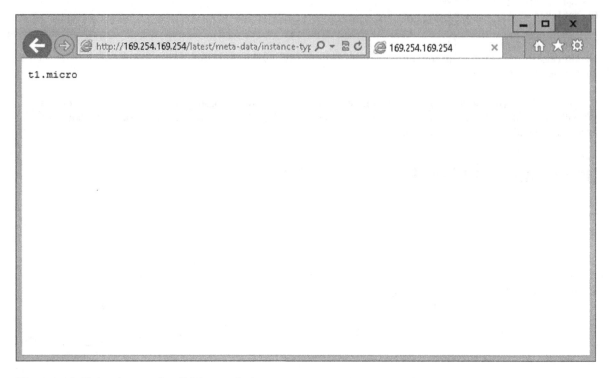

Figure 3-13. *Using the metadata URL to get the instance type*

Of course, you can also access metadata from PowerShell using the Invoke-RestMethod command and passing the metadata URL. The following script is equivalent to the earlier example:

```
Invoke-RestMethod 'http://169.254.169.254/latest/meta-data/instance-type'
```

The preceding script results in the following:

```
t1.micro
```

A common use of the metadata URL is to discover the id of the current instance and then use it call the AWS API. This way, we can write a generic script that will run on any EC2 instance. The following script uses the metadata API to discover the instance id and then calls Get-EC2Instance on it. Note that the instance id was not known ahead of time. Instead, it was discovered by the script.

```
$InstanceID = Invoke-RestMethod 'http://169.254.169.254/latest/meta-data/instance-id'
Get-EC2Instance $InstanceID
```

Using User Data

One of the options we skipped over in the section on launching new instances was user data. User data is similar to metadata, but it allows you to include any custom data you want. The user data is available via a web service call, just like the metadata in the prior section.

One common use of user data is to include information needed to "bootstrap" the instance, or configure it after launch. We will do this in the second exercise at the end of this chapter.

To include user data, simply type whatever you want into the text box at the bottom of the third page of the Request Instances Wizard (see Figure 3-14). It is common, but not required, to use XML in the User Data section. Using XML makes it easier to parse the data later. In the example in Figure 3-14, I am using a combination of free-form text and XML-formatted data.

Step 3: Configure Instance Details

▼ Advanced Details

User data ⓘ   • As text ○ As file ☐ Input is already base64 encoded

```
This is a Test!!!
<TestValue>42</TestValue>
```

Cancel   Previous   Review and Launch   Next: Add Storage

Figure 3-14. *Setting user data*

Once the instance launches, you can retrieve the data using the user-data URL, `http://169.254.169.254/latest/user-data` (see Figure 3-15).

Figure 3-15. *Retrieving user data*

Similar to the metadata URL, this URL will always return the user data for the running instance. Each instance has its own unique user data.

You can also include user data when calling New-Instance from PowerShell using the UserData parameter. AWS anticipates that the user data will include XML. Remember that the API call is also a web service that may be formatted as XML. Therefore, to avoid confusion, you must base 64 encode the user-data section. For example, the following code is equivalent to the console example shown earlier:

```
$UserData = @'
This is a Test!!!
<TestValue>42</TestValue>
'@

$UserData = [System.Convert]::ToBase64String([System.Text.Encoding]::ASCII.GetBytes($UserData))

$AMI = Get-EC2ImageByName -Name 'WINDOWS_2012_BASE'
$Reservation = New-EC2Instance -ImageId $AMI[0].ImageId -KeyName 'MyKey'
    -InstanceType 't1.micro' -MinCount 1 -MaxCount 1 -UserData $UserData
```

■ **Note**   If you are not familiar with the @'...'@ syntax, this is just a convenient way to include a multiline string in PowerShell.

You can also use the Invoke-RestMethod command that we used in the previous section to retrieve the user data from PowerShell. For example:

```
$Invoke-RestMethod 'http://169.254.169.254/latest/user-data'
```

Results in the following output:

```
This is a Test!!!
<TestValue>42</TestValue>
```

You can change the user data after launching an instance, but the instance must be stopped. From the Web Console, right-click an instance and choose View/Change User Data. Let's stop our instance and try replacing the user data with well-formed XML. For example:

```
<documentation>
  <document>
    <name>GettingStarted</name>
    <url>http://awsdocs.s3.amazonaws.com/EC2/latest/ec2-gsg.pdf</url>
  </document>
  <document>
    <name>UserGuide</name>
    <url>http://awsdocs.s3.amazonaws.com/EC2/latest/ec2-ug.pdf</url>
  </document>
  <document>
    <name>APIReference</name>
    <url>http://awsdocs.s3.amazonaws.com/EC2/latest/ec2-api.pdf</url>
  </document>
</documentation>
```

The benefit of using XML is that the `Invoke-RestMethod` command will parse the response. This means that you can interact with the response like any other object in PowerShell and you get IntelliSense in the IDE as well. Note how we can navigate the object hierarchy and format the response:

```
$Response = Invoke-RestMethod 'http://169.254.169.254/latest/user-data'
$Response.documentation.document | Format-Table
```

The preceding code results in the following output:

```
name            url
----            ---
GettingStarted  http://awsdocs.s3.amazonaws.com/EC2/latest/ec2-gsg.pdf
UserGuide       http://awsdocs.s3.amazonaws.com/EC2/latest/ec2-ug.pdf
APIReference    http://awsdocs.s3.amazonaws.com/EC2/latest/ec2-api.pdf
```

There is one other really cool feature of user ddata. You can include scripts that you want to run when the instance boots the first time. You can include Windows command shell scripts inside `<script>...</script>` or PowerShell scripts inside `<powershell>...</powershell>` tags. We will do this in the second exercise at the end of this chapter.

Working with Tags

Every object in AWS supports tags. Tags are a great way to keep track of all your instances and other objects. A tag is simply a key/value pair used to describe the object. For example, you can use a tag to record the name of an instance or which department owns it. You can use tags to record any additional information you need.

Each object can have up to 10 tags. The key can be up to 128 characters, and the value can be up to 256 characters long. Note that you can access tags on the Web Console using the Tags tab (see Figure 3-16). And, you can edit the tags using the "Add/Edit Tags" button.

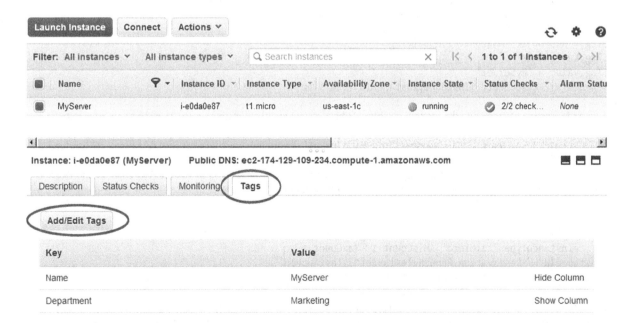

Figure 3-16. *The Tags tab*

In Powershell we can read the tags from the tag collection of any object. To get the tags for an instance, just get a reference to the instance and read the Tag property:

```
$Reservation = Get-EC2Instance -Instance i-1c242570
$Instance = $Reservation.RunningInstance[0]
$Instance.Tag
```

Here is the result:

```
Key                     Value
---                     -----
Name                    MyServer
Department              Marketing
...                     ...
```

If you want to retrieve a specific tag, use the Where-Object command to find it:

```
$Reservation = Get-EC2Instance -Instance i-38d14552
$Instance = $Reservation.RunningInstance[0]
$Tag = $Instance.Tag | Where-Object { $_.Key -eq "Name"}
$Tag.Value
```

Creating tags is a bit harder. A tag is a .Net object. There is no PowerShell command to create an EC2 tag. Instead, we use the generic New-Object command to create a .Net object of type Amazon.EC2.Model.Tag. Once we have the new tag, we simply set the Key and Value properties.

Let's use the New-EC2Instance command to create a new instance and add a few descriptive tags:

```
$AMI = Get-EC2ImageByName -Name 'WINDOWS_2012_BASE'
$Reservation = New-EC2Instance -ImageId $AMI[0].ImageId -KeyName 'MyKey'
    -InstanceType 't1.micro' -MinCount 1 -MaxCount 1
$InstanceId = $Reservation.RunningInstance[0].InstanceId
$Tag = New-Object Amazon.EC2.Model.Tag
$Tag.Key ='Name'
$Tag.Value = 'MyServer'
New-EC2Tag -ResourceId $Instance.InstanceId -Tag $Tag
```

As I mentioned, you can add a tag to anything. When you have only a few instances, it is relatively simple to keep track of everything. Once you launch 10 or more, it quickly gets very confusing.

One trick I have learned is to tag everything. Each instance has at least one volume and one network interface attached. Therefore, whenever I create a machine, I tag the instance and all of the attached resources.

AWS makes it easy to tag multiple objects at once. You simply pass all the IDs to New-EC2Tag as an array. There is no need to tell AWS what type of object each is. It can figure that out on its own.

```
$AMI = Get-EC2ImageByName -Name 'WINDOWS_2012_BASE'
$Reservation = New-EC2Instance -ImageId $AMI[0].ImageId -KeyName 'MyKey'
    -InstanceType 't1.micro' -MinCount 1 -MaxCount 1
$InstanceId = $Reservation.RunningInstance[0].InstanceId
Start-Sleep -s 60 #Wait for drives to be mounted, etc.
$Reservation = Get-EC2Instance -Instance $InstanceId
$VolumeId = $Reservation.RunningInstance[0].BlockDeviceMapping[0].EBS.VolumeId
$NetworkInterfaceId = $Reservation.RunningInstance[0].NetworkInterfaceSet[0].NetworkInterfaceId
```

```
$Tag = New-Object Amazon.EC2.Model.Tag
$Tag.Key = 'Name'
$Tag.Value = 'MyServer'
New-EC2Tag -ResourceId $InstanceId, $VolumeId, $NetworkInterfaceId  -Tag $Tag
```

Did you notice that Start-Sleep in the previous command? This is another little trick I have learned. When you create a new instance, the command may return before all of the resources have been allocated. Therefore, you may find that a volume or network interface is null.

To get around this, I have my script sleep for a few seconds. Then I query AWS for an updated copy of the instance metadata. This gives AWS enough time to allocate resources.

Working with Filters

In the previous section, we used the Where-Object command to filter a collection and find a specific tag. This same method could be applied to other objects—for example, to find all of the instances owned by a given department.

AWS provides a better solution: filters. A filter allows you to specify search criteria to be executed on the server. This way you don't have to download metadata from hundreds of instances when you are only interested in a handful.

The "Get" methods usually include a filter parameter. The filter allows you to return only those resources with a specific value for a given attribute.

For example, if you want to return a list of instances that are currently running, you can use the instance-state-code filter. A value of 16 is running. The filter names and values are not intuitive. They use the AWS CLI syntax, which may be foreign to a user of the PowerShell API. I have included a list of filters and values with each "Get" command in Appendix C.

Once again, you have to use the generic New-Object to create the filter. For example:

```
$Filter = New-Object Amazon.EC2.Model.Filter
$Filter.Name = 'instance-state-code'
$Filter.Value = 16
Get-EC2Instance -Filter $Filter
```

You can also use filters to search for custom tags. For example, assume you record the department that owns each instance. If you wanted to retrieve all of the instances that belong to the marketing department, you could use a filter that specifies Department = Marketing. For example:

```
$Filter = New-Object Amazon.EC2.Model.Filter
$Filter.Name = 'tag:Department'
$Filter.Value = 'Marketing'
Get-EC2Instance -Filter $filter
```

Note that when you filter on tags, you use the format tag: followed by the key. Remember that keys are case sensitive. If you are creating keys manually using the Web Console, be consistent.

EXERCISE 3.1: WAITING FOR AN INSTANCE TO LAUNCH

For this exercise let's assume that you often receive requests to create new instances from developers in your organization and those developers don't have access to the AWS Web Console. As AWS adoption has grown, this has become very time consuming. It would be nice to script the build in PowerShell.

You know you can create a new instance and get the password with a few lines of code. But, you still have to wait for the build to finish and then send the instance name and password to the requestor. If would be great if the script could wait for the build to finish and then automatically e-mail the password to the requestor. But, how do we know when the server is finished?

One way to determine whether the server is finished is to poll the instance to check if the password is available. We can call the Get-EC2PasswordData command to check if a password exists. This provides a convenient way to check for password availability.

Let's start by creating a new method, called GetPasswordWhenReady. This method checks once every minute until the password is ready and then returns it. The method takes three parameters. The first is the id of the instance to wait on. The second is the location of the private key used to decrypt the password. The third is the munber of minutes to wait for the password, after which the script will give up. Note that it writes a period to the screen each minute to let the user know that it is still working.

```
Function GetPasswordWhenReady()
{
    Param(
        [string][Parameter(Mandatory=$True)] $InstanceId,
        [string][Parameter(Mandatory=$True)] $PemFile,
        [Int] $TimeOut = 30
    )

    $RetryCount = $TimeOut

    Write-Host "Waiting for password" -NoNewline

    While($RetryCount -gt 1) {
        Try {
            $Password = Get-EC2PasswordData -InstanceId $InstanceId -PemFile $PemFile
            Write-Host ""
            Return $Password
        } Catch {
            $RetryCount--
            Start-Sleep -s 60 #It's not ready.  Let's wait for it.
            Write-Host "." -NoNewline #It's nice to give a little feedback now and then
        }
    }
}
```

All we need now is a method that sends e-mails. This method will take three parameters: recipient, instance name, and password. Note that I have hard-coded the from address and SMTP server name in my script. You will need to change them.

```
Function SendInstanceReadyEmail()
{
    Param(
        [string][Parameter(Mandatory=$True)] $Recipient,
        [string][Parameter(Mandatory=$True)] $InstanceName,
        [string][Parameter(Mandatory=$True)] $Password
    )
    $Message = "You can access the instance at $InstanceName.
        The administrator password is $Password."

    #Create the message
    $Email = New-Object Net.Mail.MailMessage
```

```
    $Email.From = "admin@brianbeach.com"
    $Email.ReplyTo = "admin@brianbeach.com"
    $Email.To.Add($Recipient)
    $Email.Subject = "Your Instance is Ready"
    $Email.Body = $Message

    #Send the message
    $SMTP = New-Object Net.Mail.SmtpClient('smtp.brianbeach.com')
    $SMTP.Send($Email)
}
```

Now we can test it. Here I am creating a new instance and retrieving the id. Then I wait for the password to become available. This usually takes about 10 minutes. Once the password is ready, I refresh the metadata. Remember that some attributes are not available when New-EC2Instance returns. The Public DNS of the new instance is one of these. By refreshing the metadata after the build completes, we know that all variables are present. Now we can send an e-mail to the requestor.

```
Param(
    [string][Parameter(Mandatory=$false)] $ImageID,
    [string][Parameter(Mandatory=$false)] $KeyName = 'MyKey',
    [string][Parameter(Mandatory=$false)] $PemFile = 'c:\aws\MyKey.pem',
    [string][Parameter(Mandatory=$false)] $InstanceType = 't1.micro',
    [string][Parameter(Mandatory=$true)] $EmailRecipient
)


#Create a new instance
If([System.String]::IsNullOrEmpty($ImageID)){ $ImageID = (Get-EC2ImageByName
    -Name "WINDOWS_2012_BASE")[0].ImageId}
$Reservation = New-EC2Instance -ImageId $ImageID -KeyName $KeyName
    -InstanceType $InstanceType -MinCount 1 -MaxCount 1
$InstanceId = $Reservation.RunningInstance[0].InstanceId

#Get the password to the new instance
$Password = GetPasswordWhenReady -Instance $InstanceId -PemFile $PemFile

#Get the latest meta-data including the DNS name
$Reservation = Get-EC2Instance -Instance $InstanceId
$InstanceName = $Reservation.RunningInstance[0].PublicDnsName

#Send an email with connection info
SendInstanceReadyEmail -Recipient $EmailRecipient
    -InstanceName $InstanceName -Password $Password
```

Note that I am using the PublicDnsName. Here I am assuming that we are using an EC2 Classic instance. If this were a VPC instance, we would use the internal IP address rather than public DNS. But, we have not talked about VPC instances yet. We'll get to that in Chapter 6.

EXERCISE 3.2: BOOTSTRAPPING WITH USER DATA

At this point we know how to launch and manage instances. Before we close this chapter, let's spend a minute talking about how we can customize instances. You could, of course, just log in and configure each instance manually. But the cloud is all about automation and standardization.

If we script the configuration of our server, the results will be more consistent and reproducible. Amazon thought of this, and it included the capability to run configuration scripts when a server boots. In this exercise, I am going to configure our instance for remote administration. We will use a PowerShell script in the user data to complete the configuration.

Amazon includes the EC2 Config Service in every AMI they provide. The first time an instance boots, the EC2 Config Service will check the user data for <script>...</script> or <powershell>...</powershell> tags and then execute them at the command prompt or PowerShell prompt respectively. By default, scripts are run only the first time an instance boots, but you can configure it to run every time the instance starts. (We will look at this in Chapter 7.)

We talked in the last chapter about specifying default credentials and a default region. We will use a server role to provide credentials, but remember that we still need to set the default region. We can use PowerShell in the user data to accomplish this. On the fourth tab of the Launch Instance Wizard, we can set the IAM Role and provide the user data (see Figure 3-17).

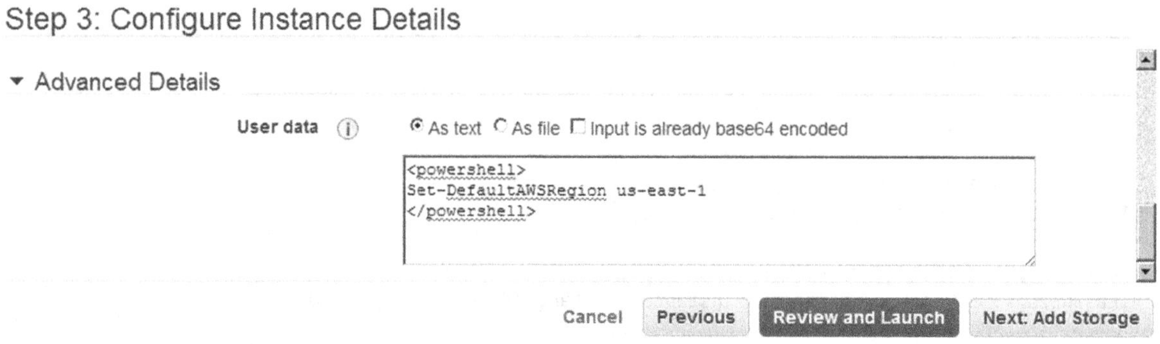

Step 3: Configure Instance Details

Figure 3-17. *Setting user data and IAM role*

When this instance launches, it will be ready to run scripts without further configuration. Before we launch it, though, let's make a few more changes—and let's use PowerShell to launch it.

It would be nice if we could interact with the instance without having to log in. Microsoft has many remote administration technologies. Let's configure PowerShell remoting for administration and Windows Management Instrumentation (WMI) for monitoring and management.

PowerShell remoting is really easy. The command is simply

```
Enable-PSRemoting
```

WMI is a bit more complicated. WMI is already running, but Windows Firewall will block external access. Fortunately, the firewall rules are already configured. They just need to be enabled. All we need to do is use the PowerShell command `Enable-NetFirewallRule`. Here I find and enable all of the WMI firewall rules:

```
Get-NetFirewallRule | Where { $_.DisplayName -like "Windows Management Instrumentation *" } |
  Enable-NetFirewallRule
```

The complete script is available with the accompanying code in a file called Bootstrap.ps1. For information on downloading the sample code, see Chapter 1. You could simply use the "as file" option on the Advanced Instance Options page of the Request Instances Wizard to open this file, but I prefer to launch the instance from PowerShell. Let's create another script that launches a new instance.

The following script will open the bootstrap script from disk. Then it will format the script for use with the AWS API. Finally, it will launch the instance, passing the script as user data.

```
param(
    [parameter(mandatory=$false)][string]$KeyName = 'MyKey',
    [parameter(mandatory=$false)][string]$RoleName = 'AdminRole',
    [parameter(mandatory=$false)][string]$UserDataFile = 'C:\AWS\Chapter3\Excercise2\Bootstrap.ps1',
    [parameter(mandatory=$false)][string]$ImageId,
    [parameter(mandatory=$false)][string]$InstanceType = 't1.micro'
)

#If no image was specified, assume 2012 base
If([System.String]::IsNullOrEmpty($ImageID)){ $ ImageID = (Get-EC2ImageByName
    -Name "WINDOWS_2012_BASE")[0].ImageId}

#Read the bootstrap script from the file specified
$BootstrapScript = Get-Content $UserDataFile

#Get-Content returns an array of strings.  Convert the array to a single string
$BootstrapScript = [System.String]::Join("`r`n", $BootstrapScript )

#Add the PowerShell tags to the script
$BootstrapScript = @"
<powershell>
$BootstrapScript
</powershell>
"@

#Base 64 encode the script
$UserData = [System.Convert]::ToBase64String([System.Text.Encoding]::ASCII.
GetBytes($BootstrapScript))

#Get the IAM Role to apply to the new instance
$Profile = Get-IAMInstanceProfile -InstanceProfileName $RoleName

#Launch the new instance with bootstrap script
$Reservation = New-EC2Instance -ImageId $ImageId  -KeyName $KeyName
    -InstanceType $InstanceType -MinCount 1 -MaxCount 1 -UserData $UserData
```

```
    -InstanceProfile_Arn $Profile.Arn
$InstanceId = $Reservation.RunningInstance[0].InstanceId
Write-Host "Launched new instance with id $InstanceId"
```

User data is a really powerful option. You can use this to make just about any customizations you need without ever logging into a server. As your adoption of AWS matures, you will likely begin to use features such as auto scaling, which deploys instances automatically in response to load. Obviously, it is critical that you can auto configure these instances. (We will talk more about auto scaling in Chapter 8.)

Summary

In this chapter we got a good introduction to instances. We learned to launch instances using both Web Console and PowerShell. We learned how to start, stop, and terminate instances. We also learned how to discover information about our instance using both PowerShell and the metadata URL. Next, we learned how to include custom data with user data and tags. Then we discussed how to use filters to find specific instances. In the examples we created a complete script to managing launching instances. Then we learned how to customize our instance using user data.

In the next chapter, we will discuss storage including volumes and snapshots. Volumes are the disks that are attached to an instance, and snapshots are point-in-time backups of your volumes.

CHAPTER 4

■ ■ ■

Elastic Block Storage

In the last chapter, we learned how to launch and manage instances. In this chapter we will focus on the volumes, or disks, attached to the instance. We will learn how to customize and add additional volumes at launch. Then we will look at modifying the volumes after launch.

This chapter will also cover snapshots. Snapshots are a point-in-time copy of a volume, often used for backups. Snapshots can be used to create copies of volumes or to recover from a disaster. We will talk about using snapshots to create a backup of a volume and how to restore a volume when a disaster occurs.

Let's start with a little background. Volumes are based on a technology Amazon calls *Elastic Block Storage (EBS)*. EBS is network-attached storage used by EC2 instances. Like iSCSI in a traditional data center, EBS shares bandwidth with other network traffic. This means performance is affected by network load. I will show you how to configure quality of service to guarantee the performance of your volumes.

EBS volumes are redundant within an availability zone. Therefore, there is no need to create RAID arrays of EBS disks within the operating system. Remember that an availability zone is a single data center. Despite the redundancy EBS provides, it is possible to lose an entire availability zone in a disaster. Therefore, you still need to back up your volumes using snapshots.

Snapshots are backups of volumes stored in the Simple Storage Service (S3). (We will talk about S3 in detail in Chapter 10.) Each snapshot is stored in multiple availability zones within a region to provide very high durability. In addition, I will show you how to copy snapshots from one region to another.

Let's get started by building on our experience in Chapter 3. In the next section, we will extend our launch scripts to control volumes at launch.

Managing Volumes at Launch

In the last chapter, we discussed launching a new EC2 instance. If you remember, we skipped over a few of the screens in the wizard. Let's return to the wizard and look at the Storage Device Configuration screen. This screen allows us to specify the number, size, and performance characteristics of the volumes that will be attached to the instance.

Open the AWS Management Console and click the Launch Instance button on the EC2 dashboard. Navigate through the wizard and stop on the Storage Device Configuration screen (see Figure 4-1). This screen lists the default volumes that come with the Amazon Machine Image (AMI) you choose. Remember that an AMI is the template that describes an instance. Most Windows images include a 30GB root volume. SQL images are larger, and most Linux distributions are significantly smaller.

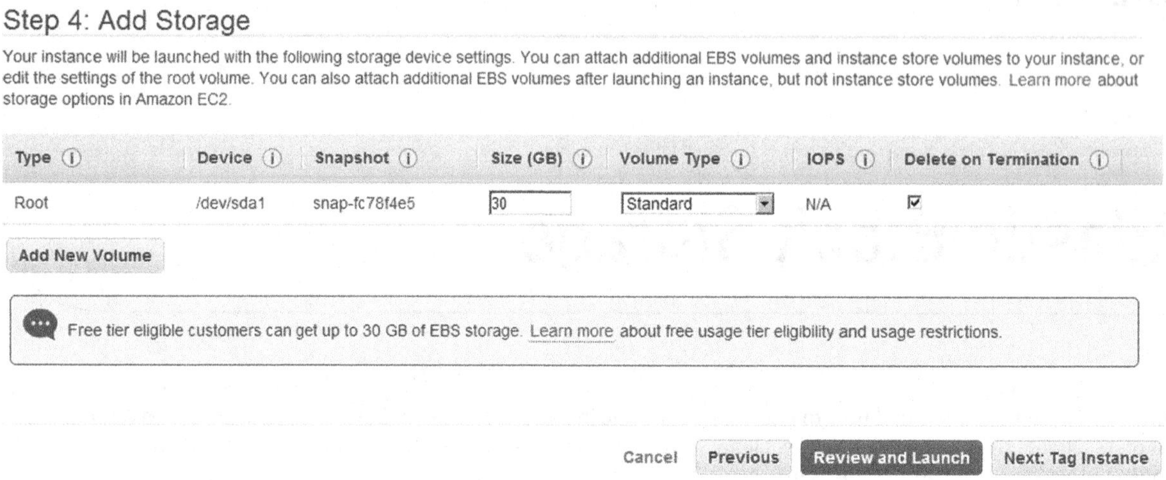

Step 4: Add Storage

Your instance will be launched with the following storage device settings. You can attach additional EBS volumes and instance store volumes to your instance, or edit the settings of the root volume. You can also attach additional EBS volumes after launching an instance, but not instance store volumes. Learn more about storage options in Amazon EC2.

Type ⓘ	Device ⓘ	Snapshot ⓘ	Size (GB) ⓘ	Volume Type ⓘ	IOPS ⓘ	Delete on Termination ⓘ
Root	/dev/sda1	snap-fc78f4e5	30	Standard ▾	N/A	☑

Add New Volume

💬 Free tier eligible customers can get up to 30 GB of EBS storage. Learn more about free usage tier eligibility and usage restrictions.

Cancel **Previous** **Review and Launch** **Next: Tag Instance**

Figure 4-1. *Storage device configuration*

You can change the size of the root volume by simply typing into textbox under the heading Size (GB). Thirty GB is good enough for most Windows applications, but some applications, such as SQL Server, require more room. A volume can be between 1GB and 1TB. In addition, you can configure the IO Operations per Second (IOPS). (We will talk about provisioned IOPS later in this chapter.)

You can also choose to delete the volume on termination. If you check this box, the volume will be automatically deleted when you terminate the instance. In general, the root volume is configured to auto delete, and any additional volumes you attach are not.

WHAT'S A GIBIBYTE (GIB)?

If you look closely at Figure 4-2 you may notice the Volume Size is measured in GiB, which is the abbreviation for Gibibyte. A Gibibyte (GiB) is closely related to, but not equal to, a Gigabyte (GB).

You have probably heard that 1KB = 1024 bytes. Of course, in other scientific disciplines 1K = 1000. Computer scientists prefer 1024 because it is a power of 2 ($2^{10} = 1024$).

Amazon is using the unambiguous Gibibyte. I'm going to stick to the old GB, but I really mean GiB.

Manipulating the root volume in PowerShell is verbose, but straightforward. PowerShell uses .Net objects to describe the drive configuration. You simply pass the .Net object to the New-EC2Instance we used in Chapter 3.

First, we use the Amazon.EC2.Model.EbsBlockDevice object to describe the volume. Here I want a 55GB standard volume, which does not use provisioned IOPS. In addition, I want the volume to be deleted when I terminate the instance.

```
$Volume = New-Object Amazon.EC2.Model.EbsBlockDevice
$Volume.VolumeSize = 55
$Volume.VolumeType = 'standard'
$Volume.DeleteOnTermination = $True
```

Next, we use the Amazon.EC2.Model.BlockDeviceMapping object to describe how the volume should be attached to the instance. The root volume is always attached to "/dev/sda1". Notice that I am passing the EbsBlockDevice object created by the preceding code.

```
$Mapping = New-Object Amazon.EC2.Model.BlockDeviceMapping
$Mapping.DeviceName = '/dev/sda1'
$Mapping.Ebs = $Volume
```

Finally, we call New-EC2Instance and include the BlockDeviceMapping parameter describing how we want the volume configured.

```
$AMI = Get-EC2ImageByName -Name 'WINDOWS_2012_BASE'
$Reservation = New-EC2Instance -ImageId $AMI[0].ImageId -KeyName 'MyKey'
    -InstanceType 't1.micro' -MinCount 1 -MaxCount 1 -BlockDeviceMapping $Mapping
$Instance = $Reservation.RunningInstance[0]
```

You can also add additional volumes to your instance. See Figure 4-2. Windows instances will support up to 16 volumes. The New Instance Wizard allows you to add additional volumes using the EBS Volumes tab of the Storage Device Configuration page. Most of these options are the same as the root volume with a couple of additions, described next.

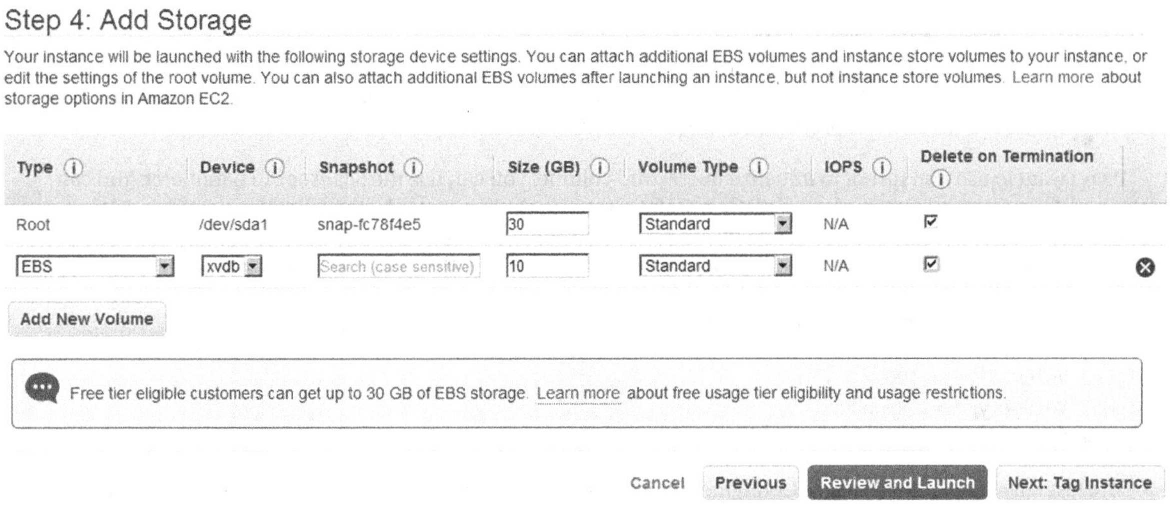

Step 4: Add Storage

Your instance will be launched with the following storage device settings. You can attach additional EBS volumes and instance store volumes to your instance, or edit the settings of the root volume. You can also attach additional EBS volumes after launching an instance, but not instance store volumes. Learn more about storage options in Amazon EC2.

Type (i)	Device (i)	Snapshot (i)	Size (GB) (i)	Volume Type (i)	IOPS (i)	Delete on Termination (i)	
Root	/dev/sda1	snap-fc78f4e5	30	Standard	N/A	☑	
EBS ▾	xvdb ▾	Search (case sensitive)	10	Standard	N/A	☑	✕

Add New Volume

💬 Free tier eligible customers can get up to 30 GB of EBS storage. Learn more about free usage tier eligibility and usage restrictions.

Cancel   **Previous**   **Review and Launch**   **Next: Tag Instance**

Figure 4-2. *EBS volumes*

You can choose to use a snapshot to initialize your disk. Recall that a snapshot is a copy of a volume at a specific point in time. The root volume always uses the snapshot specified by the AMI, but additional volumes can use any snapshot. You can choose your own snapshot, or there are numerous interesting data sets available that other users have made available.

You can also set an attachment point. The attachment point describes how the volume is attached to the instance. This is similar to describing which port the disk is plugged into on a physical machine. For Windows instances you should use xvd[f-z]. Just use them in order: xvdf, xvdg, xvdh, etc.

Additional volumes are handled just like the root volume in PowerShell. We just create two EbsBlockDevice objects and two BlockDeviceMapping objects. Note that the root volume is attached at "/dev/sda1" and the second disk is attached at "xvdf". Also, note that I have chosen to delete the root volume when the instance is terminated, but keep the second volume. You separate the mapping objects by commas when calling New-EC2Instance to create an array of mappings.

```
$Volume1 = New-Object Amazon.EC2.Model.EbsBlockDevice
$Volume1.DeleteOnTermination = $True
$Volume1.VolumeSize = 30
$Volume1.VolumeType = 'standard'

$Mapping1 = New-Object Amazon.EC2.Model.BlockDeviceMapping
$Mapping1.DeviceName = '/dev/sda1'
$Mapping1.Ebs = $Volume1

$Volume2 = New-Object Amazon.EC2.Model.EbsBlockDevice
$Volume2.DeleteOnTermination = $False
$Volume2.VolumeSize = 100
$Volume2.VolumeType = 'standard'

$Mapping2 = New-Object Amazon.EC2.Model.BlockDeviceMapping
$Mapping2.DeviceName = 'xvdf'
$Mapping2.Ebs = $Volume2

$AMI = Get-EC2ImageByName -Name 'WINDOWS_2012_BASE'
$Reservation = New-EC2Instance -ImageId $AMI[0].ImageId -KeyName 'MyKey'
    -InstanceType 't1.micro' -MinCount 1 -MaxCount 1 -BlockDeviceMapping $Mapping1, $Mapping2
$Instance = $Reservation.RunningInstance[0]
```

If you want to use a snapshot to initialize the second volume, you can use the SnapshotId parameter. You can use a snapshot you created or use one of the many already available. For example, the following partial code example will attach the Windows 2012 installation media in Northern Virginia. Note that there are no CD/DVD drives in EC2 instances. (Later in this chapter we will talk more about discovering the numerous snapshots available with AWS.)

```
$Volume2 = New-Object Amazon.EC2.Model.EbsBlockDevice
$Volume2.DeleteOnTermination = $False
$Volume2.VolumeSize = 100
$Volume2.VolumeType = 'standard'
$Volume2.SnapshotId = 'snap-9470c3e7'
```

The last tab of the Storage Device Configuration is for Instance Store (or ephemeral) Volumes. Ephemeral volumes allow you to access the disks in the host server. While EBS volumes are network-attached storage, ephemeral volumes are directly attached storage.

There can be significant performance gains using the directly attached ephemeral volumes–specifically, if you choose an instance that has SSD drives in it. But, this approach comes with a big limitation. The ephemeral drives are not persisted when the instance is stopped. The data is simply deleted. Therefore, ephemeral drives are good only for temporary storage such as a cache or similar item.

If you selected a micro instance, there are no ephemeral volumes. In Figure 4-3, I have chosen an m1.small. Note that all the drives are attached by default. You can remove them if you want, but you don't pay anything extra for them. Just be careful that you're not using the ephemeral drives when you think you're using an EBS volume.

Step 4: Add Storage

Your instance will be launched with the following storage device settings. You can attach additional EBS volumes and instance store volumes to your instance, or edit the settings of the root volume. You can also attach additional EBS volumes after launching an instance, but not instance store volumes. Learn more about storage options in Amazon EC2.

Figure 4-3. Ephemeral volumes

When you create an instance using PowerShell, the ephemeral drives are also attached automatically. There is no reason to remove them, but if you want to you can do so by creating a `BlockDeviceMapping` with `NoDevice=true`. Note in the following partial code example that there is no `EbsBlockDevice` object in this case.

```
$Mapping = New-Object Amazon.EC2.Model.BlockDeviceMapping
$Mapping.DeviceName = 'xvdca'
$Mapping.NoDevice = $true
```

Figure 4-4 shows the disk configuration of a Windows Server 2012 instance with all three volume types: a 30GB root volume, one additional 100GB EBS volume, and a 160GB ephemeral volume. Note that not all instance types have 160GB ephemeral volumes. Some, such as the t1.micro, have none. Others have as much as 48TB of ephemeral storage. Still others have 2-4TB of high performance SSD.

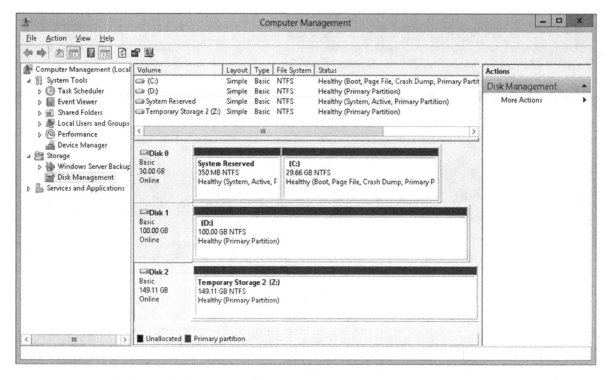

Figure 4-4. *EBS and ephemeral volumes as seen by Windows*

As we have seen, Amazon makes it really easy to manage volumes when launching an instance. Unfortunately, we don't always know exactly what the volumes should look like. We do our best to estimate how big each volume needs to be, but requirements change. New software is installed, usage patterns change, etc. In the next section, we will discuss how to add volumes to a running instance, and in Exercise 4.1 we will resize a volume.

Adding a Volume to a Running Instance

Often you want to add a volume after the instance is already running. You can create a new volume and attach it to a running instance at any time.

To create an instance in the Web Console, click Create Volume on the Volumes page of the EC2 Service. You will need to specify all of the options we discussed earlier, plus the Availability Zone (see Figure 4-5). Remember from Chapter 1 that an availability zone is one of many data centers in a region. Obviously, you can only attach a volume to an instance in the same availability zone.

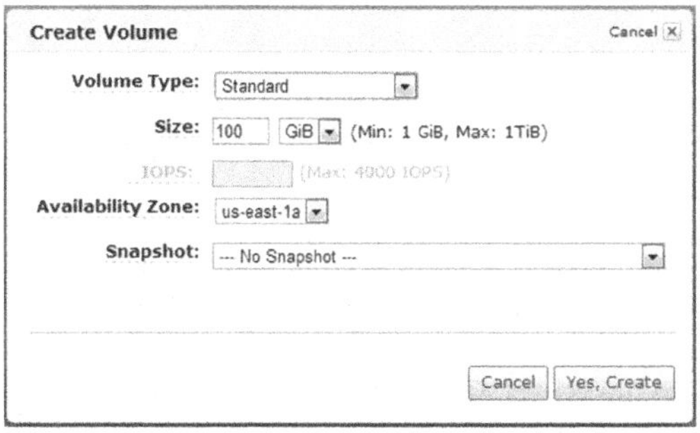

Figure 4-5. *Creating a new volume*

Creating a volume in PowerShell is really simple. The following example creates a new 100GB volume:

```
$Volume = New-EC2Volume -Size 100 -AvailabilityZone us-east-1a -VolumeType standard
```

If you wanted to use a snapshot to initialize your volume, just specify the snapshot ID. This example creates a new 4GB volume with the Windows 2012 install media on it:

```
$Volume = New-EC2Volume -Size 4 -SnapshotId snap-9470c3e7
    -AvailabilityZone us-east-1a -VolumeType standard
```

Once the volume is created, you can attach it to an instance using the Add-EC2Volume command. But, you have to wait for the instance to finish initializing. In the following example, I use a while loop to wait for the volume to become available. Then I attach it to an instance using Add-EC2Volume.

```
$Volume = New-EC2Volume -Size 4 -SnapshotId snap-9470c3e7
    -AvailabilityZone us-east-1a -VolumeType standard
While($Volume.Status -ne 'available') {$Volume = Get-EC2Volume
    -VolumeId $Volume.VolumeId; Start-Sleep -Seconds 15 }
Add-EC2Volume -VolumeId $Volume.VolumeId -InstanceId i-2143eb59 -Device 'xvdg'
```

Once you are done with the volume, you can detach it from the instance using Dismount-EC2Volume. If you no longer need the volume, you can also delete it using Remove-EC2Volume, but you have to wait a few seconds between calls to ensure the dismount is complete.

```
Dismount-EC2Volume -VolumeId $Volume.VolumeId
Start-Sleep -Seconds 60
Remove-EC2Volume -VolumeId $Volume.VolumeId -Force
```

Managing Quality of Service

Some instances–database servers, for example—are more IO intensive than others. AWS offers two options for managing storage quality of service (QoS): EBS-optimized instances and provisioned IOPS. Note that both options result in additional charges.

Remember that EBS volumes are shared network storage. Obviously, there are many AWS tenants competing for the same resources. In addition, the EBS traffic is typically competing for bandwidth with the other network traffic to and from your own instance. EBS-optimized instances get guaranteed network bandwidth between the instance and the EBS volumes. This ensures that you get the expected performance regardless of how congested the network gets.

To create an EBS-optimized instance, add the EbsOptimized flag to the New-EC2Instance command. This setting must be specified at launch and cannot be changed later. In addition, note that not all instance types support EBS optimization. In the following example, I am launching an m1.large with EBS optimization enabled.

```
$AMI = Get-EC2ImageByName -Name 'WINDOWS_2012_BASE'
$Reservation = New-EC2Instance -ImageId $AMI[0].ImageId -KeyName 'MyKey' -InstanceType
    'm1.large' -MinCount 1 -MaxCount 1 -EbsOptimized:$true
$Instance = $Reservation.RunningInstance[0]
```

Provisioned IOPS allows you to specify the number of IO operations per second the EBS disks provide. Remember that in addition to the network, EBS disks are also shared. If you create a standard disk, you get the best performance available at that time. When you choose provisioned IOPS, you can specify the performance you need from the disks. You can specify between 100 and 4000 IOPS, but you cannot change it after the volume is created.

To specify IOPS at launch time, use the EbsBlockDevice object. Simply, set the volume type to "io1" and specify the IOPS desired. In the following example, I am launching a new EBS-optimized instance with a root volume provisioned at 300 IOPS.

```
$Volume = New-Object Amazon.EC2.Model.EbsBlockDevice
$Volume.DeleteOnTermination = $True
$Volume.VolumeSize = 30
$Volume.VolumeType = 'io1'
$volume.IOPS = 300

$Mapping = New-Object Amazon.EC2.Model.BlockDeviceMapping
$Mapping.DeviceName = '/dev/sda1'
$Mapping.Ebs = $Volume

$AMI = Get-EC2ImageByName -Name 'WINDOWS_2012_BASE'
$Reservation = New-EC2Instance -ImageId $AMI[0].ImageId -KeyName 'MyKey'
    -InstanceType 'm1.large' -MinCount 1 -MaxCount 1 -BlockDeviceMapping $Mapping
    -EbsOptimized:$true
$Instance = $Reservation.RunningInstance[0]
```

You can also create a new volume with provisioned IOPS and attach it to an existing instance:

```
$Volume = New-EC2Volume -Size 100 -AvailabilityZone us-east-1a -VolumeType io1 -IOPS 300
```

You could attach this volume to an instance the same way we did in the previous section:

```
Add-EC2Volume -VolumeId $Volume.VolumeId -InstanceId i-2143eb59 -Device 'xvdf'
```

Now we know how to create and manage volumes. We can add volumes when launching a new instance or add a volume to a running instance. We can also manage the quality of service to guarantee performance. Next, we will talk about snapshots. As you will see, snapshots allow us to take a point-in-time copy of a volume.

Working with Snapshots

Snapshots are used to create a point-in-time copy a volume often used for backup and recovery. Creating a new snapshot is really simple. Just call New-EC2Snapshot and pass the ID of the volume. You can also add an optional description. For example, let's assume you are about to do a risky upgrade and you want to take a snapshot of an instance. First, create the snapshot. Note that your volume will have a different ID.

```
$Snapshot = New-EC2Snapshot -VolumeId vol-c3605d89 -Description 'Before upgrade to version 3.22'
```

Now, let's assume that our suspicions were correct, and we need to roll back the change. You already know how to restore a snapshot. We did it in the last section. You just create a new volume using the snapshot. Make sure that you restore the volume in the same availability zone as the instance you want to restore.

```
$Volume = New-EC2Volume -Size 30 -AvailabilityZone us-east-1a -VolumeType standard
    -SnapshotId $Snapshot.SnapshotId
```

You cannot overwrite the contents of an existing volume. A restore always creates a new volume. Therefore, to replace the volume of an existing instance, you have to delete the current volume and replace it with the restored one. Let's delete the volume with the failed install and replace it with the restored volume. Note that this is the root volume and the instance should be stopped first.

```
Dismount-EC2Volume -VolumeId vol-c3605d89
Start-Sleep -Seconds 60
Remove-EC2Volume -VolumeId vol-c3605d89 -Force
Add-EC2Volume -VolumeId $Volume.VolumeId -InstanceId i-2143eb59 -Device '/dev/sda1'
```

Now, just boot the instance, and you are back where you were before the upgrade.

Let's assume the upgrade works the second time, and we want to delete the snapshot. Just use Remove-EC2Snapshot:

```
Remove-EC2Snapshot -SnapshotId $Snapshot.SnapshotId -Force
```

Before we move on, let's talk about backup strategy. You are probably accustomed to taking tape backups each night and storing them offsite. Can a snapshot replace offsite tape backups? Absolutely!

Snapshots are stored in the AWS S3. S3 data is replicated three times across multiple availability zones within a region. This provides 99.999999999% durability.

But, let's say you have a truly critical application that cannot stand an outage. It is possible that an entire region will suffer a power outage or other catastrophe that will bring your application down temporarily. You can optionally copy the snapshot to another region using snapshot copy.

Let's assume we have an application running in Northern Virginia (us-east-1) and want to copy it to Northern California (us-west-1). The copy is always initiated from the destination region. Again, your snapshot ID will be different.

```
Copy-EC2Snapshot -SourceRegion 'us-east-1' -SourceSnapshotId 'snap-9d33c193' -Region 'us-west-1'
    -Description 'Copied from Northern Virginia'
```

Now, in the unlikely case that the all the data in the Northern Virginia region was destroyed, we could recover our application in Northern California.

Managing Public Snapshots

At the beginning of this chapter, we created a volume that included the Windows 2012 install media from a public snapshot. There are numerous snapshots available for your use. You can get a list by running Get-EC2Snapshot, but be warned that there are a lot of snapshots to sift through, and not all of them are from trustworthy sources.

To get a list of snapshots from Amazon, use a filter on owner-alias. This will narrow the list considerably. In the following example, I use a where clause to further filter the list looking for Windows 2012 media.

```
$Filter = New-Object Amazon.EC2.Model.Filter
$Filter.Name = 'owner-alias'
$Filter.Value = 'amazon'
Get-EC2Snapshot -Filter $Filter | Where-Object { $_.Description -like '*Windows 2012*' }
```

In addition to software, Amazon has numerous datasets that can be used for testing. For example, the following command will return U.S. Census data.

```
$Filter = New-Object Amazon.EC2.Model.Filter
$Filter.Name = 'owner-alias'
$Filter.Value = 'amazon'
Get-EC2Snapshot -Filter $Filter | Where-Object { $_.Description -eq '1990 US Census (Windows)' }
```

If you find that you have an interesting dataset that you want to make available to others, you can share your snapshots. You can choose to share with a specific AWS account or with all AWS accounts.

If you want to share your snapshot with everyone, you call Edit-EC2SnapshotAttribute with the UserGroup attribute.

```
Edit-EC2SnapshotAttribute -SnapshotId 'snap-9d33c193' -Attribute 'createVolumePermission'
    -OperationType 'add' -UserGroup 'all'
```

If you prefer to share with a specific account, use the UserId attribute and supply the account number. Note that you must remove the dashes from your account number, for example, if your account number is 1234-1234-1234.

```
Edit-EC2SnapshotAttribute -SnapshotId 'snap-9d33c193' -Attribute 'createVolumePermission'
    -OperationType 'add' -UserId '123412341234'
```

If you want to remove a permission, just set the operation type to "remove." For example:

```
Edit-EC2SnapshotAttribute -SnapshotId 'snap-9d33c193' -Attribute 'createVolumePermission'
    -OperationType 'remove' -UserId '123412341234'
```

And, if you want to remove all permissions to a snapshot, use the Reset-EC2SnapshotAttribute. For example:

```
Reset-EC2SnapshotAttribute -SnapshotId 'snap-9d33c193' -Attribute 'createVolumePermission'
```

In this chapter we learned about volumes and snapshots. We learned how to add volumes to an instance and make copies of a volume using snapshots. In the first exercise, we will build a script to resize a volume. In the second example, we will build a script to back up all the volumes in an account.

EXERCISE 4.1: RESIZING A VOLUME

Over time, you may find that a volume is not big enough, and you need to resize it. You cannot resize a volume, per se, but you can create a copy on a larger volume and then replace it. In this example we will build a script that automates the process.

The script takes two parameters: the id of the volume we want to resize and the new size.

```
Param(
    [string][Parameter(Mandatory=$True)] $VolumeId,
    [int][Parameter(Mandatory=$True)] $NewSize
)
```

Before we start, let's get a reference to the volume so we know how it is attached and what instance it is attached to.

```
$OldVolume = Get-EC2Volume -Volume $VolumeId
$Attachment = $OldVolume.Attachment[0]
```

Next, let's check a few prerequisites. First, we cannot make the volume smaller, or there will not be room for the snapshot when we restore it. Second, the instance must be stopped. Actually, this is not always true, but it is usually a bad idea to remove a volume from a running instance.

```
If($NewSize -lt $OldVolume.Size) { Throw "New volume must be larger than current" }
If($Attachment.InstanceId -ne $null){
    If((Get-EC2InstanceStatus $Attachment.InstanceId) -ne $null){
        Throw "Instance must be stopped"
    }
}
```

Now, we can create a new snapshot of the old volume. Remember to wait until the snapshot completes before you try to restore it.

```
$Snapshot = New-EC2Snapshot -VolumeId $OldVolume.VolumeId
While($Snapshot.Status -ne 'completed') {$Snapshot = Get-EC2Snapshot
    -SnapshotId $Snapshot.SnapshotId; Start-Sleep -Seconds 15 }
```

Next, create a new volume from the snapshot. Notice that I am checking if the old volume is using provisioned IOPS and creating a new volume with the same settings. Once again, remember to wait for the new volume to become available.

```
If($OldVolume.VolumeType -eq 'standard')
{$NewVolume = New-EC2Volume -Size $NewSize -SnapshotId $Snapshot.SnapshotId
    -AvailabilityZone $OldVolume.AvailabilityZone -VolumeType 'standard'}
Else
{$NewVolume = New-EC2Volume -Size $NewSize -SnapshotId $Snapshot.SnapshotId
    -AvailabilityZone $OldVolume.AvailabilityZone -VolumeType 'io1' -IOPS
    $OldVolume.IOPS}
While($NewVolume.Status -ne 'available') {$NewVolume = Get-EC2Volume
    -VolumeId $NewVolume.VolumeId; Start-Sleep -Seconds 15 }
```

If the volume is attached to an instance, let's remove the old volume and attach the new one.

```
If($Attachment.InstanceId -ne $null){
    Dismount-EC2Volume -VolumeId $OldVolume.VolumeId
    Start-Sleep -Seconds 15
    Add-EC2Volume -VolumeId $NewVolume.VolumeId -InstanceId $Attachment.InstanceId
        -Device $Attachment.Device
}
```

Finally, we can delete the old volume and the temporary snapshot we created.

```
Remove-EC2Volume -VolumeId $OldVolume.VolumeId -Force
Remove-EC2Snapshot -SnapshotId $Snapshot.SnapshotId -Force
```

The script is complete, but we are not quite done yet. The EBS volume has been resized, but the Windows partition has not. See Figure 4-6 for a visualization. To extend the partition, log into Windows and start the Computer Management MMC. On the Disk Management page, right-click the partition and select Extend Volume. Just accept the defaults to extend it to its maximum size.

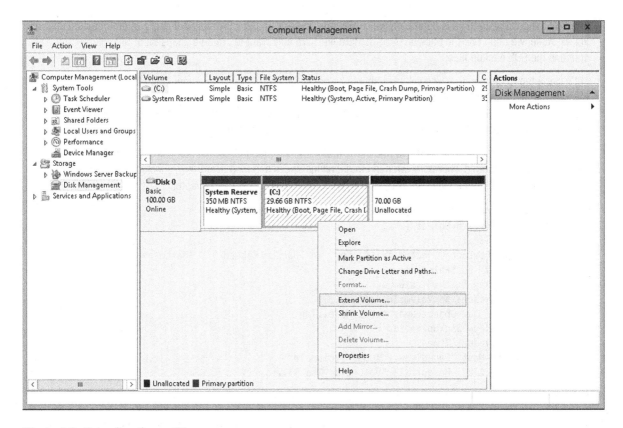

Figure 4-6. *Extending the partition*

In this exercise we resized a volume. Note that AWS does not have native support for resizing. Instead, we created a larger copy of the volume and deleted the original. This is a common pattern with AWS. In Chapter 8 we will use a similar method to resize an instance. In the next exercise, we will create a script to back up all the volumes in your account on a schedule.

EXERCISE 4.2: CREATING A BACKUP AGENT

AWS gives you the tools to back up and recover a volume on demand. This is a good start, but not enough. We really need scheduled backups and the ability to delete snapshots after a specified retention period. Let's create a script that will back up every volume in our AWS account.

Our script will take two parameters: a type parameter used to differentiate backup sets and the number of days to keep the backups. These parameters allow you to run multiple instances of the script with different configurations. For example, I run a daily backup retained for two weeks and a weekly backup retained for 90 days.

```
param(
    [parameter(mandatory=$false)][string]$Type = 'Daily',
    [parameter(mandatory=$false)][string]$RetentionDays = 14
)
```

The first thing we need to do is determine which volumes to back up. We may not want every volume backed up. For example, we don't want to back up our SQL data files. We only want to create a snapshot of the volume that contains the SQL backup files.

Let's use a tag to determine which volumes should be backed up. We will create a new tag, named BackupEnabled. I would prefer to back up all volumes by default. Therefore, the first part of the script will look for any volumes that have not been tagged. If it finds any, it will assume they should be backed up, and set the BackupEnabled tag to true. If you don't want a volume backed up, just change the tag to false.

Unfortunately, you can only use a filter to find items that have been tagged. You cannot use a filter to find items that have not been tagged. Therefore, we need to get all instances and loop over them, checking for the tag. If it does not exist, we add it using the New-EC2Tag we learned about in the last chapter.

```
#First, find any new volumes that have not been marked for backup
Get-EC2Volume | ForEach-Object {
        $HasKey = $False
        $_.Tag | ForEach-Object { If ($_.Key -eq 'BackupEnabled') { $HasKey = $True } }
        If($HasKey -eq $False) {
            #Add Tag to this volume
            $VolumeId = $_.VolumeId
            $Tag = New-Object amazon.EC2.Model.Tag
            $Tag.Key='BackupEnabled'
            $Tag.Value='True'
            Write-Host "Found new volume: $VolumeId"
            New-EC2Tag -ResourceId $VolumeId -Tag $Tag
        }
}
```

Now that our volumes are tagged, we can use a filter find all the volumes that need to be backed up. Then we can loop over the volumes and take a snapshot.

```
$Filter = New-Object Amazon.EC2.Model.Filter
$Filter.Name = 'tag:BackupEnabled'
$Filter.Value = 'True'
Get-EC2Volume -Filter $Filter | ForEach-Object {
        #Backup routine goes here
}
```

If there is a disaster, we may not be able to access the metadata about which snapshot came from which instance. Therefore, if the volume is currently attached to an instance, we should record the name and attachment information in the snapshot description. The following code uses the Get-EC2Instance command we learned about in the last chapter to get information about the instance.

```
if($_.Attachment){
        $Device = $_.Attachment[0].Device
        $InstanceId = $_.Attachment[0].InstanceId
        $Reservation = Get-EC2Instance $InstanceId
        $Instance = $Reservation.RunningInstance |
                Where-Object {$_.InstanceId -eq $InstanceId}
        $Name = ($Instance.Tag | Where-Object { $_.Key -eq 'Name' }).Value
        $Description = "Currently attached to $Name as $Device;"
}
```

Now, we can create the snapshot as discussed earlier in the chapter.

```
$Volume = $_.VolumeId
Write-Host "Creating snapshot of volume: $Volume; $Description"
$Snapshot = New-EC2Snapshot $Volume -Description "$Type backup of volume $Volume;
    $Description"
```

We should also tag the snapshots so we know which were created by our script. We don't want our script to delete snapshots it didn't create. For example, if a developer takes a snapshot before rolling out a new version of an application, he may not want that to be deleted after two weeks. Let's add a tag called BackupType used to differentiate scheduled backups from any others.

```
#Add a tag so we can distinquish this shanpshot from all the others
$Tag = New-Object amazon.EC2.Model.Tag
$Tag.Key='BackupType'
$Tag.Value=$Type
New-EC2Tag -ResourceId $Snapshot.SnapshotID -Tag $Tag
```

Great! The routine to create a snapshot is done. Now we just have to create a routine to delete old backups after the retention period expires. In this routine, I find all of the snapshots that were created by the backup agent, using the BackupType tag. Then, I check how old it is. If it is older than the retention period, the snapshot is deleted.

```
Function PurgeBackups($Type, $RetentionDays)
{
    #Delete and snapshots created by this tool, that are older than the specified number of days
    $Filter = New-Object Amazon.EC2.Model.Filter
    $Filter.Name = 'tag:BackupType'
    $Filter.Value = $Type
    $RetentionDate = ([DateTime]::Now).AddDays(-$RetentionDays)
    Get-EC2Snapshot -Filter $filter | Where-Object { [datetime]::Parse($_.StartTime)
                        -lt $RetentionDate} | ForEach-Object {
        $SnapshotId = $_.SnapshotId
        Write-Host "Removing snapshot: $SnapshotId"
        Remove-EC2Snapshot -SnapshotId $SnapshotId -Force
    }
}
```

At this point all we have to do is schedule the script to run once a day. I have this script deployed on an AWS instance. The instance is configured with an IAM role (as we discussed in Chapter 2), and I saved the script as C:\AWS\DailyBackup.ps1.

To schedule the job, log into the instance that is going to run the script and open Task Scheduler. Then follow these steps:

1. Click the Create a Basic Task link.

2. Name the task "DailyBackup" and click Next.

3. Choose Daily, and click Next.

4. Pick a time of day for the script to run and click Next.

5. Choose Start a Program and click Next.

6. Fill in the next screen, as shown in Figure 4-7, and click Next.

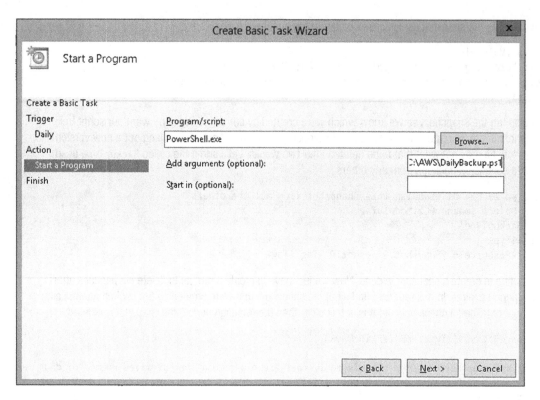

Figure 4-7. *Configure a scheduled task*

7.   Check the "Open the properties dialog . . ." option and click Finish.

8.   Click the Change User or Group button.

9.   Change the user to NETWORK SERVICE, as shown in Figure 4-8, and click OK.

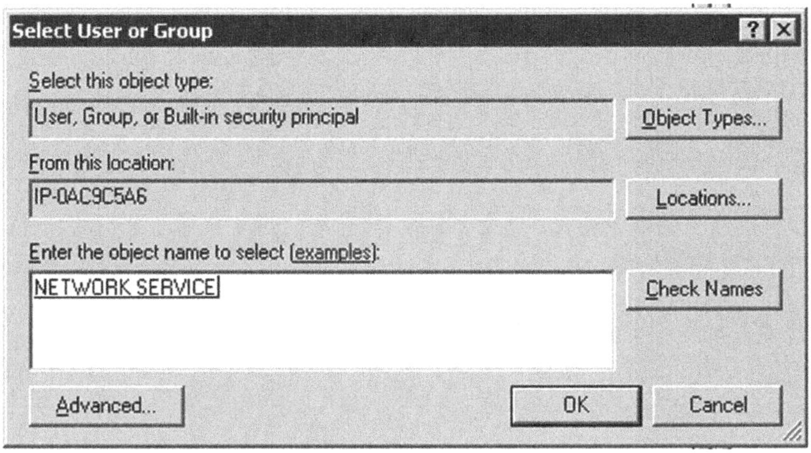

Figure 4-8. *Configure user or group*

10. Click OK to close the wizard.

In this chapter we created a scheduled task that uses snapshots to create a backup of all volumes. Let's stop and reflect on how easy that was. A few lines of code just replaced backup tapes forever. You don't need an operator on staff after hours to put tapes in servers. You don't need to manage tape storage and rotation. And, if you added a call to Copy-EC2Snapshot, you will never have to ship tapes to an offsite storage location again.

Summary

In this chapter we examined volumes and snapshots. We learned how to customize and add additional volumes at launch as well modify volumes after launch. We learned how to back up and restore a volume using highly durable snapshots and copy snapshots to another region for even greater durability.

In the first example, we created a script to resize a volume. You can use this script anytime you are running out of space on an existing instance. In the second example, we created a scheduled task that backs up all the volumes in your account. You can use this script to replace tape backups.

In the next chapter, we will learn how to configure a Virtual Private Cloud (VPC). VPC allows you to create your own private network configuration in the cloud. We will discuss subnets, routing, and security.

CHAPTER 5

■ ■ ■

Virtual Private Cloud

In this chapter we are going to discuss Virtual Private Cloud (VPC). VPC allows you to configure a custom network topology, as well as manage IP routing and security. A network topology is the structure of the network and controls how data flows between nodes.

This chapter will be a bit different from the prior ones. On one hand, the commands are relatively simple. Most only have one or two parameters. On the other hand, these primitive commands can be woven together in countless ways to create a seemingly endless combination of network topologies.

Throughout this chapter, we will continue to explore the Web Console and the individual PowerShell commands. In previous chapters, each section stood alone. All the sections in this chapter will build upon each other and come together at the end to produce a single solution, pictured in Figure 5-1.

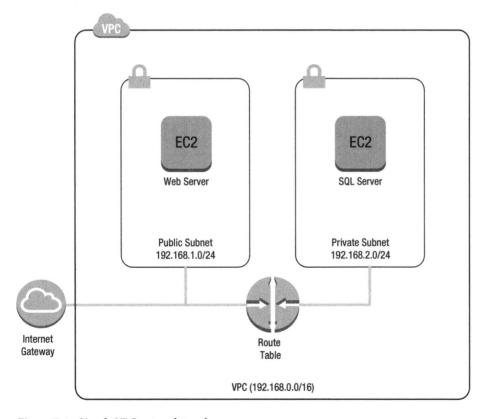

Figure 5-1. *Simple VPC network topology*

Figure 5-1 shows a simple network with two subnets. The public subnet is Internet accessible. We would use the public subnet to host our web servers. The private subnet is not connected to the Internet and is used to host our database. This is a common pattern in IT. Typically we put the web servers in the "DMZ" and keep the database behind the firewall.

■ **Note**   This chapter often takes a roundabout solution in order to show you each command. For example, I could have created a new route table for the public subnet rather than altering the Main route table and then creating a new main table. But, then I would not have reason to talk about deleting route tables and altering associations. If you want a streamlined script, exercise 5.1 includes a complete script that will build the network pictured in Figure 5-1 in a much more direct manner than I followed throughout the chapter.

Let's get started with the first step in this process: creating a VPC.

Creating a VPC

VPC allows you to create one or more networks of EC2 instances. Note that each account can have up to five VPCs per region. For example, you can implement a layered security approach or span multiple availability zones for high availability. This chapter and Chapter 6 focus on security while Chapter 8 focuses on high availability.

As usual, let's start in the Web Console and then move to PowerShell. In the Web Console, from the Services dropdown at the top of the screen, choose VPC. We will build up our VPC in stages so we can discuss each piece. Note that AWS offers a VPC wizard, which we are not going to use. The second option in the VPC wizard, "VPC with Public and Private Subnets," is similar to the network we are going to create in this chapter.

To create a new VPC, navigate to the Your VPCs page and click the Create VPC button. The Create VPC dialog has only one tab (see Figure 5-2). Enter the CIDR range you wish to use.

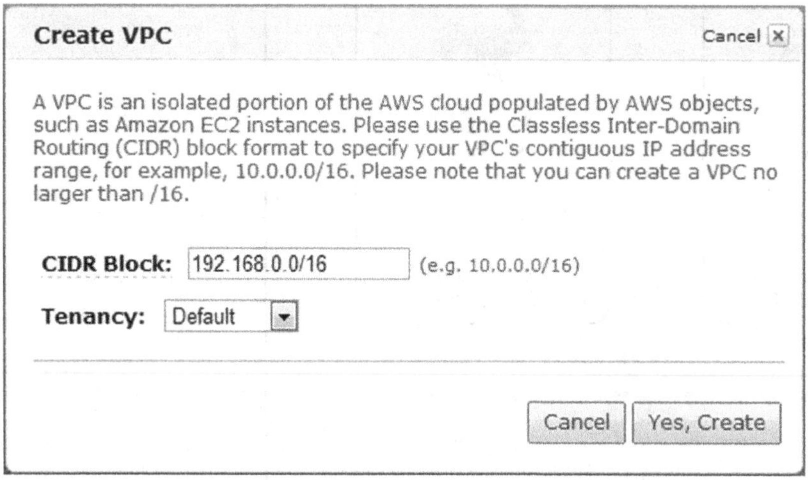

Figure 5-2. *The Create VPC dialog box*

You can provision a CIDR block up to a "/16." A "/16" network will give you about 65,535 hosts. You can use any network, but note that VPC addresses are not Internet accessible. Your hosts will access the Internet using Network Address Translation (NAT). Therefore, you should use a private (non-routable) segment such as 10.0.0.0/8, 172.16.0.0/12, or 192.168.0.0/16.

Most organizations are already using the 10.0.0.0 network. Therefore, I tend to use 10.0.0.0 for any VPC that will be attached to the corporate network. AWS uses 172.16.0.0 for the default VPC that is replacing EC2 Classic in some regions. That leaves 192.168.0.0. I like to use 192.168.0.0 for VPCs that are neither attached to the corporate network nor the default VPC. This makes it easy to tell which VPC is which later.

The Tenancy option allows you to provision a dedicated VPC. If you choose a dedicated VPC, you can only launch dedicated instances into that VPC. A dedicated instance runs on dedicated hardware that is not shared with other AWS clients. This is an expensive option and not one I have used often.

The equivalent PowerShell is equally simple.

```
$VPC = New-EC2Vpc -CidrBlock '192.168.0.0/16'
$VPC.VpcId
```

As you can see, creating a VPC is really easy. Before we can launch a machine into the VPC, we need to carve it up into multiple subnets. In the next section we will create a subnet.

Creating a Subnet

Now that we have our VPC created, we want to carve it up into multiple subnets to host our instances. (We will add hosts to the subnet in Chapter 6.)

Each subnet is assigned to an availability zone. Remember from Chapter 1 that an availability zone is one of multiple data centers that comprise a region. We can use multiple availability zones to ensure high availability. (I will cover high availability in Chapter 8.)

Each subnet is also assigned a subset of the VPC's address space, again using CIDR notation. Here I am using a "/24." This will divide the VPC into 256 subnets of about 256 hosts each.

RESERVED IPS

In reality, we will not get 256 hosts per subnet when using "/24." The first four and last addresses are reserved. The reserved addresses are used as follows:

First - Network ID

Second - Gateway

Third - DHCP and DNS services

Fourth - Reserved for future use

Last - Network Broadcast

Creating a subnet using the Web Console is relatively easy. You simply identify the availability zone and CIDR range (see Figure 5-3).

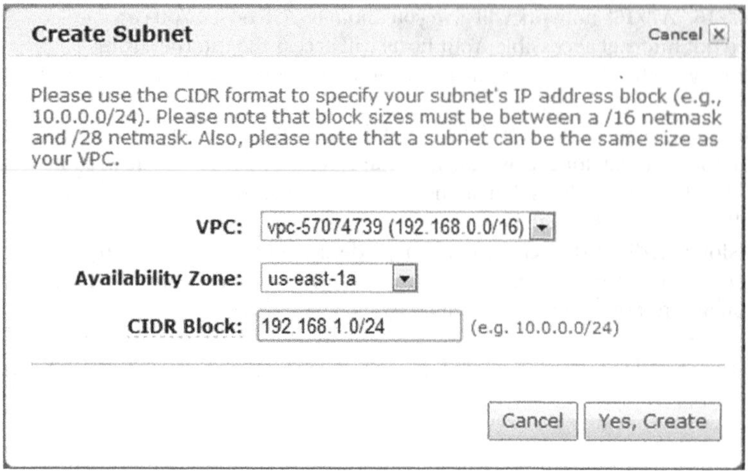

Create Subnet   Cancel ⊠

Please use the CIDR format to specify your subnet's IP address block (e.g., 10.0.0.0/24). Please note that block sizes must be between a /16 netmask and /28 netmask. Also, please note that a subnet can be the same size as your VPC.

           VPC: vpc-57074739 (192.168.0.0/16) ▼

Availability Zone: us-east-1a ▼

   CIDR Block: 192.168.1.0/24   (e.g. 10.0.0.0/24)

                              Cancel   Yes, Create

Figure 5-3. *The Create Subnet dialog box*

Creating a subnet with PowerShell is equally easy. Just use New-EC2Subnet. This command takes the same parameters as the Web Console: the VPC, availability zone, and CIDR block.

```
New-EC2Subnet -VpcId 'vpc-57074739' -CidrBlock '192.168.2.0/24' -AvailabilityZone 'us-east-1a'
```

You can list the subnets with the Get-EC2Subnet command. Unfortunately, Get-EC2Subnet does not have a VPC parameter. This is true of all the VPC-related commands. If you want to list the subnets in a given VPC you have to use a filter. For example:

```
$VPCFilter = New-Object Amazon.EC2.Model.Filter
$VPCFilter.Name = 'vpc-id'
$VPCFilter.Value = 'vpc-57074739'
Get-EC2Subnet -Filter $VPCFilter
```

Of course you can delete a subnet using the Remove-EC2Subnet command. Note that if the subnet has instances assigned, the remove command will fail.

```
Remove-EC2Subnet -SubnetId 'subnet-0a9ace64' -Force
```

At this point we have a VPC with a single subnet. We could launch an instance into this subnet, but you would not be able to connect to the instance because our VPC has no connection to the outside world. In the next section, we will add an Internet gateway, which is a connection to the Internet.

Creating an Internet Gateway

At this point your VPC is isolated from the world. You can launch an instance, but it cannot connect to the Internet. More importantly, you cannot connect to it either. To create a connection to the Internet, you need an Internet gateway.

Think of the Internet gateway like your router at home. It connects all of the instances in your VPC to the Internet using Network Address Translation (NAT). While your home network probably only has only one public IP address, the EC2 Internet Gateway allows you to assign a public IP address to each instance. These public IP addresses are known as Elastic IP addresses. (We will be assigning Elastic IP addresses in Chapter 6.)

The process of creating an Internet gateway is the same using the Web Console or PowerShell. First you create a new gateway and then you connect it to a VPC. In PowerShell it looks like this:

```
$InternetGateway = New-EC2InternetGateway
Add-EC2InternetGateway -InternetGatewayId $InternetGateway.InternetGatewayId -VpcId
    'vpc-57074739'
```

Despite the two-step process you can only connect the gateway to one VPC at a time. If necessary, you can disconnect the gateway from VPC and connect it to another.

At this point you have a VPC with a subnet and Internet connection. In the next section we will configure routing within the VPC.

Managing Route Tables

Now that we have an Internet connection, we need to tell instances how to find that connection. We use routes to do this. Every subnet is associated with a route table that tells an instance the best way to reach a given destination.

■ **Note**   Routing is a fairly complicated topic. If you are not familiar with IP routing, I recommend reading up on the basics.

When we create the VPC, AWS created a default route table (see Figure 5-4). Notice that the route table is associated with 0 subnets; this is deceiving. The route table is not explicitly associated with any subnets, but it is identified as the Main route table in the VPC. Subnets will use the Main route table unless you explicitly configure them to use another route table. Therefore, all of the subnets in our VPC are using this route table.

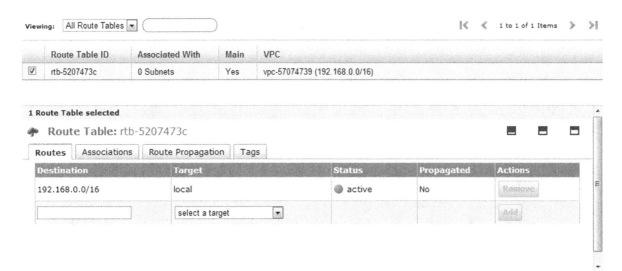

Figure 5.4. *Sample route table displayed in the Web Console*

The Main route table has only one route by default. This route says that all traffic destined for 192.168.0.0/16 should stay local. Remember that our VPC is using the range 192.168.0.0/16. In other words, only local traffic is configured by default; there is no route to the Internet.

To list route tables in PowerShell, use Get-EC2RouteTable. If you have more than one VPC, use a filter to display only those route tables in a given VPC.

```
$VPCFilter = New-Object Amazon.EC2.Model.Filter
$VPCFilter.Name = 'vpc-id'
$VPCFilter.Value = 'vpc-57074739'
Get-EC2RouteTable -Filter $VPCFilter
```

Each route table has a Routes property that contains a list of the individual routes. It is easier to read if you pipe the list to Format-Table:

```
$VPCFilter = New-Object Amazon.EC2.Model.Filter
$VPCFilter.Name = 'vpc-id'
$VPCFilter.Value = 'vpc-57074739'
 (Get-EC2RouteTable -Filter $VPCFilter).Routes | Format-Table
```

If you want to get a reference to the Main route table, use the association.main filter with a value of true. Note that true will be passed as a string and must be specified in lower case.

```
$VPCFilter = New-Object Amazon.EC2.Model.Filter
$VPCFilter.Name = 'vpc-id'
$VPCFilter.Value = 'vpc-57074739'
$IsDefaultFilter = New-Object Amazon.EC2.Model.Filter
$IsDefaultFilter.Name = 'association.main'
$IsDefaultFilter.Value = 'true'
$DefaultRouteTable = Get-EC2RouteTable -Filter $VPCFilter, $IsDefaultFilter
$DefaultRouteTable.Routes | Format-Table
```

Now we want to tell our instances about the Internet gateway. To do this, we add a new route to the route table. In Figure 5-5, I am adding a route to 0.0.0.0/0 to the Internet gateway we created.

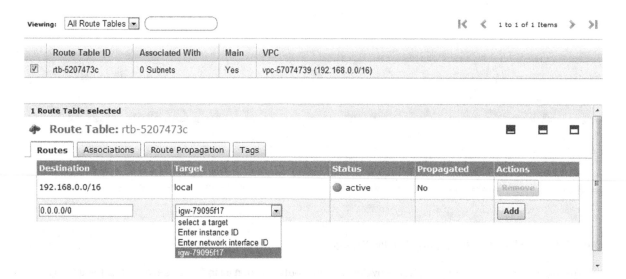

Figure 5-5. *Adding a new route to a route table*

The route table works like this. Whenever a request is received, AWS looks at the route table to determine what to do with it. It tries to match the request with the most specific route. The larger the number after the forward slash, the more specific the route. Since the rule we just added has a zero after the slash, this rule will be evaluated last.

For example, assume a request is destined for www.google.com at 173.194.43.2. AWS will first check it against the most specific rule. In this case the 192.168.0.0/16 is the most specific. The rule says to check if the first 16 bits of the destination (e.g., 173.194) match the route (192.168). Since they do not match, AWS tries the next route. The next route has a zero after the slash. Since there are zero bits to match, this rule always matches (this is called the default route). Therefore, AWS routes the request to the Internet gateway.

To add a new route to the route table using PowerShell, use the New-EC2Route command.

```
New-EC2Route -RouteTableId 'rtb-52007473c' -DestinationCidrBlock '0.0.0.0/0'
    -GatewayId 'igw-79095f17'
```

You can also create a route that points to a specific instance. You might do this if you want to take specific actions on the traffic. For example, you might want to run a software firewall or web proxy on an EC2 instance. AWS offers many such virtual appliances in the marketplace. There is an example of this in the exercises at the end of Chapter 6.

To route traffic to a specific instance in PowerShell, use InstanceId rather than GatewayId.

```
New-EC2Route -RouteTableId 'rtb-52007473c'  -DestinationCidrBlock '0.0.0.0/0' -InstanceId
    'i-12345678'
```

Not all subnets in a VPC need to use the same route table. You can create a custom route table for each subnet. A common use of this is to create a private subnet that does not have Internet connectivity, and a public subnet that does. Security standards often require that databases be hosted in a private subnet without Internet connectivity.

Let's create a new route table that does not have Internet connectivity.

```
New-EC2RouteTable -VpcId 'vpc-57074739'
```

Now that we have more than one route table, we need to associate the subnet with a route table. To this we use a route table association.

```
Register-EC2RouteTable -RouteTableId 'rtb-d65006b8' -SubnetId 'subnet-334e185d'
```

At this point, we have two route tables in our VPC. Remember that we added Internet connectivity to our Main route. This is the route that will be used by default. It would be better security practice to have our Main route table be private. This way, if we create a new subnet, it defaults to the subnet without Internet access and only gets it if we explicitly assign it to the public subnet.

Changing the Main route table is less than intuitive because there is no command to change the Main route table. First, you have to find the Main route table using filters. Then, you find the Main route table association. Typically, an association maps a route table to a subnet, but the main association is special in that the subnet is blank.

```
$VPCFilter = New-Object Amazon.EC2.Model.Filter
$VPCFilter.Name = 'vpc-id'
$VPCFilter.Value = 'vpc-57074739'
$IsDefaultFilter = New-Object Amazon.EC2.Model.Filter
$IsDefaultFilter.Name = 'association.main'
$IsDefaultFilter.Value = 'true'
$MainRouteTable = Get-EC2RouteTable -Filter $VPCFilter, $IsDefaultFilter
$Association = $MainRouteTable.Associations | Where-Object {$_.Main -eq $True}
$Association
```

This command returns:

```
RouteTableAssociationId   RouteTableId   SubnetId   Main
-----------------------   ------------   --------   ----
rtbassoc-5307473d         rtb-5207473c              True
```

Since there is no command to change the Main route table, we have to reassign the existing association to a new route table using the Set-EC2RouteTableAssociation command.

```
Set-EC2RouteTableAssociation -AssociationId $Association.RouteTableAssociationId
    -RouteTableId 'rtb-d65006b8'
```

I know that was a lot of material very quickly. I strongly recommend that you work through the examples at the end of this chapter to better understand EC2 routing. Let's review our progress so far. We created a VPC, added a subnet and Internet gateway, and configured routing. In the next section, we will configure network security.

Managing Network ACLs

Network Access Control Lists (ACLs) allow you to control what types of traffic can enter and leave a subnet. Each ACL contains an ordered list of inbound and outbound rules. If you have worked with EC2 Classic in the past, you are likely familiar with Security Groups. ACLs and Security Groups are similar in that they allow you to filter traffic on the network. (We will cover security groups in Chapter 6.) The main differences are the following:

1. ACLs are applied to a network segment, while security groups are applied to individual instances.

2. Security Groups are stateful while ACLs are stateless. This means ACLs require a rule for both the request and response, while security groups only require a request rule.

AWS creates a default ACL for each new VPC. As you can see in Figure 5-6, the default ACL contains two rules. The first allows all traffic to anywhere and second denies all traffic to anywhere. Rules are executed in order. Therefore, the first rule is always applied and the default behavior is to allow all traffic to and from anywhere. Obviously it is a good idea to create more conservative rules.

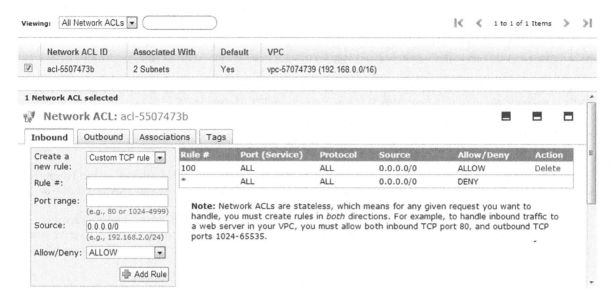

Figure 5-6. *Network ACLs*

To get the same list using PowerShell, use the `Get-EC2NetworkACL` command. Again, I am using a filter to only return the ACLs from one VPC because you may have more than one VPC in a given region. Notice that there are both inbound (egress=false) and outbound (egress=true) rules. Figure 5-6 was displaying the inbound rules only.

```
$VPCFilter = New-Object Amazon.EC2.Model.Filter
$VPCFilter.Name = 'vpc-id'
$VPCFilter.Value = 'vpc-57074739'
$ACL = Get-EC2NetworkAcl -Filter $VPCFilter
$ACL.Entries | Format-Table
```

This code returns the following output:

```
RuleNumber Protocol RuleAction Egress CidrBlock Icmp PortRange
---------- -------- ---------- ------ --------- ---- ---------
100        -1       allow      True   0.0.0.0/0
32767      -1       deny       True   0.0.0.0/0
100        -1       allow      False  0.0.0.0/0
32767      -1       deny       False  0.0.0.0/0
```

As you can see from the two rules numbered 100, the default ACL allows all traffic into and out of the subnet. Now let's learn how to modify the default rules.

Securing the Public Subnet

It is bad practice to allow all traffic into our network. Let's assume that we are running a web site). The public subnet hosts a web server and the private subnet hosts a database. We want to allow the minimum set of traffic possible into each subnet.

75

First let's remove the rule 100 that allows all traffic. Note that I am removing both the inbound and outbound rules.

```
Remove-EC2NetworkAclEntry -NetworkAclId acl-5507473b -RuleNumber 100 -Egress $true -Force
Remove-EC2NetworkAclEntry -NetworkAclId acl-5507473b -RuleNumber 100 -Egress $false -Force
```

Now let's add rules for the public subnet. First, we need to allow HTTP traffic from the Internet. Remember that 0.0.0.0/0 means traffic from anywhere. Also, HTTP uses port 80 and TCP is protocol 6.

```
New-EC2NetworkAclEntry -NetworkAclId acl-5507473b -RuleNumber 100 -CidrBlock '0.0.0.0/0'
    -Egress $False -PortRange_From 80 -PortRange_To 80 -Protocol 6 -RuleAction 'Allow'
```

Remember that ACLs are stateless. This means that we need to create separate rules for the request and response. Security groups on the other hand are stateful. You only need to create a rule for the request, and AWS takes care of the response.

When the browser makes a request to our web server, the destination port is 80. But, there is also a source port, called the ephemeral port. The ephemeral port is chosen at random in the range 49152 to 65535. The web server sends its reply back to the ephemeral port the request was received from. Therefore, we need a corresponding egress rule for the reply:

```
New-EC2NetworkAclEntry -NetworkAclId 'acl-5507473b' -RuleNumber 100 -CidrBlock '0.0.0.0/0'
    -Egress $True -PortRange_From 49152 -PortRange_To 65535 -Protocol 6 -RuleAction 'Allow'
```

The web server also needs to talk to the database. Let's assume the database server is running Microsoft SQL Server and is located in the private subnet. SQL Server uses port 1433 and the CIDR range for the private subnet is 192.168.2.0/24. Therefore, we need to allow the request on port 1433, and the response in the ephemeral range.

```
New-EC2NetworkAclEntry -NetworkAclId 'acl-5507473b' -RuleNumber 200 -CidrBlock '192.168.2.0/24'
    -Egress $True -PortRange_From 1433 -PortRange_To 1433 -Protocol 6 -RuleAction 'Allow'
```

```
New-EC2NetworkAclEntry -NetworkAclId 'acl-5507473b' -RuleNumber 200 -CidrBlock '192.168.2.0/24'
    -Egress $False -PortRange_From 49152 -PortRange_To 65535 -Protocol 6 -RuleAction 'Allow'
```

Notice that I have incremented the rule number by 100. It is common to increment by 100 to allow room to insert additional rules later. Remember that the rules are always executed in order, until a rule is found that either allows or denies the traffic. Before moving on to the private subnet, let's spend a minute looking at deny rules.

You may have noticed that we allow HTTP traffic from any source (i.e., 0.0.0.0/0). This includes the private subnet. This is not really what we intended. We wanted to allow traffic from the Internet, but not within the VPC. We can block this by adding a deny rule that fires before rule 100.

```
New-EC2NetworkAclEntry -NetworkAclId 'acl-5507473b' -RuleNumber 50 -CidrBlock '192.168.0.0/16'
    -Egress $False -PortRange_From 80 -PortRange_To 80 -Protocol 6 -RuleAction 'Deny'
```

```
New-EC2NetworkAclEntry -NetworkAclId 'acl-5507473b' -RuleNumber 50 -CidrBlock '192.168.0.0/16'
    -Egress $True -PortRange_From 49152 -PortRange_To 65535 -Protocol 6 -RuleAction 'Deny'
```

In the preceding example, I have added a new rule with rule number 50. This rule will fire first. If a request is received from within the VPC, the request will be denied and processing will stop. If the request is received from outside the VPC, this rule will not match and rule 100 will fire next. Rule 100 will then allow the request and processing will stop.

Now let's look at what would happen if we received a request we didn't anticipate. We didn't plan for HTTPS requests. If we received a request on port 443, rules 50, 100, and 200 would again fire in order, but none would match because none of the existing rules are for port 443. Next, rule 32767 would fire and deny the request. Rule 32767 is the max rule number. It is always present and cannot be deleted. In other words, if none of the rules that we create match, the traffic is always denied.

FINDING THE NEXT ACL RULE NUMBER

When you create new rules, you often need to know the largest rule number in the list so you can use the next number. Here is a quick script to find the largest egress rule in PowerShell.

```
$MaxAcl = ((Get-EC2NetworkAcl -NetworkAclId acl-5507473b).Entries | Where-Object
    {$_.Egress -and $_.RuleNumber -lt 32767 } | Measure-Object RuleNumber
    -Maximum).Maximum
$NextAcl = $MaxAcl + 100
```

Now that we have the public subnet configured, let's look at the private subnet.

Securing the Private Subnet

At this point we have our public subnet locked down, but we have ignored our private subnet. Even worse, we have been applying the rules to the only access control list in the VPC. This means that the rules we applied to the public subnet have also been applied to the private one that is going to host our database server. Let's fix this.

First, let's create a new access control list for the private subnet. In PowerShell, we use the New-EC2NetworkAcl command.

```
$ACL = New-EC2NetworkAcl -VpcId 'vpc-57074739'
$ACL.Entries | Format-Table
```

This code returns the following output:

```
RuleNumber Protocol RuleAction Egress CidrBlock Icmp PortRange
---------- -------- ---------- ------ --------- ---- ---------
32767      -1       deny       True   0.0.0.0/0
32767      -1       deny       False  0.0.0.0/0
```

Notice that the list is effectively empty. The only entries are the default deny rules. This is different from the ACL that was created when we created the VPC. That ACL allowed all traffic, and this one denies all traffic.

Let's add rules to allow all traffic in and out of our private subnet. This may seem like we are cutting corners. Why don't we create specific rules like we did for the public subnet? We could, and we probably should, but remember that the public subnet is Internet accessible. The public subnet is much more likely to be attacked. It is common to put much stronger controls on the public subnets and leave the private subnets free to communicate among one another. Think of this like your house. You likely have a much better lock on your front door than you do on your bedroom. For now let's keep it simple and allow all traffic.

```
New-EC2NetworkAclEntry -NetworkAclId $ACL.NetworkAclId -RuleNumber 100 -CidrBlock '0.0.0.0/0'
    -Egress $True -Protocol '-1' -RuleAction 'Allow'
New-EC2NetworkAclEntry -NetworkAclId $ACL.NetworkAclId -RuleNumber 100 -CidrBlock '0.0.0.0/0'
    -Egress $False -Protocol '-1' -RuleAction 'Allow'
```

Now, all we have to do is attach this ACL to the private subnet. The process is similar to changing the Main route table. First, we use a filter to find the ACL associated with the subnet. Then, we get a reference to the association for the ACL. Next, we get a reference to the new ACL we want to assign to the subnet. Finally, we use the Set-EC2NetworkAclAssociation to point the association to the new ACL.

```
$SubnetFilter = New-Object Amazon.EC2.Model.Filter
$SubnetFilter.Name = 'association.subnet-id'
$SubnetFilter.Value = 'subnet-334e185d'
$OldACL = Get-EC2NetworkAcl -Filter $SubnetFilter
$OldAssociation = $OldACL.Associations | Where-Object { $_.SubnetId -eq 'subnet-334e185d' }
Set-EC2NetworkAclAssociation -AssociationId $OldAssociation.NetworkAclAssociationId
    -NetworkAclId acl- db9dc0b5'
```

Working with ACLs can be very tedious. You must very careful to identify the traffic in both directions. In Chapter 6 we will discuss security groups, which offer a much easier solution to filter traffic to and from individual instances. Before we end this chapter, let's have a quick look at configuring DHCP.

Managing DHCP

VPC uses Dynamic Host Configuration Protocol (DHCP) to configure the instances in the VPC. Although you are likely familiar with DHCP, it works a bit differently at AWS.

First, IP addresses are assigned to the instance for life. Once a primary IP address is assigned, it cannot be changed, and cannot be assigned to another instance until the instance is terminated. (Note that you can add and remove secondary IP addresses, which we will do in Chapter 6.)

Second, you cannot change the network configuration from within the instance. AWS does not use layer two broadcasts to discover network configuration changes. Rather it depends on the instance metadata to make forwarding decisions. If you change an IP address from within Windows, AWS will not learn of the change, and traffic will not be forwarded to the server.

In addition to managing IP addresses, DHCP is also used to configure DNS, NetBIOS, and Network Time Protocol (NTP). AWS offers DNS and NTP services, but if you prefer, you can choose to override the default settings to use another service.

Let's imagine that we are going to launch an Active Directory (AD) server into our private subnet. Our AD instance will be assigned the IP address 192.168.2.10. The domain name is brianbeach.com. We want AD to be the primary DNS, NetBIOS, and NTP server. Using the Web Console, you simply create a new option set and then associate it with a VPC (see Figure 5-7).

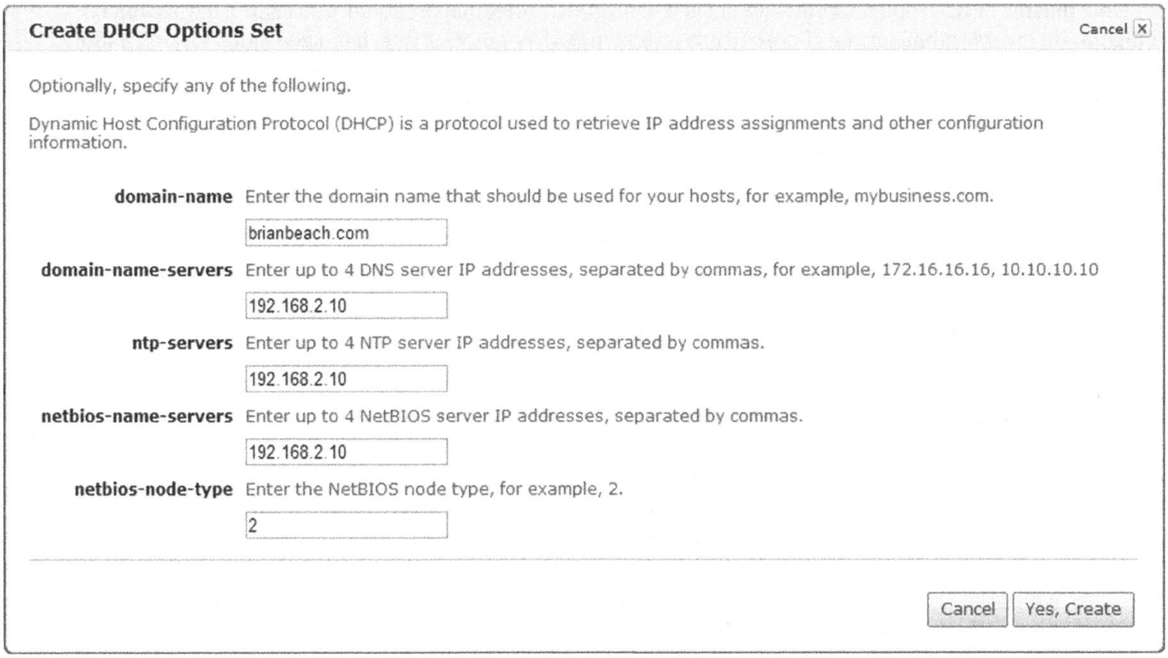

Create DHCP Options Set   Cancel [X]

Optionally, specify any of the following.

Dynamic Host Configuration Protocol (DHCP) is a protocol used to retrieve IP address assignments and other configuration information.

domain-name	Enter the domain name that should be used for your hosts, for example, mybusiness.com.
	brianbeach.com
domain-name-servers	Enter up to 4 DNS server IP addresses, separated by commas, for example, 172.16.16.16, 10.10.10.10
	192.168.2.10
ntp-servers	Enter up to 4 NTP server IP addresses, separated by commas.
	192.168.2.10
netbios-name-servers	Enter up to 4 NetBIOS server IP addresses, separated by commas.
	192.168.2.10
netbios-node-type	Enter the NetBIOS node type, for example, 2.
	2

Cancel   Yes, Create

Figure 5-7. *Creating a new DHCP option set*

To change the DHCP configuration using PowerShell, we first create an array of configuration options. Then, we use New-EC2DHCPOption to create a new option set. Finally, we associate to the new option set with our VPC using Register-EC2DhcpOption:

```
$Domain = New-Object Amazon.EC2.Model.DhcpConfiguration
$Domain.Key = 'domain-name'
$Domain.Value = 'brianbeach.com'
$DNS = New-Object Amazon.EC2.Model.DhcpConfiguration
$DNS.Key = 'domain-name-servers'
$DNS.Value = '192.168.2.10'
$NTP = New-Object Amazon.EC2.Model.DhcpConfiguration
$NTP.Key = 'ntp-servers'
$NTP.Value = '192.168.2.10'
$NetBios= New-Object Amazon.EC2.Model.DhcpConfiguration
$NetBios.Key = 'netbios-name-servers'
$NetBios.Value = '192.168.2.10'
$NetBiosType = New-Object Amazon.EC2.Model.DhcpConfiguration
$NetBiosType.Key = 'netbios-node-type'
$NetBiosType.Value = '2'
$DHCP = New-EC2DHCPOption -DhcpConfiguration $Domain, $DNS, $NTP, $NetBios, $NetBiosType
Register-EC2DhcpOption -DhcpOptionsId $DHCP.DhcpOptionsId -VpcId 'vpc-57074739'
```

Note that the DHCP configuration is associated with a VPC rather than a subnet. You cannot have a different configuration in each subnet. If you choose to use your own DNS or other service, it is a good idea to launch more than one of each service for high availability. For instance, you might have two AD servers. One uses IP 192.168.2.10, and one uses 192.168.12.10. To configure this, just include both in the Options array. For example:

```
$Domain = New-Object Amazon.EC2.Model.DhcpConfiguration
$Domain.Key = 'domain-name'
$Domain.Value = 'brianbeach.com'
$DNS1 = New-Object Amazon.EC2.Model.DhcpConfiguration
$DNS1.Key = 'domain-name-servers'
$DNS1.Value = '192.168.2.10'
$DNS2 = New-Object Amazon.EC2.Model.DhcpConfiguration
$DNS2.Key = 'domain-name-servers'
$DNS2.Value = '192.168.12.10'
$DHCP = New-EC2DHCPOption -DhcpConfiguration $Domain, $DNS1, $DNS2
```

In the preceding example, note that not all options are required. You can choose to configure only some options. If you choose to omit DNS, be sure to include a reference to AmazonProvidedDNS or you will not be able to resolve any DNS names. Here is an example if you want to change the default domain name, but use Amazon's DNS:

```
$Domain = New-Object Amazon.EC2.Model.DhcpConfiguration
$Domain.Key = 'domain-name'
$Domain.Value = 'brianbeach.com'
$DNS = New-Object Amazon.EC2.Model.DhcpConfiguration
$DNS.Key = 'domain-name-servers'
$DNS.Value = 'AmazonProvidedDNS'
$DHCP = New-EC2DHCPOption -DhcpConfiguration $Domain, $DNS
```

Wow, that was a lot of content to get through. I'm glad you made it! At this point your VPC is complete. In the next chapter we will launch a few instances into the new VPC. But, before we do, let's look at this chapter's exercises. In the first exercise, we will build a streamlined script that creates a new VPC identical to the one described in this chapter. In the second example, we will use a Virtual Private Gateway to connect the VPC to a local office.

EXERCISE 5.1: CREATING A VIRTUAL PRIVATE CLOUD

In this exercise, we will create an end-to-end script to provision a Virtual Private Cloud (see Figure 5-8). The VPC wizard, available in the Web Console, does a good job of creating a VPC, but you want more control. In addition, you want the process to run unattended. Therefore, you decide to script the build in PowerShell.

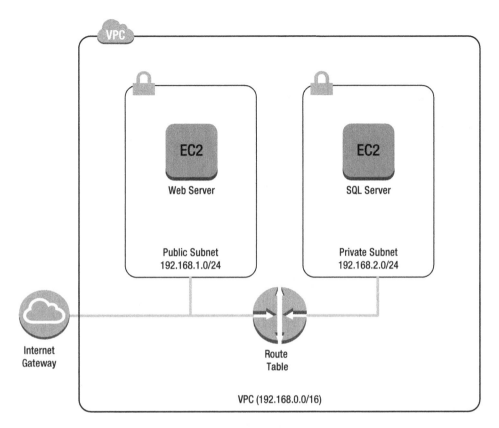

Figure 5-8. *Simple VPC (Note: Our script will not add instances.)*

In continuous integration, you want to start fresh to ensure that manual changes made the day before do not impact the results of testing. In the cloud, we can truly start from the ground up every day. Imagine how difficult this would be with physical switches and routers. AWS makes continuous integration really easy.

This exercise will create and configure the VPC shown in Figure 5-8. I assume our application is a simple web application with an SQL database. The script will create a public subnet for the web server and a private subnet for the SQL Server. Note that the script will not launch the instances. We will build on this recipe in later chapters. Here are the main components of our script:

- Create a VPC
- Create a DHCP option set
- Create subnets
- Add an Internet gateway
- Configure a routing table
- Configure ACLs

Our script takes a few parameters. First, it requires a domain name (e.g., brianbeach.com). Second, it takes the CIDR range of the VPC and two subnets.

```
param
(
    [string][parameter(mandatory=$true)]$DomainName,
    [string][parameter(mandatory=$false)]$VPCCIDR = '192.168.0.0/16',
    [string][parameter(mandatory=$false)]$PublicSubnetCIDR = '192.168.1.0/24',
    [string][parameter(mandatory=$false)]$PrivateSubnetCIDR = '192.168.2.0/24'
)
```

Next, we create a new VPC. I wait a few seconds to avoid errors. The Create Subnet command below will fail if the VPC has not been created.

```
$VPC = New-EC2Vpc -CidrBlock $VPCCIDR
Start-Sleep -s 15 #This can take a few seconds
```

Then, we configure the DHCP options. Here I am using the default DNS provider.

```
#Configure the DHCP Options
$Domain = New-Object Amazon.EC2.Model.DhcpConfiguration
$Domain.Key = 'domain-name'
$Domain.Value = $DomainName
$DNS = New-Object Amazon.EC2.Model.DhcpConfiguration
$DNS.Key = 'domain-name-servers'
$DNS.Value = 'AmazonProvidedDNS'
$DHCP = New-EC2DHCPOption -DhcpConfiguration $Domain, $DNS
Register-EC2DhcpOption -DhcpOptionsId $DHCP.DhcpOptionsId -VpcId $VPC.VpcId
```

Now we can create our two subnets. The web servers will be hosted in the public subnet and have Internet access. The SQL server will be hosted in the private subnet and will not have Internet access.

```
#Pick the first availability zone in the region.
$AvailabilityZones = Get-EC2AvailabilityZone
$AvailabilityZone = $AvailabilityZones[0].ZoneName

#Create and tag the Public subnet.
$PublicSubnet = New-EC2Subnet -VpcId $VPC.VpcId
    -CidrBlock $PublicSubnetCIDR -AvailabilityZone $AvailabilityZone
Start-Sleep -s 15 #This can take a few seconds
$Tag = New-Object Amazon.EC2.Model.Tag
$Tag.Key = 'Name'
$Tag.Value = 'Public'
New-EC2Tag -ResourceId $PublicSubnet.SubnetId  -Tag $Tag

#Create and tag the Private subnet.
$PrivateSubnet = New-EC2Subnet -VpcId $VPC.VpcId
    -CidrBlock $PrivateSubnetCIDR -AvailabilityZone $AvailabilityZone
Start-Sleep -s 15 #This can take a few seconds
$Tag = New-Object Amazon.EC2.Model.Tag
```

```
$Tag.Key = 'Name'
$Tag.Value = 'Private'
New-EC2Tag -ResourceId $PrivateSubnet.SubnetId  -Tag $Tag
```

Now, we add an Internet gateway and configure the route table.

```
#Add an Internet Gateway and attach it to the VPC.
$InternetGateway = New-EC2InternetGateway
Add-EC2InternetGateway -InternetGatewayId $InternetGateway.InternetGatewayId -VpcId $VPC.
VpcId

#Create a new routeTable and associate it with the public subnet
$PublicRouteTable = New-EC2RouteTable -VpcId $VPC.VpcId
New-EC2Route -RouteTableId $PublicRouteTable.RouteTableId -DestinationCidrBlock '0.0.0.0/0'
    -GatewayId $InternetGateway.InternetGatewayId
$NoEcho = Register-EC2RouteTable -RouteTableId $PublicRouteTable.RouteTableId
    -SubnetId $PublicSubnet.SubnetId
```

Finally, we configure the ACLs.

```
#Create a new Access Control List for the public subnet
$PublicACL = New-EC2NetworkAcl -VpcId $VPC.VpcId
New-EC2NetworkAclEntry -NetworkAclId $PublicACL.NetworkAclId -RuleNumber 50
    -CidrBlock $VPCCIDR -Egress $false -PortRange_From 80
    -PortRange_To 80 -Protocol 6 -RuleAction 'Deny'
New-EC2NetworkAclEntry -NetworkAclId $PublicACL.NetworkAclId -RuleNumber 50
    -CidrBlock $VPCCIDR -Egress $true -PortRange_From 49152
    -PortRange_To 65535 -Protocol 6 -RuleAction 'Deny'
New-EC2NetworkAclEntry -NetworkAclId $PublicACL.NetworkAclId -RuleNumber 100
    -CidrBlock '0.0.0.0/0' -Egress $false -PortRange_From 80
    -PortRange_To 80 -Protocol 6 -RuleAction 'Allow'
New-EC2NetworkAclEntry -NetworkAclId $PublicACL.NetworkAclId -RuleNumber 100
    -CidrBlock '0.0.0.0/0' -Egress $true -PortRange_From 49152
    -PortRange_To 65535 -Protocol 6 -RuleAction 'Allow'
New-EC2NetworkAclEntry -NetworkAclId $PublicACL.NetworkAclId -RuleNumber 200
    -CidrBlock $PrivateSubnetCIDR -Egress $true -PortRange_From 1433
    -PortRange_To 1433 -Protocol 6 -RuleAction 'Allow'
New-EC2NetworkAclEntry -NetworkAclId $PublicACL.NetworkAclId -RuleNumber 200
    -CidrBlock $PrivateSubnetCIDR -Egress $false -PortRange_From 49152
    -PortRange_To 65535 -Protocol 6 -RuleAction 'Allow'
New-EC2NetworkAclEntry -NetworkAclId $PublicACL.NetworkAclId -RuleNumber 300
    -CidrBlock '0.0.0.0/0' -Egress $false -PortRange_From 3389
    -PortRange_To 3389 -Protocol 6 -RuleAction 'Allow'

#Associate the ACL to the public subnet
$VPCFilter = New-Object Amazon.EC2.Model.Filter
$VPCFilter.Name = 'vpc-id'
$VPCFilter.Value = $VPC.VpcId
$DefaultFilter = New-Object Amazon.EC2.Model.Filter
$DefaultFilter.Name = 'default'
$DefaultFilter.Value = 'true'
```

```
$OldACL = (Get-EC2NetworkAcl -Filter $VPCFilter, $DefaultFilter )
$OldAssociation = $OldACL.Associations | Where-Object { $_.SubnetId -eq $PublicSubnet.
SubnetId }
$NoEcho = Set-EC2NetworkAclAssociation -AssociationId $OldAssociation.NetworkAclAssociationId
    -NetworkAclId $PublicACL.NetworkAclId

#Log the most common IDs
Write-Host "The VPC ID is" $VPC.VpcId
Write-Host "The public subnet ID is" $PublicSubnet.SubnetId
Write-Host "The private subnet ID is" $PrivateSubnet.SubnetId
```

As you can see, it is easy to create and re-create a VPC. The examples in the next chapter will build on this VPC. Feel free to use the script to create a new VPC for each exercise in Chapter 6. In the next example, we will build a new VPC that is attached to our corporate network.

EXERCISE 5.2: CREATING A VIRTUAL PRIVATEGATEWAY

In this exercise, we will use a VPN connection to extend a company's private network directly to the VPC. This will allow you to connect to the private instance in your VPC and allow VPC instances to access resources on your local network. We will create a Virtual Private Gateway and connect our offices to Amazon using an IPSec Tunnel.

Figure 5-9 provides an overview of the configuration. Our corporate LAN is using the private IP range 10.0.0.0/0. We have decided to allocate a section of this, 10.200.0.0/16, for use at AWS.

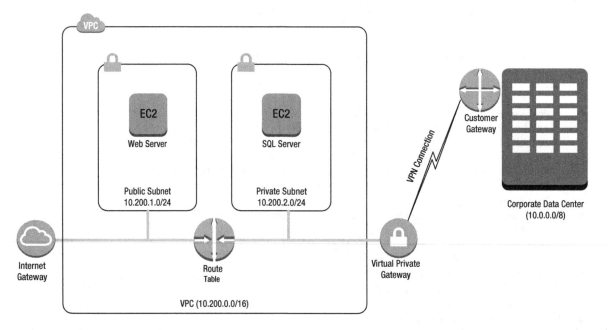

Figure 5-9. *VPC with a virtual private gateway*

I'm going to assume that you know how to create the VPC, subnets, etc. Let's get right to configuring the VPN connection. Note that you will be charged for the VPN connection as soon as you create the virtual private gateway, even if you never connect the local side of the VPN connection.

The first step is describing your customer gateway to AWS. The customer gateway is your side of the tunnel. If you have multiple office locations, you can connect up to five customer gateways to each VPC. You need to tell AWS your public IP address to connect to and the type of tunnel you want to create. At this time, IPSec is the only type of tunnel supported. The PowerShell command is New-EC2CustomerGateway.

```
$CustomerGateway = New-EC2CustomerGateway -Type 'ipsec.1' -IpAddress '198.51.100.12'
```

The next thing you need to do is to create the virtual private gateway. This is Amazon's side of the tunnel. You simply tell AWS which availability zone to use and the type of tunnel you want to create. Then you attach it to an existing VPC.

```
$VpnGateway = New-EC2VpnGateway -Type 'ipsec.1' -AvailabilityZone $AvailabilityZone
Add-EC2VpnGateway -VpnGatewayId $VpnGateway.VpnGatewayId  -VpcId $VpcId
```

Now that we have both sides of the tunnel established, we create a new connection between them by calling New-EC2VpnConnection. You need to pass the ID of the customer gateway and the virtual private gateway as well as passing the type of tunnel one more time.

```
$VPNConnection = New-EC2VpnConnection -Type 'ipsec.1' -CustomerGatewayId
    $CustomerGateway.CustomerGatewayId -VpnGatewayId $VpnGateway.VpnGatewayId
    -StaticRoutesOnly $true
```

Note that I have configured this tunnel to use static routes. This means that you need to tell AWS what networks are available on your side of the tunnel. You could also use dynamic routing and allow Border Gateway Protocol (BGP) to learn the routes. BGP is beyond the scope of this book.

Before we can add static routes, we need to wait for the configuration to complete. I am using the loop below to wait for the VPN connection to come online.

```
While ($VPNConnection.VpnConnectionState -eq 'pending') {
    #Wait for the VPN connection to become available
    Start-Sleep -s 15
    $VPNConnection = Get-EC2VpnConnection
        -VpnConnectionId  $VPNConnection.VpnConnectionId
}
```

Now that the tunnel is up, we have to configure the static routing. We need to tell AWS that the rest of the private network is available on the other side of the tunnel. The rule below tells AWS that it can find the 10.0.0.0/8 network by sending traffic over the tunnel. Note that AWS already knows that 10.200.0.0/16 is the local network. Remember that the most specific route (the one with the largest number after the slash) is chosen first.

```
New-EC2VpnConnectionRoute -VpnConnectionId $VPNConnection.VpnConnectionId
    -DestinationCidrBlock '10.0.0.0/8'
```

We could also choose to have traffic from our private instances bound for the Internet go over the tunnel rather than using a NAT gateway from the prior section. The benefit of this is that we can configure the traffic to use all of existing network appliances such as black lists, data loss prevention, etc. The downside is that we introduce a lot of latency, specifically when accessing an Internet address hosted in the Amazon data center such as S3.

```
New-EC2VpnConnectionRoute -VpnConnectionId $VPNConnection.VpnConnectionId
    -DestinationCidrBlock '0.0.0.0/0'
```

The last thing we need to do is configure the route tables for the individual subnets in our VPC. Let's assume that we want our private instances to access the public Internet over the VPN tunnel and our public instances to use the Internet gateway. Both subnets will have access to the rest of the private network over the VPN tunnel.

My private route table looks like this. Note that the default route (0.0.0.0/0) is pointed to the virtual gateway.

```
(Get-EC2RouteTable -RouteTableId $PrivateRouteTableID)[0].routes | Format-Table
===
DestinationCidrBlock GatewayId      InstanceId State
-------------------- ---------      ---------- ------
10.200.0.0/16        local                     active
10.0.0.0/8           vgw-e424c48d              active
0.0.0.0/0            vgw-e424c48d              active
```

And, my public route table looks like this. Note that the default route (0.0.0.0/0) is pointed to the Internet gateway.

```
(Get-EC2RouteTable -RouteTableId $PublicRouteTableID)[0].routes | Format-Table
===
DestinationCidrBlock GatewayId      InstanceId State
-------------------- ---------      ---------- ------
10.200.0.0/16        local                     active
10.0.0.0/8           vgw-e424c48d              active
0.0.0.0/0            igw-79095f17              active
```

Of course, you would want to configure your ACLs as well, but I think we have spent enough time on ACLs in the chapter. I'll leave that up to you.

Please note that the VPN configuration above is for Amazon. You will also need to configure your side of the tunnel on whatever device you are using. The process is different on each device type, but Amazon will help you by autogenerating a script for common hardware types.

From the Web Console, go to the VPN service, click VPN connection from the left navigation, and click the Download Configuration button. Now choose your hardware configuration (see Figure 5-10) and click "Yes, Download" to download a script for your device.

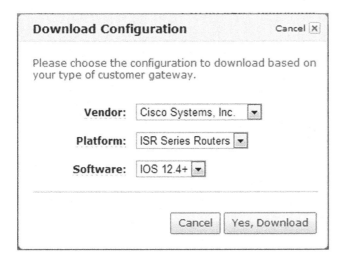

Figure 5-10. *Downloading a VPN configuration for your local device*

Once the VPN tunnel is established, you will be able to communicate with the AWS instances as if they were on the local network.

Summary

In this chapter, we learned about networking with AWS. We learned to create a VPC, add subnets, and control how traffic is routed and filtered. As you can see, VPC is very powerful and very simple. You can quickly build network topologies that would take weeks to implement with physical equipment.

In addition, we saw how easy it was to script the build. When used with continuous integration, a scripted VPC can be used to wipe and rebuild the entire environment on a daily basis.

In the next chapter, I will show you how to launch instances into our new VPC and manage their behavior. We will learn how to configure IP addresses and network interfaces and security groups. Grab a cup of coffee and keep reading!

■ ■ ■

CHAPTER 6

Advanced Instance Management

In the last chapter, we created a Virtual Private Cloud (VPC). In this chapter we are going to discuss configuring instances in the VPC.

Before launching an instance we first need to configure security groups. Security groups are similar to the network access control lists ACLs we discussed in Chapter 5, but are enforced at the instance rather than subnet. I'll show you how to create and manage rules, discuss the differences between security groups and traditional firewalls, and show you how to add servers to a security group.

Once we have the security groups configured, we can launch a VPC instance. We will discuss managing private IP addresses and assigning public IP addresses. Then, I will talk about elastic network interfaces and how we manage them.

Managing Security Groups

We start out this chapter by discussing security groups. A security group is similar to a firewall. Traditionally, a firewall is used to separate a network into security zones. For example, a firewall may be used to protect the private network from the Internet, but the machines on the private network have no restrictions when communicating with other machines on the private network.

In recent years, the cost of a firewall has decreased, and we have begun to use them to protect much smaller segments of the network. For example, we may use a firewall to separate the finance department from the rest of the organization or to protect a single application that hosts sensitive data. EC2 security groups take this idea to the extreme. An EC2 security group is like having a firewall in front of each instance. No two instances can communicate without traversing a firewall, even if they are in the same subnet. In other words, the security group is part of an instance rather than part of the network.

■ **Note** When I was writing this book, I debated discussing security groups in Chapter 5 along with ACLs. In the end, I felt they were best discussed here to emphasize the difference between security groups and a traditional firewall.

A security group allows you to control what traffic is allowed to flow to and from an instance. You can control the type of traffic (e.g., TCP, UDP, and ICMP), which ports are open, and the source and destination. While there were security groups in EC2 Classic, you could filter inbound traffic only. In a VPC, security groups allow you to filter both inbound and outbound traffic.

By default all instances are added to the default security group when launched from PowerShell. The default group allows an instance to communicate freely with any other instance in the default security group. Note that if you used the Wizard in the AWS Management Console, it will create a new security group for each instance rather than adding the instance to the default group.

Displaying Security Groups

Let's start by looking at the default security group in the Web Console. I assume that you have created a VPC. If not, use exercise 1 from Chapter 5 to create one. In Figure 6-1 you can see that there is only one inbound rule.

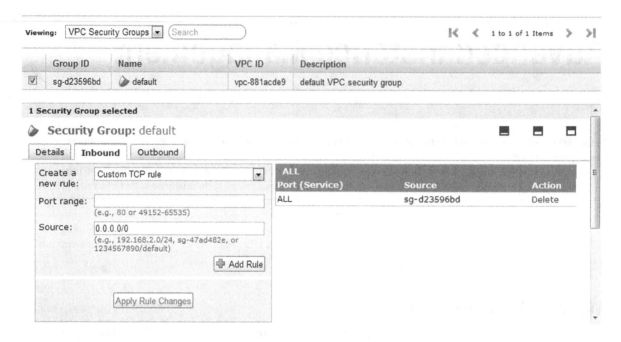

Figure 6-1. *Inbound security group rules*

Notice that this rule allows all traffic on any port from the security group sg-d23596bd. Note that sg-d23596bd is the security group we are already looking at. In other words, this rule allows any instance in the security group to communicate with any other instance in the group. All other traffic is blocked by default.

Now let's look at the outbound rules in Figure 6-2. Again there is only a single rule. This rule allows outbound traffic on any protocol and any port to any destination. In other words, all outbound traffic is allowed by default.

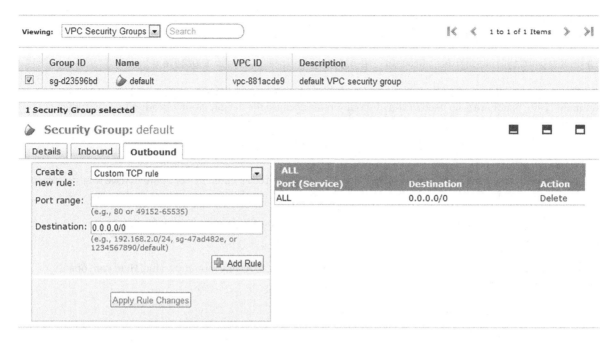

Figure 6-2. *Outbound security group rules*

Unlike traditional firewall rules, we are not specifying individual instances by IP address. In fact, we don't even have an instance in our VPC yet. The security architect can define all of the rules necessary before adding instances. You can then give the developers permission to add instances to security groups that have been predefined, and they don't have to wait for a change request to be approved to open the firewall ports later.

Returning to PowerShell, you can list the security groups using the Get-EC2SecurityGroup command.

```
Get-EC2SecurityGroup | Format-Table
```

Notice that this command returns security groups for all VPCs. Make note of the GroupID of the default group in your VPC. We will be using it to modify the security group in the next section.

```
OwnerId        VpcId          GroupId       GroupName ...
-----------    ------------   ----------    --------- ...
928041546250                  sg-033e6b6b   default   ...
928041546250   vpc-881acde9   sg-d23596bd   default   ...
```

Adding and Removing Rules

Let's add a rule to the default VPC security group to allow Remote Desktop Protocol (RDP) access to our Windows instances. To add inbound rules to the group we use the now-common pattern of creating a .Net object to describe the rule, and then call Grant-EC2SecurityGroupIngress. Note that FromPort and ToPort are used to specify a range of destination ports, not the source and destination port. RDP runs on TCP port 3389; therefore, the PowerShell command is the following:

```
$RDPRule = New-Object Amazon.EC2.Model.IpPermission
$RDPRule.IpProtocol='tcp'
$RDPRule.FromPort = 3389
```

```
$RDPRule.ToPort = 3389
$RDPRule.IpRanges = '0.0.0.0/0'

Grant-EC2SecurityGroupIngress -GroupId 'sg-d23596bd' -IpPermissions $SQLRule
```

The process to add an outbound rule is almost identical, but you use the `Grant-EC2SecurityGroupEgress` command. Note that there is no need to add outbound rules because the default group already allows all traffic outbound.

```
Grant-EC2SecurityGroupEgress -GroupId 'sg-d23596bd' -IpPermissions $Rule
```

You can easily create a security group using the `New-EC2SecurityGroup` command. For example, if we were developing a web application, we might create a security group that allowed HTTP and HTTPS requests from the Internet.

```
$GroupId = New-EC2SecurityGroup -VpcId 'vpc-881acde9' -GroupName 'Web' -GroupDescription
    "Allows HTTP/S traffic from the internet."
```

A new group allows all outbound traffic by default, but does not allow any inbound traffic. Here I am opening port 80 (HTTP) and 443 (HTTPS):

```
$HTTPRule = New-Object Amazon.EC2.Model.IpPermission
$HTTPRule.IpProtocol='tcp'
$HTTPRule.FromPort = 80
$HTTPRule.ToPort = 80
$HTTPRule.IpRanges = '0.0.0.0/0'

$HTTPSRule = New-Object Amazon.EC2.Model.IpPermission
$HTTPSRule.IpProtocol='tcp'
$HTTPSRule.FromPort = 443
$HTTPSRule.ToPort = 443
$HTTPSRule.IpRanges = '0.0.0.0/0'

Grant-EC2SecurityGroupIngress -GroupId $GroupId -IpPermissions $HTTPRule, $HTTPSRule
```

You can also remove inbound and outbound rules using `Revoke-EC2SecurityGroupIngress` and `Revoke-EC2SecurityGroupEgress`, respectively. For example, you might want to remove the default rule that allows all outbound traffic from our web group.

Unlike ACLs, security groups are stateful. That means that you do not need to explicitly add a rule to allow return traffic. The security group knows that the HTTP request is going to have a corresponding response and will allow it automatically. We only need the outbound rule when the instance is acting as the client. Therefore, the default outbound rule is not needed. Let's remove it.

```
$Rule = New-Object Amazon.EC2.Model.IpPermission
$Rule.IpProtocol='-1'
$Rule.IpRanges = '0.0.0.0/0'

Revoke-EC2SecurityGroupEgress -GroupId $GroupId -IpPermissions $Rule
```

Note that I used an `IpProtocol` of `"-1."` Security groups allow you to add rules for any IP protocol number. ICMP, TCP, and UDP can all be referred to by name or number (1, 6, and 17, respectively). The less-common protocols must be referenced by number. A value of `"-1"` means all protocols.

As we saw in Figure 6-1 we can create rules based on other security groups. For example, imagine our web application has an SQL database. The web servers must be able to access the SQL server. But, the number of web servers will change throughout the day depending on the load.

Let's create a new SQL group for our SQL servers. Then we will grant access to any instance in the web security group we created earlier. My web security group has ID sg-0c3b9863. Note that SQL server uses TCP port 1433.

```
$GroupId = New-EC2SecurityGroup -VpcId vpc-881acde9 -GroupName SQL -GroupDescription
    "Allows SQL Queries from the web server."

$WebGroup = New-Object Amazon.EC2.Model.UserIdGroupPair
$WebGroup.GroupId = 'sg-0c3b9863'

$SQLRule = New-Object Amazon.EC2.Model.IpPermission
$SQLRule.IpProtocol='tcp'
$SQLRule.FromPort = 1433
$SQLRule.ToPort = 1433
$SQLRule.UserIdGroupPair = $WebGroup

Grant-EC2SecurityGroupIngress -GroupId $GroupId -IpPermissions $SQLRule
```

With this new security group in place, all we have to do is add web servers to the web security group and AWS will grant access to the SQL server. There is no need to update the security group rules when a new instance is launched.

Before we close this section, let's imagine that you want to be able to ping all of your instances.

■ **Caution**   This example poses a security risk, but I want to show you how ICMP rules work. I don't recommend that you allow ping from outside the VPC.

Let's add a new rule to the default security group that allows ICMP Echo Request messages from anywhere. ICMP uses message types rather than ports. To enable an ICMP message you use an IpProtocol of "icmp" and then put the message type in FromPort. For example, an ICMP Echo Request is message type 8. Note that the ToPort is not used and should be set to -1.

```
$PingRule = New-Object Amazon.EC2.Model.IpPermission
$PingRule.IpProtocol='icmp'
$PingRule.FromPort = 8
$PingRule.ToPort = -1
$PingRule.IpRanges = '0.0.0.0/0'

Grant-EC2SecurityGroupIngress -GroupId sg-d23596bd -IpPermissions $PingRule
```

In this section we discussed security groups. We saw that a security group is similar to a firewall, but is enforced at the instance rather than network segment. We also looked at how to create various security group rules. Now, let's move on and launch an instance into our VPC.

Launching Instances into a VPC

VPC gives you considerable control over network configuration of your EC2 instances. Let's start by launching a new instance into the VPC we created in Chapter 5. If you have not created a VPC, use the script from Exercise 5.1.

Once again let's begin by looking at the Request Instances Wizard. Notice the network configuration options at the bottom of page 3 in the Wizard shown in Figure 6-3. This page allows you to control the number of network interfaces your instance has. It also allows you to choose a subnet and specify an IP address. In addition, you can add secondary IP addresses to the instance.

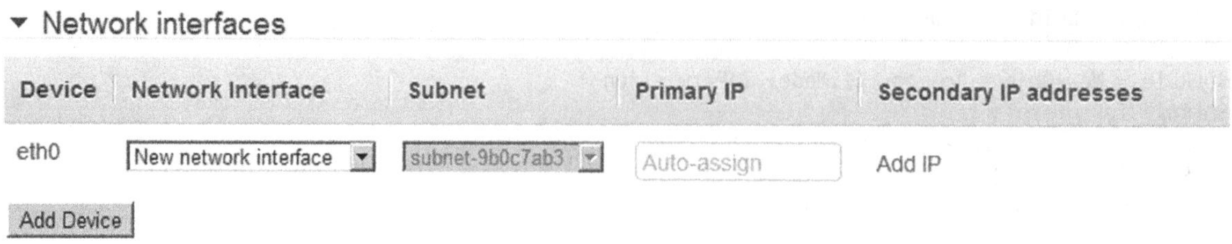

▼ Network interfaces

Device	Network Interface	Subnet	Primary IP	Secondary IP addresses
eth0	New network interface ▼	subnet-9b0c7ab3 ▼	Auto-assign	Add IP

Add Device

Figure 6-3. *Network options in the Request Instances Wizard*

Creating a VPC instance with PowerShell is almost identical to creating an EC2 Classic instance. Once again we use the New-EC2Instance command, but we add one new parameter: the id of the subnet you want to launch the instance into. Note that you can only connect to instances in a public subnet so I recommend that you use the public subnet here.

```
$AMI = Get-EC2ImageByName -Name 'WINDOWS_2012_BASE'
New-EC2Instance -ImageId $AMI[0].ImageId -KeyName 'MyKey' -InstanceType 't1.micro' -MinCount 1
    -MaxCount 1 -SubnetId subnet-7922ea18
```

That's all it takes to launch a VPC instance. But, there are many new options available that did not exist in EC2. For example, the machine we just launched has a randomly assigned IP address within the CIDR range of the subnet we specified. Unlike EC2 Classic, you can control the IP address of the instance. To specify an IP address at launch, use the PrivateIPAddress parameter.

```
$AMI = Get-EC2ImageByName -Name 'WINDOWS_2012_BASE'
New-EC2Instance -ImageId $AMI[0].ImageId -KeyName 'MyKey' -InstanceType 't1.micro' -MinCount 1
    -MaxCount 1 -SubnetId subnet-7922ea18 -PrivateIpAddress 192.168.1.5
```

Note that the IP address is immutable. You can set it when you launch a new instance, but you cannot change it once the machine is running. Also, remember that the first four IP addresses of each subnet are reserved.

Of course, you can also specify the security groups when you launch an instance. Notice, in Figure 6-4, that you can select more than one security group. For example, I can make my new instance a member of the web and default groups that we discussed in the prior section. The web group will allow HTTP traffic and the default group will allow RDP.

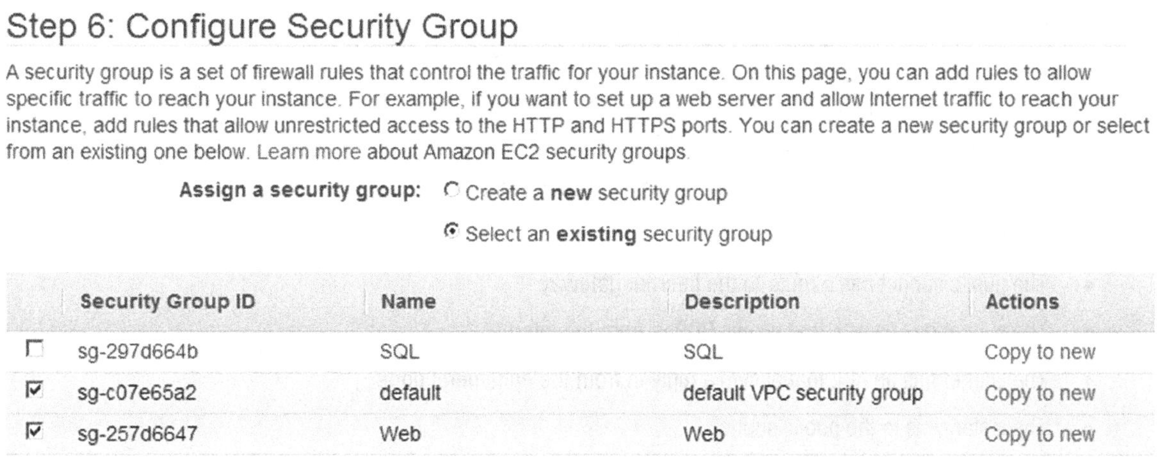

Step 6: Configure Security Group

A security group is a set of firewall rules that control the traffic for your instance. On this page, you can add rules to allow specific traffic to reach your instance. For example, if you want to set up a web server and allow Internet traffic to reach your instance, add rules that allow unrestricted access to the HTTP and HTTPS ports. You can create a new security group or select from an existing one below. Learn more about Amazon EC2 security groups.

Assign a security group: ○ Create a **new** security group

                               ⦿ Select an **existing** security group

	Security Group ID	Name	Description	Actions
☐	sg-297d664b	SQL	SQL	Copy to new
☑	sg-c07e65a2	default	default VPC security group	Copy to new
☑	sg-257d6647	Web	Web	Copy to new

Figure 6-4. *Security groups in the Request Instances Wizard*

To add an instance to a security group using PowerShell use the SecurityGroupId parameter and pass an array of security group IDs.

```
$AMI = Get-EC2ImageByName -Name 'WINDOWS_2012_BASE'
New-EC2Instance -ImageId $AMI[0].ImageId -KeyName 'MyKey' -InstanceType 't1.micro' -MinCount 1
    -MaxCount 1 -SubnetId subnet-7922ea18 -SecurityGroupId sg-d23596bd, sg-0c3b9863
```

As we have just seen, running instances in a VPC gives you the ability to control the private network configuration of the instance. We launched an instance into our public subnet and enabled HTTP and RDP traffic from the Internet using security groups. But, so far, we have assigned a private IP address only. Without a public IP address there is no way to access the instance from the Internet. To add a public IP, we need an elastic IP address.

Managing Elastic IP Addresses

So far our instances have a private IP address only. An instance needs a public IP address to communicate with the Internet. AWS allows you to associate a public IP address – called an elastic IP (EIP) – with your instance.

In earlier chapters, when we were using EC2 Classic or the default VPC, every instance had a public IP address assigned automatically. That meant that every instance was publicly addressable. In a VPC, we can choose which instances are public and which are private.

To be public, an instance must be in a public subnet (one with a route to the Internet gateway) and have an EIP address associated with it. AWS uses network address translation (NAT) to map traffic between the private IP and the EIP. The NAT is implemented in the Internet gateway.

To create an EIP address we use New-EC2Address. You also have to tell AWS that the EIP will be used in a VPC instance rather than an EC2 Classic instance. For example:

```
$EIP = New-EC2Address -Domain vpc
```

AWS will randomly assign you an EIP. In order to associate the EIP to your instance, use Register-EC2PrivateIpAddress.

```
Register-EC2Address -InstanceId $Instance.InstanceId -AllocationId $EIP.AllocationId
```

LOGGING INTO A VPC INSTANCE

At this point you can log in to the instance using REMOTE DESKTOP. Open the Web Console, decrypt the password, and click the Connect link. If you don't remember how, jump back to Chapter 3.

If you have an issue, review the configuration. You should check that

- The VPC has an Internet gateway
- The public subnet has a route to the Internet gateway
- The subnet has an ACL that allows RDP in from the Internet
- The subnet has an ACL that allows a reply in from the ephemeral ports
- The instance is in the public subnet
- The default security group allows RDP in from the Internet
- The instance is a member of the default security group
- The instance has an EIP address assigned

VPC is a powerful offering that gives you a lot of control over your environment, but as a result, it is also complicated. Don't worry; you will get very good at diagnosing these issues.

It is common to reassign an EIP as part of a disaster recovery plan. If the EIP is already assigned to another instance you will get an error when you try to reassign it. You must include the AllowReassign attribute to reassign an EIP that is assigned to another instance.

```
Register-EC2Address -InstanceId $Instance.InstanceId -AllocationId $EIP.AllocationId
    -AllowReassociation:$true
```

You can remove the EIP address from an instance using the Unregister-EC2Address command. First, get a reference to the EIP using Get-EC2Address. Then, call Unregister-EC2Instance and pass the association id.

```
$EIP = Get-EC2Address -PublicIp '54.208.194.131'
Unregister-EC2Address -AssociationId $EIP.AssociationId
```

Note that AWS will charge you a fee for an EIP that is not attached to a running instance. If you are no longer using an EIP, you can use the Remove-EC2Address command to abandon it and avoid the fees.

```
$EIP = Get-EC2Address -PublicIp '54.208.194.131'
Remove-EC2Address -AllocationId $EIP.AllocationId -Force
```

If you know when you are launching an instance that will need an EIP, you can automatically assign one by using the AssociatePublicIp attribute of the New-EC2Instance command.

```
$AMI = Get-EC2ImageByName -Name 'WINDOWS_2012_BASE'
New-EC2Instance -ImageId $AMI[0].ImageId -KeyName 'MyKey' -InstanceType 't1.micro' -MinCount 1
    -MaxCount 1 -SubnetId subnet-7922ea18 -AssociatePublicIp:$true
```

Public EIPs are a critical component of most applications. Now that we know how to manage public IPs, let's look more closely at private IP addresses. As you will see in the next section, spending a little extra time planning can make your application easier to manage.

Managing Private IPs

In the previous sections we referred to the private IP as an attribute of an instance. This was oversimplification. In reality, an instance can have many network interfaces and each interface can have many IP addresses. We will look at adding network interfaces in the next section. For now let's focus on IP addresses.

When AWS displays the private IP address of an instance, it really means the first IP address of the first network interface. Earlier, I mentioned that the private IP address of an instance could not be changed. What I really meant was that you cannot change the first IP address of a network interface. You can, however, add additional IP addresses to an interface.

One common use is disaster recovery. The secondary IP can be easily moved between instances. If you have a critical application that relies on a single instance, you may want to keep a second instance on standby. If you detect a failure in the primary instance, you could move the IP address to a secondary instance.

To add a secondary IP address to an instance, first find the network interface. All of the network interfaces are available from the `NetworkInterfaces` property of the `Instance` object.

```
$Reservation = Get-EC2Instance -Instance i-b67722cd
$Instance = $Reservation.RunningInstance[0]
$ENI = $Instance.NetworkInterfaces[0]
```

Now that we have the network interface we can use the `Register-EC2PrivateIpAddress` method to add a secondary IP address. For example:

```
Register-EC2PrivateIpAddress -NetworkInterfaceId $ENI.NetworkInterfaceId
    -PrivateIpAddresses '192.168.1.6'
```

Unfortunately, DHCP will not configure the secondary IP addresses. In order to use secondary IPs, you must disable DHCP and configure the network interface manually. Luckily there are PowerShell commands for this. The following example will configure an instance with a static network configuration.

Note You must log in to the instance you want to configure and execute these commands locally.

```
#Disable DHCP
Set-NetIPInterface -InterfaceAlias 'Ethernet' -Dhcp Disabled

#Configure the primary IP
New-NetIPAddress -InterfaceAlias 'Ethernet' -IPAddress '192.168.1.5' -PrefixLength 24
    -DefaultGateway '192.168.1.1'

#Configure DNS
Set-DnsClientServerAddress -InterfaceAlias 'Ethernet' -ServerAddresses '192.168.0.2'

#Add the secondary IP address
New-NetIPAddress -InterfaceAlias 'Ethernet' -IPAddress '192.168.1.6' -PrefixLength 24
```

━━━

■ **Caution** A static network configuration can be dangerous. You must be careful to ensure that the IP addresses assigned within Windows match those assigned in AWS. Remember that the security groups are implemented at the instance level. This means that if you assign a different IP address, the security groups will not allow traffic to flow to the instance. I recommend that you take a snapshot before manually configuring the security groups.

━━━

Now that we know how to manage IP addresses let's take a closer look at the network interfaces.

Managing Elastic Network Interfaces

As I mentioned, an instance can have multiple network interfaces. Amazon calls these interfaces elastic network interfaces (ENIs). The maximum number of interfaces varies with the instance type. Unlike secondary IP addresses, network interfaces can be deployed in separate subnets. See Figure 6-5.

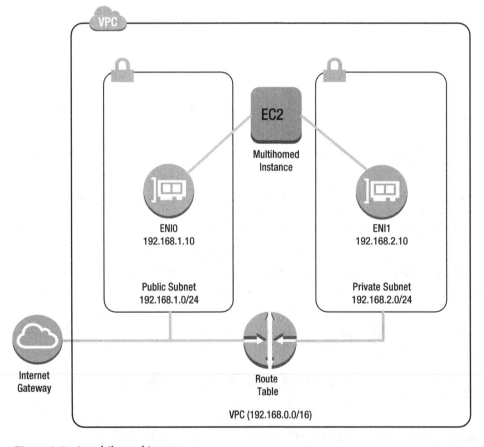

Figure 6-5. *A multihomed instance*

Every instance has at least one ENI, but you can add additional interfaces when you launch an instance. Remember that the SubnetId, PrivateIpAddress, SecurityGroupId attributes of the New-EC2Instance command act on the default ENI. You cannot use these parameters to launch instances with multiple interfaces.

If you want to add multiple interfaces to an instance, use a .Net object to describe them. Then, pass an array of interfaces to the New-EC2Instance command using the NetworkInterfaces attribute. Each ENI has its own IP address and can be in a different subnet. In addition, each ENI can be in a different set of security groups. To launch the instance pictured in Figure 6-5, I used the following PowerShell script:

```
$ENI0 = New-Object Amazon.EC2.Model.InstanceNetworkInterfaceSpecification
$ENI0.PrivateIpAddress = '192.168.1.10'
$ENI0.SubnetId = 'subnet-7922ea18'
$ENI0.DeviceIndex = 0
$ENI0.Groups.Add('sg-e775d688')

$ENI1 = New-Object Amazon.EC2.Model.InstanceNetworkInterfaceSpecification
$ENI1.PrivateIpAddress = '192.168.2.10'
$ENI1.SubnetId = 'subnet-2f22ea4e'
$ENI1.DeviceIndex = 1
$ENI1.Groups.Add('sg-e775d688')

$AMI = Get-EC2ImageByName -Name 'WINDOWS_2012_BASE'
New-EC2Instance -ImageId $AMI[0].ImageId -KeyName 'MyKey' -InstanceType 't1.micro' -MinCount 1
    -MaxCount 1 -NetworkInterfaces $ENI0, $ENI1
```

Unfortunately, the reservation returned from New-EC2Instance does not include the network interfaces. The command returns asynchronously, and it takes a few seconds for the interfaces to attach. If you want to check the details, you have to wait a few seconds and then run Get-EC2Instance to refresh your copy of the metadata. For example:

```
$Reservation = Get-EC2Instance -Instance i-b67722cd
$Instance = $Reservation.RunningInstance[0]
$Instance.NetworkInterfaces | Format-Table
```

This command returns:

```
NetworkInterfaceId SubnetId         MacAddress       PrivateIpAddress
------------------ ---------------  ---------------- ----------------
eni-cc478fad       subnet-7922ea18  2a:5b:de:70:8... 192.168.1.10
eni-cf478fae       subnet-2f22ea4e  2a:5b:de:7b:8... 192.168.2.10
```

If you want to add an interface to an existing instance you can. First, create a new ENI using the New-EC2NetworkInterface command. Then, attach it to an instance using the Add-EC2NetworkInterface command. For example:

```
$NIC = New-EC2NetworkInterface -SubnetId subnet-1619ce77 -PrivateIpAddress 192.168.1.15
    -GroupId sg-d23596bd
Add-EC2NetworkInterface -NetworkInterfaceId $NIC.NetworkInterfaceId -InstanceId i-c829b8b3
    -DeviceIndex 1
```

If you want to remove an ENI you can detach it using `Dismount-EC2NetworkInterface`. First, get the attachment id and then pass that to the `Dismount-EC2NetworkInterface` command.

```
$NIC = Get-EC2NetworkInterface eni-c00ad7a1
Dismount-EC2NetworkInterface -AttachmentId $NIC.Attachment.AttachmentId
```

There are a few reasons that you might choose to add multiple interfaces to a server. On physical machines we often include multiple interfaces to increase reliability and bandwidth. In EC2, and all virtual machine environments, the interfaces all share the same physical interface in the hypervisor. Therefore, there is no real reliability or bandwidth gain.

The other reason we include multiple interfaces it to allow our machine to span multiple subnets. Again there are multiple reasons we may choose this. One common practice is to have a management subnet used for administration and backup that is separate from the primary subnet. Again, this is likely not valuable with EC2. Security groups allow us to control administrative traffic and backups do not use our private network.

We might choose to span subnets to allow our instance to route traffic from one subnet to another. You could launch an application firewall that does traffic inspection or data loss prevention. The instance would have an interface in the private and public subnets, and you would configure the route table to route all Internet traffic through the application firewall.

Note that if you want use an instance to route traffic you must disable the source/destination check. Typically, AWS will discard any traffic sent to an instance where the instance's IP address is not the source or destination. In order for the instance to forward traffic, you must disable this check. (We will do this in Exercise 6-1.)

```
Edit-EC2NetworkInterfaceAttribute -NetworkInterfaceId eni-c00ad7a1 -SourceDestCheck:$false
```

One other reason to use multiple interfaces is disaster recovery. Just as you might move a secondary IP from the primary to standby instance, you could move the ENI. There are two advantages of moving an ENI rather than a secondary IP. First, route tables refer to the interface rather than IP. If your disaster recovery plan involves an instance that is routing traffic, you should use an ENI. Second, DHCP can be used to configure multiple ENIs, but not multiple IP addresses on the same interface.

At this point you know how to manage security groups, private IPs, EIPs, and ENIs. Now let's test our knowledge with a couple of examples.

EXERCISE 6.1: MANAGING PRIVATE INSTANCES

In Chapter 5 we created a private subnet. Remember that instances in a private subnet are not accessible from the Internet. While this is a good security practice, it introduces some new challenges.

The obvious issue is how we administer the private instances. How do we log in to a private instance to configure it, debug issues, etc.? One way to address this is to launch a remote desktop gateway (RDG) server in the public subnet and use it as a proxy to access the private instances.

In addition, the private instances are not able to access the Internet. This means that they cannot connect to the Internet resources to get patches, antivirus definitions, etc. A common solution to this problem is to launch a proxy server in the public subnet and configure the route table to route traffic from the private subnet through this proxy.

Figure 6-6 describes the complete solution. We will launch two new instances in a new subnet. Administrative traffic comes in through the RDP gateway, and outbound web traffic goes out through the NAT gateway.

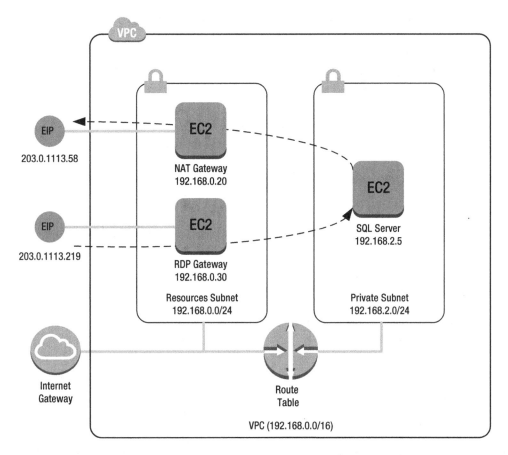

Figure 6-6. *VPC with a NAT gateway and RDP gateway*

Note that this example is, by far, the most complicated example in the book. Don't worry if you have to read through it more than once. I could have simply put all the instances in a public subnet or left the ACLs and security groups open to all traffic. But, I wanted to give you a pattern for a real-world VPC that implemented security controls likely to please an enterprise security architect.

Let's begin by altering our network configuration. This exercise assumes you already have a VPC. If you don't have a VPC, you can use Exercise 5.1 to create one. We are going to add a new public subnet to host our resources (the NAT and RDP gateways) with the CIDR block 192.168.0.0/24.

First, we define a few variables including the VPCID, CIDR Block, and the AMIs to use.

```
param
(
    [string][parameter(mandatory=$true)]$VPCID,
    [string][parameter(mandatory=$false)]$ResourcesSubnetCIDR = '192.168.0.0/24',
    [string][parameter(mandatory=$false)]$NAT_AMI,
    [string][parameter(mandatory=$false)]$RDP_AMI
)
```

If the user does not provide an AMI, let's assume he or she wants the default NAT and 2008R2.

```
If([System.String]::IsNullOrEmpty($NAT_AMI)){ $NAT_AMI =
(Get-EC2ImageByName -Name 'VPC_NAT')[0].ImageId}

If([System.String]::IsNullOrEmpty($RDP_AMI)){ $RDP_AMI =
(Get-EC2ImageByName -Name 'WINDOWS_2008_BASE')[0].ImageId}
```

Next, we choose an availability zone. I simply get the first availability zone in the region.

```
$VPC = Get-EC2VPC -VpcID $VPCID
$AvailabilityZones = Get-EC2AvailabilityZone
$AvailabilityZone = $AvailabilityZones[0].ZoneName
```

Now we create the resources subnet which will use a route table configured just like the public subnet that we created in Chapter 5.

```
$ResourcesSubnet = New-EC2Subnet -VpcId $VPCID -CidrBlock $ResourcesSubnetCIDR
    -AvailabilityZone $AvailabilityZone
$ResourcesRouteTable = New-EC2RouteTable -VpcId $VPC.VpcId
$VPCFilter = New-Object Amazon.EC2.Model.Filter
$VPCFilter.Name = 'attachment.vpc-id'
$VPCFilter.Value = $VPCID
$InternetGateway = Get-EC2InternetGateway -Filter $VPCID
New-EC2Route -RouteTableId $ResourcesRouteTable.RouteTableId -DestinationCidrBlock
    '0.0.0.0/0' -GatewayId $InternetGateway.InternetGatewayId
Register-EC2RouteTable -RouteTableId $ResourcesRouteTable.RouteTableId -SubnetId
    $ResourcesSubnet.SubnetId
```

Next we need to configure the ACLs for our new subnet. First, we will allow traffic in to configure the NAT and RDP gateway servers. The NAT instance is running Linux and requires port SSH port 22. The RDP instance is running Windows and requires RDP port 3389. In addition, we need to remember to open the ephemeral ports to allow the return traffic.

```
$ACL = New-EC2NetworkAcl -VpcId $VPCID
New-EC2NetworkAclEntry -NetworkAclId $ACL.NetworkAclId -RuleNumber 100 -CidrBlock
    '0.0.0.0/0' -Egress $false -PortRange_From 22 -PortRange_To 22 -Protocol 6
    -RuleAction Allow
New-EC2NetworkAclEntry -NetworkAclId $ACL.NetworkAclId -RuleNumber 110 -CidrBlock
     '0.0.0.0/0' -Egress $false -PortRange_From 3389 -PortRange_To 3389 -Protocol 6
    -RuleAction Allow
New-EC2NetworkAclEntry -NetworkAclId $ACL.NetworkAclId -RuleNumber 120 -CidrBlock
    '0.0.0.0/0' -Egress $true  -PortRange_From 49152 -PortRange_To 65535 -Protocol 6
    -RuleAction Allow
```

Second, the NAT gateway will be used to download patches over HTTP and HTTPS. Therefore, we need to allow traffic on 80 and 443 from our private subnets, through the resources subnet, and out to the Internet.

```
New-EC2NetworkAclEntry -NetworkAclId $ACL.NetworkAclId -RuleNumber 200 -CidrBlock
    $VPC.CidrBlock -Egress $false -PortRange_From 80 -PortRange_To 80 -Protocol 6
    -RuleAction Allow
```

```
New-EC2NetworkAclEntry -NetworkAclId $ACL.NetworkAclId -RuleNumber 210 -CidrBlock
     $VPC.CidrBlock -Egress $false -PortRange_From 443 -PortRange_To 443 -Protocol 6
     -RuleAction Allow
New-EC2NetworkAclEntry -NetworkAclId $ACL.NetworkAclId -RuleNumber 230 -CidrBlock
     $VPC.CidrBlock -Egress $true -PortRange_From 49152 -PortRange_To 65535 -Protocol 6
     -RuleAction Allow
New-EC2NetworkAclEntry -NetworkAclId $ACL.NetworkAclId -RuleNumber 240 -CidrBlock
     '0.0.0.0/0' -Egress $true -PortRange_From 80 -PortRange_To 80 -Protocol 6
     -RuleAction Allow
New-EC2NetworkAclEntry -NetworkAclId $ACL.NetworkAclId -RuleNumber 250 -CidrBlock
     '0.0.0.0/0' -Egress $true -PortRange_From 443 -PortRange_To 443 -Protocol 6
     -RuleAction Allow
New-EC2NetworkAclEntry -NetworkAclId $ACL.NetworkAclId -RuleNumber 260 -CidrBlock
     '0.0.0.0/0' -Egress $false -PortRange_From 49152 -PortRange_To 65535 -Protocol 6
     -RuleAction Allow
```

Third, we also need to allow RDP traffic in through our RDP gateway. The RDP gateway creates an SSL tunnel (port 443) from the client to the gateway. Then it uses RDP (port 3389) from the gateway to the server. Again, we need to remember the ephemeral ports.

```
New-EC2NetworkAclEntry -NetworkAclId $ACL.NetworkAclId -RuleNumber 300 -CidrBlock
     '0.0.0.0/0' -Egress $false -PortRange_From 443 -PortRange_To 443 -Protocol 6
     -RuleAction Allow
New-EC2NetworkAclEntry -NetworkAclId $ACL.NetworkAclId -RuleNumber 310 -CidrBlock
     '0.0.0.0/0' -Egress $true -PortRange_From 49152 -PortRange_To 65535 -Protocol 6
     -RuleAction Allow
New-EC2NetworkAclEntry -NetworkAclId $ACL.NetworkAclId -RuleNumber 320 -CidrBlock
     $VPC.CidrBlock -Egress $true -PortRange_From 3389 -PortRange_To 3389 -Protocol 6
     -RuleAction Allow
New-EC2NetworkAclEntry -NetworkAclId $ACL.NetworkAclId -RuleNumber 330 -CidrBlock
     $VPC.CidrBlock -Egress $false -PortRange_From 49152 -PortRange_To 65535 -Protocol 6
     -RuleAction Allow
```

Next, we have to create security groups to protect the instances we are going to launch in the resources subnet. First, we will create a security group for administration. This will allow SSH port 22 and RDP port 3389 to configure the servers.

```
$RDPRule = New-Object Amazon.EC2.Model.IpPermission
$RDPRule.IpProtocol='tcp'
$RDPRule.FromPort = 3389
$RDPRule.ToPort = 3389
$RDPRule.IpRanges = '0.0.0.0/0'
$SSHRule = New-Object Amazon.EC2.Model.IpPermission
$SSHRule.IpProtocol='tcp'
$SSHRule.FromPort = 22
$SSHRule.ToPort = 22
$SSHRule.IpRanges = '0.0.0.0/0'
$AdminGroupId = New-EC2SecurityGroup -VpcId $VPCID -GroupName 'Admin' -GroupDescription
     "Allows RDP and SSH for configuration."
Grant-EC2SecurityGroupIngress -GroupId $AdminGroupId -IpPermissions $RDPRule, $SSHRule
```

Second, we will create a security group to allow HTTP and HTTPS traffic from anywhere in the VPC to the NAT gateway.

```
$HTTPRule = New-Object Amazon.EC2.Model.IpPermission
$HTTPRule.IpProtocol='tcp'
$HTTPRule.FromPort = 80
$HTTPRule.ToPort = 80
$HTTPRule.IpRanges = $VPC.CidrBlock
$HTTPSRule = New-Object Amazon.EC2.Model.IpPermission
$HTTPSRule.IpProtocol='tcp'
$HTTPSRule.FromPort = 443
$HTTPSRule.ToPort = 443
$HTTPSRule.IpRanges = $VPC.CidrBlock
$NatGroupId = New-EC2SecurityGroup -VpcId $VPCID -GroupName 'NATGateway'
    -GroupDescription "Allows HTTP/S from the VPC to the internet."
Grant-EC2SecurityGroupIngress -GroupId $NatGroupId -IpPermissions $HTTPRule, $HTTPSRule
```

Third, we will create a security group to allow RDP over SSL from the Internet to the RDP gateway.

```
$RDPRule = New-Object Amazon.EC2.Model.IpPermission
$RDPRule.IpProtocol='tcp'
$RDPRule.FromPort = 443
$RDPRule.ToPort = 443
$RDPRule.IpRanges = '0.0.0.0/0'
$RdpGroupId = New-EC2SecurityGroup -VpcId $VPCID -GroupName 'RDPGateway'
    -GroupDescription "Allows RDP over HTTPS from the internet."
Grant-EC2SecurityGroupIngress -GroupId $RdpGroupId -IpPermissions $RDPRule
```

Fourth, we must allow RDP traffic from the RDP gateway to the instances in the default subnet.

```
$VPCFilter = New-Object Amazon.EC2.Model.Filter
$VPCFilter.Name = 'vpc-id'
$VPCFilter.Value = $VPCID
$GroupFilter = New-Object Amazon.EC2.Model.Filter
$GroupFilter.Name = 'group-name'
$GroupFilter.Value = 'default'
$DefaultGroup = Get-EC2SecurityGroup -Filter $VPCFilter, $GroupFilter
$RDPGatewayGroup = New-Object Amazon.EC2.Model.UserIdGroupPair
$RDPGatewayGroup.GroupId = $RdpGroupId
$RDPRule = New-Object Amazon.EC2.Model.IpPermission
$RDPRule.IpProtocol='tcp'
$RDPRule.FromPort = 3389
$RDPRule.ToPort = 3389
$RDPRule.UserIdGroupPair = $RDPGatewayGroup
Grant-EC2SecurityGroupIngress -GroupId $DefaultGroup.GroupId -IpPermissions $RDPRule
```

Now we associate the resource subnet we created with the new ACL.

```
$VPCFilter = New-Object Amazon.EC2.Model.Filter
$VPCFilter.Name = 'vpc-id'
$VPCFilter.Value = $VPCID
```

```
$DefaultFilter = New-Object Amazon.EC2.Model.Filter
$DefaultFilter.Name = 'default'
$DefaultFilter.Value = 'true'
$OldACL = (Get-EC2NetworkAcl -Filter $VPCFilter, $DefaultFilter )
$OldAssociation = $OldACL.Associations | Where-Object { $_.SubnetId -eq
    $ResourcesSubnet.SubnetId }
$NoEcho = Set-EC2NetworkAclAssociation -AssociationId $
    OldAssociation.NetworkAclAssociationId -NetworkAclId $ACL.NetworkAclId
```

Next, we launch a NAT gateway to serve as an outbound proxy. A NAT gateway is simply a Red Hat Linux instance that forwards traffic to the Internet. There are numerous other proxies available in the AWS marketplace that can do advanced inspection, but they are all relatively expensive. The NAT gateway is offered by Amazon as an inexpensive (you pay only for the instance) solution.

```
$Reservation = New-EC2Instance -ImageId $NAT_AMI -KeyName 'MyKey' -InstanceType
    't1.micro' -MinCount 1 -MaxCount 1 -SubnetId $ResourcesSubnet.SubnetId
$NATInstance = $Reservation.RunningInstance[0]
$Tag = New-Object Amazon.EC2.Model.Tag
$Tag.Key = 'Name'
$Tag.Value = 'NATGateway'
New-EC2Tag -ResourceId $NATInstance.InstanceID  -Tag $tag
```

You must wait for the instance to boot before moving on. This is different from the exercise in Chapter 3. Here I am just waiting for the instance to boot. We do not have to wait for the initialization to complete and the password to be available.

```
Start-Sleep -s 60
While ((Get-EC2InstanceStatus -InstanceId $NATInstance.InstanceID).InstanceState.name
    -ne 'running')
{
    Start-Sleep -s 60
    $NATInstance = (Get-EC2Instance -Instance $NATInstance.InstanceID).RunningInstance[0]
}
```

In order for the NAT instance to route traffic, we need to disable the source/destination check on the network interface. Usually an instance must be either the source or destination of any traffic that it sends or receives. To disable the check we use the Edit-EC2NetworkInterfaceAttribute command.

```
$NIC = $NATInstance.NetworkInterfaces[0]
Edit-EC2NetworkInterfaceAttribute -NetworkInterfaceId $NIC.NetworkInterfaceId
    -SourceDestCheck:$false
```

Next, we assign the instance an EIP. Remember that the Internet gateway uses NAT to translate private IP addresses to Internet IP addresses. Therefore, traffic from an instance in a private subnet to the Internet gets translated twice. First, the NAT gateway translates the private IP of the sender to its own private IP. Second, the Internet gateway translates from the private IP of the NAT gateway to its corresponding EIP.

```
$EIP = New-EC2Address -Domain 'vpc'
Register-EC2Address -InstanceId $NATInstance.InstanceID -AllocationId $EIP.AllocationId
```

Finally, we find the Main route table for the VPC and set the default route to the NAT gateway. I assume here that all of your private subnets are using the Main route table.

```
#Find the Main Route Table for this VPC
$VPCFilter = New-Object Amazon.EC2.Model.Filter
$VPCFilter.Name = 'vpc-id'
$VPCFilter.Value = $VPC.VpcId
$IsDefaultFilter = New-Object Amazon.EC2.Model.Filter
$IsDefaultFilter.Name = 'association.main'
$IsDefaultFilter.Value = 'true'
$MainRouteTable = (Get-EC2RouteTable -Filter $VPCFilter, $IsDefaultFilter)

#Replace the default route with reference to the NAT gateway
$MainRouteTable.Routes | Where-Object { $_.DestinationCidrBlock -eq '0.0.0.0/0'} | %
    {Remove-EC2Route -RouteTableId $MainRouteTable.RouteTableId -DestinationCidrBlock
$_.DestinationCidrBlock -Force}
New-EC2Route -RouteTableId $MainRouteTable.RouteTableId  -DestinationCidrBlock
    '0.0.0.0/0' -InstanceId $NATInstance.InstanceId
```

That takes care of the outbound traffic. Instances on the private subnets will route their traffic out through the NAT gateway, which will, in turn, route it through the Internet gateway. Now let's move on to the RDP gateway.

RDP is a Windows feature available on Windows server 2008R2 and 2012. It allows the RDP client to connect securely over the public Internet using HTTPS to instances on a remote private network. The complete configuration of RDP gateway requires purchasing SSL certificates and is beyond the scope of this book. (For more details about the configuration of RDP gateway, see: http://technet.microsoft.com/en-us/library/dd983941(v=ws.10).aspx.) For now, let's use the user data section we learned about in Chapter 3 to enable the RDP gateway feature after the instance launches.

```
#Create a user data script to configure the RDP Gateway
$UserData = @'
<powershell>
Add-WindowsFeature -Name RDS-Gateway -IncludeAllSubFeature
</powershell>
'@
$UserData =
    [System.Convert]::ToBase64String([System.Text.Encoding]::ASCII.GetBytes($UserData))
```

Now let's launch the instance. Remember to include the subnet and pass the user data script to execute after launch.

```
$Reservation = New-EC2Instance -ImageId $RDP_AMI -KeyName 'MyKey' -InstanceType
    't1.micro' -MinCount 1 -MaxCount 1 -SubnetId $ResourcesSubnet.SubnetId -UserData
    $UserData
$RDPInstance = $Reservation.RunningInstance[0]
$Tag = New-Object Amazon.EC2.Model.Tag
$Tag.Key = 'Name'
$Tag.Value = 'RDPGateway'
New-EC2Tag -ResourceId $RDPInstance.InstanceID  -Tag $tag
```

Now, we wait for the instance to boot and allocate an additional EIP for the NAT instance and we are done.

```
Start-Sleep -s 60
While ((Get-EC2InstanceStatus -InstanceId $RDPInstance.InstanceID).InstanceState.name
    -ne 'running')
{
    Start-Sleep -s 60
    $RDPInstance = (Get-EC2Instance -Instance $RDPInstance.InstanceID).RunningInstance[0]
}
$EIP = New-EC2Address -Domain 'vpc'
Register-EC2Address -InstanceId $RDPInstance.InstanceID -AllocationId $EIP.AllocationId
```

If you have completed the configuration of the RDP gateway, you should be able to connect to a private instance and attempt to run Windows Update. In order to connect to an instance in the private network, you need to tell your remote desktop client about the gateway server. See Figure 6-7. From the Advanced tab, click the Settings button, and enter the name of the server gateway. Now you can connect to the VPC instances as if they were publicly accessible.

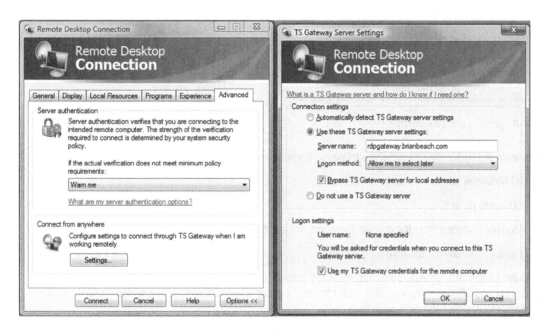

Figure 6-7. *Remote desktop connection with an RDP gateway*

EXERCISE 6.2: LEAST PRIVILEGE SECURITY GROUPS

So far we have been placing all of our private instances in the default group. The default group allows unrestricted communications between all the group members. While this makes configuration really easy, it is not as secure as it could be.

In information security, the principle of least privilege requires that a system only have access to the resources it requires to do its job. In this example, we will build a set of security groups that allows the minimum set of permissions required for a simple application. Our simple application, shown in Figure 6-8, consists of a web server and SQL server, both of which are members of an active directory domain.

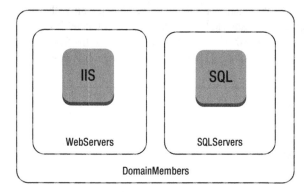 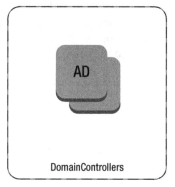

Figure 6-8. *Least privilege security groups*

At a high level, our application requires the following traffic flows:

- HTTP/S from the Internet to the IIS server
- TDS from IIS to SQL
- Multiple protocols from the domain members (IIS and SQL) to the domain controllers
- Replication between the domain controllers

Note that the IIS and SQL servers are members of two groups. Rather than adding the domain member rules to the WebServer and SQLServer groups, it is better to have a group of each distinct role a server can hold. This will make it easier to maintain the rules over time.

First, we have to create the four groups pictured in Figure 6-8.

```
$DomainMembersGroupId = New-EC2SecurityGroup -GroupName 'DomainMembers' -GroupDescription
    "Domain Members" -VpcId $VPCID
$DomainControllersGroupId = New-EC2SecurityGroup -GroupName 'DomainControllers'
    -GroupDescription "Domain controllers" -VpcId $VPCID
$WebServersGroupId = New-EC2SecurityGroup -GroupName 'WebServers' -GroupDescription "Web
    servers" -VpcId $VPCID
$SQLServersGroupId = New-EC2SecurityGroup -GroupName 'SQLServers' -GroupDescription "SQL
    Servers" -VpcId $VPCID
```

Next, we add rules to the web group. The web group will allow HTTP (port 80) and HTTPS (port 443) from anywhere on the Internet.

```
#First, the Web instances must allow HTTP/S from the internet
$HTTPRule = New-Object Amazon.EC2.Model.IpPermission
$HTTPRule.IpProtocol='tcp'
$HTTPRule.FromPort = 80
$HTTPRule.ToPort = 80
$HTTPRule.IpRanges = '0.0.0.0/0'
$HTTPSRule = New-Object Amazon.EC2.Model.IpPermission
$HTTPSRule.IpProtocol='tcp'
$HTTPSRule.FromPort = 443
$HTTPSRule.ToPort = 443
$HTTPSRule.IpRanges = '0.0.0.0/0'
Grant-EC2SecurityGroupIngress -GroupId $WebServersGroupId
    -IpPermissions $HTTPRule, $HTTPSRule
```

Then, we add rules to the SQL group. The SQL server should only be accessed from the web server. SQL uses a protocol called Tabular Data Stream (TDS) that runs on port 1433. In addition, applications are increasingly using SQL FileStream to store attachments. FileStream requires NetBIOS (port 139) and SMB (port 445) to stream the attachments to and from the SQL server.

```
$WebGroup = New-Object Amazon.EC2.Model.UserIdGroupPair
$WebGroup.GroupId = $WebServersGroupId
$SQLRule = New-Object Amazon.EC2.Model.IpPermission
$SQLRule.IpProtocol='tcp'
$SQLRule.FromPort = 1433
$SQLRule.ToPort = 1433
$SQLRule.UserIdGroupPair = $WebGroup
$NetBIOSRule = New-Object Amazon.EC2.Model.IpPermission
$NetBIOSRule.IpProtocol='tcp'
$NetBIOSRule.FromPort = 139
$NetBIOSRule.ToPort = 139
$NetBIOSRule.UserIdGroupPair = $WebGroup
$SMBRule = New-Object Amazon.EC2.Model.IpPermission
$SMBRule.IpProtocol='tcp'
$SMBRule.FromPort = 445
$SMBRule.ToPort = 445
$SMBRule.UserIdGroupPair = $WebGroup
Grant-EC2SecurityGroupIngress -GroupId $SQLServersGroupId -IpPermissions $SQLRule,
    $NetBIOSRule, $SMBRule
```

Now, we add rules to the DomainMembers group. The DomainMembers group is really simple. The only traffic it allows is ping from the domain controllers. The domain controllers will occasionally ping the domain members to check that they are still running. In addition, the DomainMembers group is used as the source of all the rules in the DomainControllers group.

```
$DCGroup = New-Object Amazon.EC2.Model.UserIdGroupPair
$DCGroup.GroupId = $DomainControllersGroupId
$PingRule = New-Object Amazon.EC2.Model.IpPermission
$PingRule.IpProtocol='icmp'
```

```
$PingRule.FromPort = 8
$PingRule.ToPort = -1
$PingRule.UserIdGroupPair = $DCGroup
Grant-EC2SecurityGroupIngress -GroupId $DomainMembersGroupId -IpPermissions $PingRule
```

Finally, we add rules to the DomainControllers group. This group has a lot of rules. I'll break them down by IP protocol.

First, assuming you have more than one domain controller, they must be able to replicate data between each other. Therefore, I am allowing unrestricted communications between the controllers.

```
$AllRule = New-Object Amazon.EC2.Model.IpPermission
$AllRule.IpProtocol='-1'
$AllRule.UserIdGroupPair = $DCGroup
Grant-EC2SecurityGroupIngress -GroupId $DomainControllersGroupId -IpPermissions $AllRule
```

Second, the domain controllers allow ping from any of the domain members.

```
$DMGroup = New-Object Amazon.EC2.Model.UserIdGroupPair
$DMGroup.GroupId = $DomainMembersGroupId
$PingRule = New-Object Amazon.EC2.Model.IpPermission
$PingRule.IpProtocol='icmp'
$PingRule.FromPort = 8
$PingRule.ToPort = -1
$PingRule.UserIdGroupPair = $DMGroup
Grant-EC2SecurityGroupIngress -GroupId $DomainControllersGroupId -IpPermissions $PingRule
```

Third, the domain controller must allow an array of TCP communication types from the domain members. These include:

- 53 - DNS Queries. Note DNS uses both TCP and UDP.

- 88 - Kerberos Authentication. Note Kerberos uses both TCP and UDP.

- 135 - Remote Procedure Calls. Note: RPC will also use a port in the range 49152-65535.

- 137–139 - NetBOIS. Note Kerberos uses both TCP and UDP.

- 389 & 636 - Lightweight Directory Access Protocol (LDAP).

- 445 - Server Message Block (SMB).

- 464 - Password Reset. Note that it uses both TCP and UDP.

- 3268 - Microsoft Global Catalogue.

```
#Domain controllers must allow numerous TCP protocols from domain members
$DNSRule = New-Object Amazon.EC2.Model.IpPermission
$DNSRule.IpProtocol='tcp'
$DNSRule.FromPort = 53
$DNSRule.ToPort = 53
$DNSRule.UserIdGroupPair = $DMGroup
```

```
$KerberosRule = New-Object Amazon.EC2.Model.IpPermission
$KerberosRule.IpProtocol='tcp'
$KerberosRule.FromPort = 88
$KerberosRule.ToPort = 88
$KerberosRule.UserIdGroupPair = $DMGroup
$NetBIOSRule = New-Object Amazon.EC2.Model.IpPermission
$NetBIOSRule.IpProtocol='tcp'
$NetBIOSRule.FromPort = 137
$NetBIOSRule.ToPort = 139
$NetBIOSRule.UserIdGroupPair = $DMGroup
$RPCRule = New-Object Amazon.EC2.Model.IpPermission
$RPCRule.IpProtocol='tcp'
$RPCRule.FromPort = 135
$RPCRule.ToPort = 135
$RPCRule.UserIdGroupPair = $DMGroup
$LDAPRule = New-Object Amazon.EC2.Model.IpPermission
$LDAPRule.IpProtocol='tcp'
$LDAPRule.FromPort = 389
$LDAPRule.ToPort = 389
$LDAPRule.UserIdGroupPair = $DMGroup
$SMBRule = New-Object Amazon.EC2.Model.IpPermission
$SMBRule.IpProtocol='tcp'
$SMBRule.FromPort = 445
$SMBRule.ToPort = 445
$SMBRule.UserIdGroupPair = $DMGroup
$PasswordRule = New-Object Amazon.EC2.Model.IpPermission
$PasswordRule.IpProtocol='tcp'
$PasswordRule.FromPort = 464
$PasswordRule.ToPort = 464
$PasswordRule.UserIdGroupPair = $DMGroup
$LDAPSRule = New-Object Amazon.EC2.Model.IpPermission
$LDAPSRule.IpProtocol='tcp'
$LDAPSRule.FromPort = 636
$LDAPSRule.ToPort = 636
$LDAPSRule.UserIdGroupPair = $DMGroup
$ADRule = New-Object Amazon.EC2.Model.IpPermission
$ADRule.IpProtocol='tcp'
$ADRule.FromPort = 3268
$ADRule.ToPort = 3269
$ADRule.UserIdGroupPair = $DMGroup
$RpcHpRule = New-Object Amazon.EC2.Model.IpPermission
$RpcHpRule.IpProtocol='tcp'
$RpcHpRule.FromPort = 49152
$RpcHpRule.ToPort = 65535
$RpcHpRule.UserIdGroupPair = $DMGroup
Grant-EC2SecurityGroupIngress -GroupId $DomainControllersGroupId -IpPermissions $DNSRule,
    $KerberosRule, $RPCRule, $LDAPRule, $PasswordRule, $LDAPSRule, $ADRule, $RpcHpRule
```

Fourth, the domain controller must allow an array of UDP communication types from the domain members. These include:

- 53 - DNS Queries. Note DNS uses both TCP and UDP.

- 88 - Kerberos Authentication. Note Kerberos uses both TCP and UDP.

- 123 - Network Time Protocol.

- 137-139 - NetBOIS. Note Kerberos uses both TCP and UDP.

- 389 - Lightweight Directory Access Protocol (LDAP).

- 464 - Password Reset. Note that it uses both TCP and UDP.

```
#Domain controllers must allow numerous TCP protocols from domain members
$DNSRule = New-Object Amazon.EC2.Model.IpPermission
$DNSRule.IpProtocol='udp'
$DNSRule.FromPort = 53
$DNSRule.ToPort = 53
$DNSRule.UserIdGroupPair = $DMGroup
$KerberosRule = New-Object Amazon.EC2.Model.IpPermission
$KerberosRule.IpProtocol='udp'
$KerberosRule.FromPort = 88
$KerberosRule.ToPort = 88
$KerberosRule.UserIdGroupPair = $DMGroup
$NTPRule = New-Object Amazon.EC2.Model.IpPermission
$NTPRule.IpProtocol='udp'
$NTPRule.FromPort = 123
$NTPRule.ToPort = 123
$NTPRule.UserIdGroupPair = $DMGroup
$NetBIOSRule = New-Object Amazon.EC2.Model.IpPermission
$NetBIOSRule.IpProtocol='udp'
$NetBIOSRule.FromPort = 137
$NetBIOSRule.ToPort = 139
$NetBIOSRule.UserIdGroupPair = $DMGroup
$LDAPRule = New-Object Amazon.EC2.Model.IpPermission
$LDAPRule.IpProtocol='udp'
$LDAPRule.FromPort = 389
$LDAPRule.ToPort = 389
$LDAPRule.UserIdGroupPair = $DMGroup
$PasswordRule = New-Object Amazon.EC2.Model.IpPermission
$PasswordRule.IpProtocol='udp'
$PasswordRule.FromPort = 464
$PasswordRule.ToPort = 464
$PasswordRule.UserIdGroupPair = $DMGroup
Grant-EC2SecurityGroupIngress -GroupId $DomainControllersGroupId -IpPermissions $DNSRule,
    $KerberosRule, $NTPRule, $NetBIOSRule, $LDAPRule, $SMBRule, $PasswordRule
```

As you can see, security groups allow you to create very specific rules to secure your resources. By writing rules that are based on other security groups, we can define our security policy before launching instances and do not have to change the rules as each instance is launched. The rules in this example are just a starting point. You will need to add additional groups and rules as your infrastructure grows.

Summary

VPC brings numerous new capabilities that were not available in EC2 Classic. We can define outbound rules in our security groups. We can control the network configuration at launch including subnet, security group, and private IP address. We can assign publicly addressable EIPs. And, we can add multiple IP address and multiple network interfaces.

All of these features allow us to create fairly complicated network configurations. In the examples, we explored advanced patterns for managing enterprise networks. First, we discussed how to manage and patch private instances using an RDP and NAT Gateway. Second, we created a series of security groups to implement least privileged access for Windows instances in an active directory domain.

While VPC brings new capabilities, it also brings complexity. In the remaining chapters on EC2 I will use a simple VPC configuration that will allow us to focus on features without the complexity discussed in Chapters 5 and 6. In the next chapter, we discuss creating our own Amazon Machine Images.

CHAPTER 7

Amazon Machine Images

In the last few chapters we have focused on creating and managing instances. This chapter is about the templates we use to create those instances. Amazon refers to these templates as Amazon Machine Images (AMIs). In this chapter we will explore the AMIs that already exist, and we will discuss how to create your own AMI and share it with others. Finally, we learn how to import a VM from VMware or Hyper-V into AWS.

Many users will never have occasion to create a custom AMI. Most users will be happy with the countless images that Amazon and its partners make available. But some users will want to have complete control over their environment. For example, you may have a corporate server image that you want to make available to your companies' employees that are using AWS.

As your experience progresses, you will likely find that you want to automate instance builds. The DevOps movement is all about scripting server builds to minimize build time and ensure consistency between builds. Assuming you want to automate the build, there are many options. Most fall on a spectrum somewhere between scripted builds and prepared images.

Working with Scripted Builds and Prepared Images

At one end of the spectrum is the scripted build. With a scripted build, you start with a generic image and use a series of scripts to configure the server as needed. For example, to create a Web Server, you might start with the Amazon Windows Server 2012 Base image. Then you could use the user data to include a custom PowerShell script that enables the Web Server role and downloads the application from source control.

At the other end of the spectrum is the prepared image. With a prepared image, you configure the server, usually manually, and then create an image. When a user needs a new server, her or she selects your server image and creates a new instance. If you choose a prepared image, be sure to update the image periodically with the latest security patches and virus definitions.

Both options have benefits and drawbacks. The scripted build is best when the application is changing often. You always get the latest code and can change the script as requirements change. The prepared image, on the other hand, is best when the application is stable. There are fewer external dependencies that can cause errors and the build is usually faster.

Of course, there are many options on the spectrum between scripted build and prepared image. The Amazon Windows AMIs provide a good example. Amazon offers a base image with nothing installed as well as Web and SQL Server images. By using these images you do not have to script the configuration of the IIS and SQL Server. You simply focus on scripting the deployment of your application.

Most of this chapter is focused on preparing images, but don't overlook scripting as an option. In the first example we will discuss the tradeoffs between scripted builds and prepared images a bit further while we will discuss a common Windows task: joining a Windows domain.

Listing AMIs

Before we create our own AMI, or simply an image, let's take a deeper look at the images that are already available. We don't want to spend time creating and maintaining an image if an identical image already exists.

■ **Caution** There are over 20,000 images available giving you a ton of options to choose from, but be careful! You should only launch images from publishers you trust. As you will see later in this chapter, anyone can publish an image.

You can find images using the Get-EC2Image command, but this command will return the complete list of over 20,000 images. Obviously, this is far too many to look through one at a time.

Limiting the Number of Instance Results

As you might expect, you can use filters to limit the number of instances. For example, if you are interested in a Windows image, you can use the platform filter. The following example will return about 1700 Windows images in the Northern Virginia region.

```
$Filter = New-Object Amazon.EC2.Model.Filter
$Filter.Name = "platform"
$Filter.Value = "windows"
Get-EC2Image -Filter $Filter | Select-Object Name
```

We can also filter by publisher using owner-alias. For example, you might list only those images that Amazon publishes. Again it is a really good idea to only use images published by an owner you trust, such as Amazon. The following example will return about 500 images.

```
$Filter = New-Object Amazon.EC2.Model.Filter
$Filter.Name = "owner-alias"
$Filter.Value = "amazon"
Get-EC2Image -Filter $Filter | Select-Object Name
```

This is still too many images to comb through one by one. Of course you can combine two or more filters. If we combine the platform and owner alias, we get a much more reasonable list of about 100 images.

```
$Filter1 = New-Object Amazon.EC2.Model.Filter
$Filter1.Name = "platform"
$Filter1.Value = "windows"
$Filter2 = New-Object Amazon.EC2.Model.Filter
$Filter2.Name = "owner-alias"
$Filter2.Value = "amazon"
Get-EC2Image -Filter $Filter1, $Filter2 | Select-Object Name
```

Finding an Instance by Name

The prior examples assume you do not yet know which image you are looking for. If you know the name of the image you want to find you can use the name filter. For example, to find the Windows Server 2012 Base image, use:

```
$Filter = New-Object Amazon.EC2.Model.Filter
$Filter.Name = "name"
$Filter.Value = "Windows_Server-2012-RTM-English-64Bit-Base-2013.09.11"
Get-EC2Image -Filter $Filter\
```

Note that Amazon updates most of its images periodically with the latest patches and updates. This causes a problem because the image name includes the publication date, and changes over time. Luckily, filters support the wildcard character (*). For example:

```
$Filter = New-Object Amazon.EC2.Model.Filter
$Filter.Name = "name"
$Filter.Value = "Windows_Server-2012-RTM-English-64Bit-Base*"
Get-EC2Image -Filter $Filter
```

So let's review. We can use a combination of the platform and owner-alias filters to discover new images from a trusted source. Then, once we know the name, we can search by name. If all of this seems cumbersome to you, I agree. Wouldn't it be great if we had a short list of the most common images?

Locating the Most Common Images

Luckily Amazon thought of the idea of getting a short list of the most common images and included another command, Get-EC2ImageByName. This command will return the images that you find on the Quick Start tab of the New Instance Wizard in the AWS Management Console. Note that the command may return an array with multiple versions of a given instance. The most recent version will be listed first in the array. See the sidebar for a list of names. For example:

```
Get-EC2ImageByName -Name "WINDOWS_2012_BASE"
```

COMMON IMAGES FOR GET-EC2IMAGEBYNAME

WINDOWS_2012_BASE - Windows Server 2012 without SQL Server

WINDOWS_2012_SQL_SERVER_EXPRESS_2012 - Windows Server 2012 with SQL Server 2012 Express Edition

WINDOWS_2012_SQL_SERVER_STANDARD_2012 - Windows Server 2012 with SQL Server 2012 Standard Edition

WINDOWS_2012_SQL_SERVER_WEB_2012 - Windows Server 2012 with SQL Server 2012 Web Edition

WINDOWS_2012_SQL_SERVER_EXPRESS_2008 - Windows Server 2012 with SQL Server 2008 R2 Express Edition

WINDOWS_2012_SQL_SERVER_STANDARD_2008 - Windows Server 2012 with SQL Server 2008 R2 Standard Edition

WINDOWS_2012_SQL_SERVER_WEB_2008 - Windows Server 2012 with SQL Server 2008 R2 Web Edition

WINDOWS_2008_BASE - Windows Server 2008 R2 without SQL Server

---

WINDOWS_2008_SQL_SERVER_EXPRESS_2012 - Windows Server 2008 R2 with SQL Server 2012 Express Edition

WINDOWS_2008_SQL_SERVER_STANDARD_2012 - Windows Server 2008 R2 with SQL Server 2012 Standard Edition

WINDOWS_2008_SQL_SERVER_WEB_2012 - Windows Server 2008 R2 with SQL Server 2012 Web Edition

WINDOWS_2008_SQL_SERVER_EXPRESS_2008 - Windows Server 2008 R2 with SQL Server 2008 R2 Express Edition

WINDOWS_2008_SQL_SERVER_STANDARD_2008 - Windows Server 2008 R2 with SQL Server 2008 R2 Standard Edition

WINDOWS_2008_SQL_SERVER_WEB_2008 - Windows Server 2008 R2 with SQL Server 2008 R2 Web Edition

VPC_NAT - This is the NAT instance we launched in Example 6.1 in Chapter 6.

Finally, if you have launched your own images, as described later in this chapter, you can find them by using the Owner parameter of the Get-EC2Image command. For example:

```
Get-EC2Image -Owner self
```

Now that we know how to find images, we can decide whether we need to create our own. Let's assume that none of the existing images meet our needs and we have decided to create our own image. Images are created using SysPrep and the EC2Config Service. Before we get started creating an image, let's look at the EC2Config Service.

Introducing the EC2Config Service

Before we move on to creating an image, I want to introduce the EC2Config Service. The EC2Config Service is a Windows service that runs on all Amazon's Windows images. We have mentioned this service a few times in prior chapters, but now is a good time to look at it in detail.

The EC2Config Service is used to configure Windows instances. The service plays a critical role in configuring an instance when it boots for the first time. For example, the EC2Config Service is responsible for encrypting the administrator password and executing scripts in the user data.

When an instance boots for the first time, the EC2 Config Service performs the following tasks.

1. Set the computer name. The instance will be renamed in the format ip-hhhhhhhh, where hhhhhhhh is the hex encoding of the private IP address.

2. Set the administrator password. A new, random password will be generated and encrypted with the specified key pair.

3. Create RDP certificate. A new self-signed host certificate is created for Remote Desktop Connection. You cannot use RDP without a certificate.

4. Extend the OS partition. Remember that you can change the size of the OS volume at launch. Therefore, the service extends the partition to fill the volume.

On subsequent boots, the EC2 Config Service performs the following tasks.

1. Activate Windows as necessary. Note that you can change the Key Management Server (KMS) server in the settings file.

2. Format disks. This mounts secondary EBS and instance store volumes, and formats them.

3. Set the clock. Note that the default is UTC time, not the local time zone of the AWS region.

4. Write event log entries to the AWS System Log. This can help debug errors that occur before RDP is available in the boot sequence.

5. Create a new wallpaper image. This includes useful information (name, type, memory, etc.) about the image.

6. Configure a few custom routes. For example, 169.254.169.250 and 169.254.169.251 are the default KMS servers and 169.254.169.254 is the meta-data URL we used in Chapter 3.

All of these actions are performed by default, but you can customize them as needed using the EC2 Config Service Settings. Log into any Windows instance and find "EC2 Config Service Settings" on the start menu. The application is organized into four tabs: General, Image, Storage, and Support.

The first tab, shown in Figure 7-1, allows you to control basic settings.

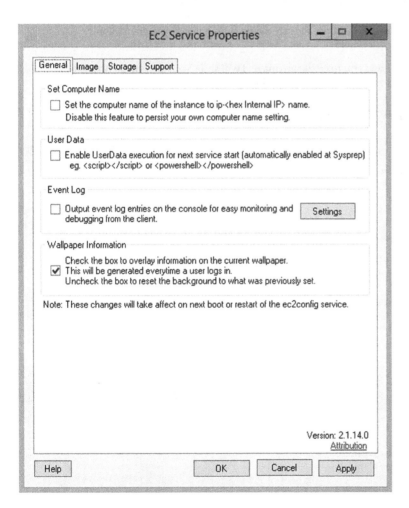

Figure 7-1. EC2 Config Service General tab

Set Computer Name will rename the instance to match the private IP address. This is enabled by default during the first boot. If you create your own image, you can disable it to use a custom naming convention.

User Data will execute <script> and <powershell> scripts included in the user data at launch. (Remember that we discussed this in Chapter 3.) By default, the user-data scripts are only executed during the first boot. You can manually enable it to run on subsequent boots. Note that during the first boot, scripts run under the administrator account. During subsequent boots, scripts run under the service account that the EC2Config Service is running under.

Event Log will write errors to the AWS System Log. You cannot connect to an instance when it is booting, and if it fails to boot you may not be able to connect at all. Therefore, it is difficult to debug issues that occur during boot. Writing errors to the system log will allow you to see them from the AWS Management Console.

Wallpaper Information writes information to the desktop. Often you will have users accessing instances that do not have access to the AWS Management Console. The wallpaper allows these users to see information about the instance they are using without needing to grant them access to the AWS console.

The second tab, shown in Figure 7-2, allows you to create an image. I will show you, step-by-step, how to create an image in the next section, but let's review a few of the key options here.

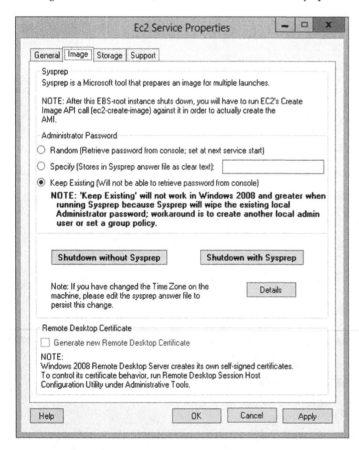

Figure 7-2. *EC2 Config Service Image tab*

Administrator Password allows you to specify the password. You can either type in a password, or allow the EC2Config Service to generate a random password for you.

Shutdown with SysPrep will prepare the image and shut down the instance. This is how we will create a new image in the next section.

Details will tell you the location of the SysPrep answer file. You can manually edit the answer file to further customize the image. For example, you can include credentials needed to join the instance to a Windows domain.

The third tab, shown in Figure 7-3, allows you to configure volumes. The options are:

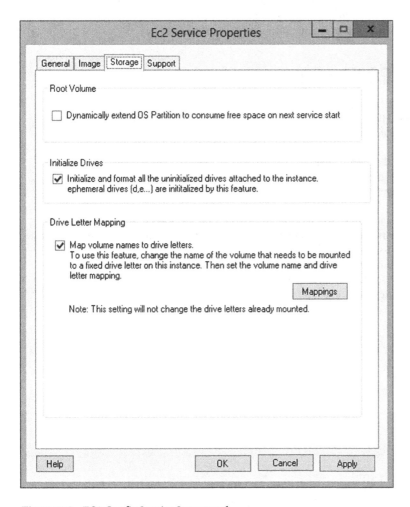

Figure 7-3. *EC2 Config Service Storage tab*

Root Volume will automatically extend the OS partition to fill the root volume. You can disable this if you want to leave free space on the root volume to create additional partitions.

Initialize Drives will automatically mount and format any secondary or instance store volumes. Disable this if you want to use a custom mount point or if you format the disk using something other than NTFS.

Drive Letter Mapping allows you to control how volumes are mapped. You specify the volume label and the drive letter you want it to use. This is useful if you are attaching multiple disks with data already on them.

The fourth tab, not pictured, provides links to a few useful debugging tools. You can explore these tools on your own.

Now that you know your way around the EC2Config Service, let's create our own image. In the next section we will customize an Amazon AMI and create a new image that includes our customizations.

Preparing an AMI Using EC2Config

In the prior section we learned about the EC2Config Service. In this section we will prepare an image of our own. To start, launch a new Windows Server 2012 Base instance that will serve as our template. You can either use the AWS Management Console or the following PowerShell script.

```
$AMI = Get-EC2ImageByName -Name 'WINDOWS_2012_BASE'
$Reservation = New-EC2Instance -ImageId $AMI[0].ImageId -KeyName 'MyKey'
    -InstanceType 't1.micro' -MinCount 1 -MaxCount 1
```

Once the instance boots, you can log in and make whatever changes you want. Let's assume we are developing a web application and we want to create a server to test it on. Our application has some complicated authentication requirements and needs a few features that were not enabled on the Amazon Windows 2012 Web Server AMI.

In Figure 7-4 I have configured the required roles and services. First, I enabled the Web Server (IIS) role. Next, I enabled the Windows Identity Foundation 3.5 feature. Finally, I enabled six of the nine Web Server Security Role Services. Obviously your configuration will depend on the applications you intend to run on the instance.

Figure 7-4. *Configuring the Web Server role*

Once you have configured your server and installed any software you want in the template, it is time to prepare the image. As I mentioned in the prior section, you use the EC2Config Service to create an image. Behind the scenes, the EC2Config Service uses SysPrep to do the heavy lifting.

A NOTE ON SQL SERVER

I want to take a minute to talk about SQL Server images. Technically SQL Server does not support SysPrep. If you SysPrep an instance that has SQL installed, the data in the master database will retain references to the original server name. This will lead to issues with some SQL components including Reporting Service and SQL Replication. The Amazon SQL images ignore this advice and use a script to fix the data in the master database.

The correct way to SysPrep SQL Server is to use the "Image preparation" option. A prepared image installs all of the application bits, but does not create the master database. You can then safely SysPrep the image and complete the installation after an instance is created from the image. For details see
http://technet.microsoft.com/en-us/library/ee210664.aspx.

■ **Caution**   Before continuing, you should take a snapshot of the instance. Once we SysPrep the image, there is no going back. If the instance fails to boot, you will have to start over from scratch.

Open the "Ec2Config Service Settings" application from the start menu on your template instance. On the General tab (see Figure 7-1 for reference) I enabled the User Data option to ensure that I can further customize any instances I create from this image. I also enabled the Event Log output option to help debugging if the image fails.

On the Storage tab (see Figure 7-3 for reference) I enabled the option to dynamically extend the OS partition. Remember that this will allow the users of our template to specify the volume size when creating an instance.

On the Image tab (see Figure 7-2 for reference) I set the administrator password to Random. This tells AWS to generate a random password and encrypt it with our key pair.

At this point you can simply click the Shutdown with SysPrep button, but before we do let's look at the SysPrep script. If you click the Details button on the Image tab, you will see the path to the SysPrep configuration file.

Editing the SysPrep Answer File

The SysPrep answer file is used to customize the setup of a new Windows instance created from an image. Click the Details button on the Image tab of the EC2Config Settings tool. Open this file in notepad.

■ **Note**   This section is optional.

The SysPrep answer file is broken into three sections that represent phases of the SysPrep and Setup process: generalize, specialize, and oobeSystem. The generalize phase occurs when you run SysPrep and is responsible for removing system-specific information from the template instance such as the server name, SID, etc. This section is fairly generic and there is little you will want to change.

The specialize phase occurs when a new instance is first booted and is responsible for configuring new system-specific information. This is your opportunity to change the machine name, join a domain, or run a custom script.

The oobeSystem or "out of the box experience" is the wizard the user is presented with when he or she logs in for the first time. You have probably seen this if you have bought a new PC. This is your opportunity to change the time zone and localization information. Remember when running at AWS, the user cannot see the Windows Console; therefore, the configuration file must provide answers to all of the questions a user would see.

Let's make a couple of changes to our answer file before running SysPrep. Note that I have included a complete SysPrep file, called sysprep2008.xml, with the example code for this chapter. First, let's change the default time zone from UTC to Eastern Standard Time. You will find this about halfway down in the oobeSystem section (and shown in bold in the following code).

```
<unattend xmlns="urn:schemas-microsoft-com:unattend">
  ...
  <settings pass="oobeSystem">
    ...
    <component name="Microsoft-Windows-Shell-Setup" ...>
      ...
      <BluetoothTaskbarIconEnabled>false</BluetoothTaskbarIconEnabled>
      <TimeZone>Eastern Standard Time</TimeZone>
```

```
        <RegisteredOrganization>Amazon.com</RegisteredOrganization>
        <RegisteredOwner>Amazon</RegisteredOwner>
      </component>
    </settings>
    ...
</unattend>
```

Next, let's add instructions to join a domain and register with DNS. I am using a domain called AWSLAB.LOCAL. You will need a username and password for a domain user that has permission to add machines to the domain. Now add the following two components to the end of the specialize section.

```
<unattend xmlns="urn:schemas-microsoft-com:unattend">
  ...
  <settings pass="specialize">
  ...
    <component name="Microsoft-Windows-DNS-Client" processorArchitecture="amd64"
      publicKeyToken="31bf3856ad364e35" language="neutral" versionScope="nonSxS"
      xmlns:wcm="http://schemas.microsoft.com/WMIConfig/2002/State"
      xmlns:xsi="http://www.w3.org/2001/XMLSchema-instance">
      <DNSDomain>awslab.local</DNSDomain>
      <UseDomainNameDevolution>true</UseDomainNameDevolution>
      <DNSSuffixSearchOrder>
        <DomainName wcm:action="add" wcm:keyValue="1"> awslab.local</DomainName>
      </DNSSuffixSearchOrder>
    </component>
    <component name="Microsoft-Windows-UnattendedJoin" processorArchitecture="amd64"
      publicKeyToken="31bf3856ad364e35" language="neutral" versionScope="nonSxS"
      xmlns:wcm="http://schemas.microsoft.com/WMIConfig/2002/State"
      xmlns:xsi="http://www.w3.org/2001/XMLSchema-instance">
      <Identification>
        <Credentials>
          <Domain>AWSLAB.LOCAL</Domain>
          <Username>DOMAIN_JOIN_USERNAME</Username>
          <Password>DOMAIN_JOIN_PASSWORD</Password>
        </Credentials>
        <JoinDomain>AWSLAB.LOCAL</JoinDomain>
        <UnsecureJoin>
        </UnsecureJoin>
      </Identification>
    </component>
    ...
  </settings>
  ...
</unattend>
```

Now, you can click the Shutdown with SysPrep button on the Image tab of the EC2Config Service Settings tool. The SysPrep process will run for a few minutes and the instance will shutdown.

The instance will begin running setup as soon as you start it, so do not start the instance again until we create an image. In the next section we will create an AMI from this instance.

Creating an AMI

The instance is now configured and waiting to run setup. We want to clone the instance in this state, so that each copy runs setup when it first boots. It's finally time to create an image. Let's look at the AWS Administration Console first, and then discuss the PowerShell commands.

In the AWS Management Console, right-click on the instance you want to create an image of and select Create Image (EBS AMI). Figure 7-5 shows the Create Image dialog box. From here you can give your image a name and description, and configure the volumes. Remember, from Chapter 4, that the user will have the option of modifying the volume configuration when he or she launches an instance of your image. If the image requires multiple volumes, you can set default values here.

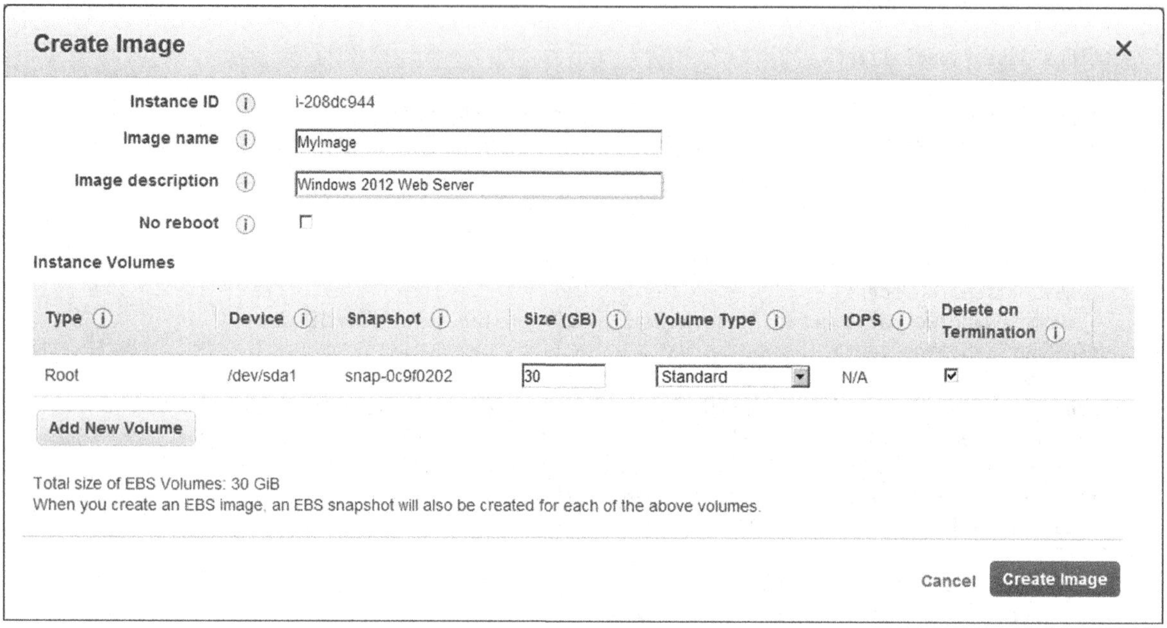

Figure 7-5. *Create Image dialog box*

The equivalent PowerShell command is New-EC2Image. The command takes the id of the instance you want to make a template from, as well as a name and description, and returns the ID of the new image. For example:

```
$AMIID = New-EC2Image -InstanceId i-208dc944
    -Name "WIN2012WEB" -Description "Windows 2012 Web Server"
```

As you might expect it takes a few minutes to create the image. You can check the ImageState to see if the image is ready. To wait for an image you can use a while loop similar to the example below.

```
$AMI = Get-EC2Image $AMIID
While($AMI.ImageState -ne "available") {
        $AMI = Get-EC2Image $AMIID
        Start-Sleep -Seconds 15
}
```

Modifying the drive configuration works just like it did when we used the `New-EC2Instance` command in Chapter 4. Let's add another 100GB volume to our image to store IIS log files. Remember that the EC2Config Service is configured to automatically mount and format any additional volumes that we attach. All we need to do is create a block device and mapping descriptor and pass it to the `New-EC2Image` command using the `BlockDeviceMapping` attribute. For example:

```
$Volume1 = New-Object Amazon.EC2.Model.EbsBlockDevice
$Volume1.DeleteOnTermination = $True
$Volume1.VolumeSize = 30
$Volume1.VolumeType = "standard"

$Mapping1 = New-Object Amazon.EC2.Model.BlockDeviceMapping
$Mapping1.DeviceName = "/dev/sda1"
$Mapping1.Ebs = $Volume1

$Volume2 = New-Object Amazon.EC2.Model.EbsBlockDevice
$Volume2.DeleteOnTermination = $False
$Volume2.VolumeSize = 100
$Volume2.VolumeType = "standard"

$Mapping2 = New-Object Amazon.EC2.Model.BlockDeviceMapping
$Mapping2.DeviceName = "xvdf"
$Mapping2.Ebs = $Volume2

$AMIID = New-EC2Image -InstanceId i-208dc944
    -Name "WIN2012WEB2" -Description "Windows 2012 Web Server 2"
    -BlockDeviceMapping $Mapping1, $Mapping2
```

At this point you have your own custom AMI and you can create instances. This same process can be used to make as many variations as you need. If you find that an image is particularly useful, you may want to share it with others. In the next section I will show you how to share your image.

Sharing an AMI

You may find that you want to share an image with other accounts. Maybe your company has multiple accounts and you want to use a single corporate image across all accounts. Or maybe you have an image that includes a trial version of your company's software and you want to share it with the world.

To share an image with another account you use the `Edit-EC2ImageAttribute` command. In the following example I am granting permission to launch an instance of an image to users of the account 1234-1234-1234. Obviously your image id and account id will be different.

```
Edit-EC2ImageAttribute -ImageId 'ami-71ebba18' -Attribute 'launchPermission'
    -OperationType 'add' -UserId '123412341234'
```

To share an image with all accounts, you grant permission to the group "all." For example:

```
Edit-EC2ImageAttribute -ImageId 'ami-71ebba18' -Attribute 'launchPermission'
    -OperationType "add" -UserGroup "all"
```

You can check which accounts and groups have access by using the Get-EC2ImageAttribute command.

```
Get-EC2ImageAttribute -ImageId 'ami-71ebba18' -Attribute 'launchPermission'
```

To revoke the launch permission from an account, use the remove operation type. For example:

```
Edit-EC2ImageAttribute -ImageId 'ami-71ebba18' -Attribute 'launchPermission'
    -OperationType 'remove' -UserId '123412341234'
```

You can revoke the launch permission from the group the same way. For example:

```
Edit-EC2ImageAttribute -ImageId 'ami-71ebba18' -Attribute 'launchPermission'
    -OperationType 'add' -UserGroup 'remove'
```

If you want to revoke the launch permission from all users and groups, you can use the Reset-EC2ImageAttribute command. For example:

```
Reset-EC2ImageAttribute  -ImageId 'ami-71ebba18' -Attribute 'launchPermission'
```

Finally, if you are sharing images between accounts, you can list the images owned by a specific account by supplying the account number to the Get-EC2Image command. For example:

```
Get-EC2Image -Owner 123412341234
```

As you can see, AMIs are a powerful tool. You can leverage the tens of thousands of existing images, create your own images, and even share your images with others. In Exercise 7.1, I will show you an alternative to creating a prepared image: the scripted build.

EXERCISE 7.1: JOINING YOUR SERVER TO A DOMAIN

At the beginning of the chapter I talked about the difference between scripted builds and prepared images. Most of this chapter has focused on prepared images, but I want to take a minute to return to the scripted build.

When we created the image earlier we modified the SysPrep answer file to join the new instance to a domain. While this was a simple solution, it has a few flaws. Most notably the setup process generates a random server name and we have no control over it. Many companies have strict naming conventions that indicate the location and role of the server. In this example we will create a script that can act on any windows AMI to properly name the server and join it to a domain.

First, we need quite a few inputs including the server name, the domain name and credentials to join, the instance type and key pair to use, and the AMI.

```
param
(
    [string][parameter(mandatory=$true)]$ServerName,
    [string][parameter(mandatory=$true)]$SubnetId,
    [string][parameter(mandatory=$false)]$DomainName = 'AWSLAB.local',
    [string][parameter(mandatory=$false)]$DomainUser = 'AWSLAB\AWSAdmin',
    [string][parameter(mandatory=$true)]$DomainPassword,
```

```
    [string][parameter(mandatory=$false)]$InstanceType = 't1.micro',
    [string][parameter(mandatory=$false)]$KeyName = 'MyKey',
    [string][parameter(mandatory=$false)]$PemFile = 'C:\AWS\MyKey.pem',
    [string][parameter(mandatory=$false)]$AMI
)
```

If no AMI is specified we will look up the Windows 2012 AMI in the current region and use that.

```
If([System.String]::IsNullOrEmpty($AMI)){ $AMI = (Get-EC2ImageByName -Name
    "WINDOWS_2012_BASE")[0].ImageId}
```

Now is where it gets interesting. We could simply add the entire script to the user-data section before we launch. But, this will include the domain credentials. We don't want to make them available to anyone who logs into the instance. Instead, I will add a PowerShell script to the user data to enable WMI calls through Windows Firewall. Then, we can use remote WMI calls to join the server to the domain without exposing the password to users.

The script to open Windows Firewall was already discussed in Chapter 3. It simply enables the existing firewall rules.

```
$UserData = [System.Convert]::ToBase64String(
    [System.Text.Encoding]::ASCII.GetBytes(@'
<powershell>
Get-NetFirewallRule | Where { $_.DisplayName -eq "Windows Management
    Instrumentation (ASync-In)" } | Enable-NetFirewallRule
Get-NetFirewallRule | Where { $_.DisplayName -eq "Windows Management
    Instrumentation (DCOM-In)" } | Enable-NetFirewallRule
Get-NetFirewallRule | Where { $_.DisplayName -eq "Windows Management
    Instrumentation (WMI-In)" } | Enable-NetFirewallRule
</powershell>
'@))
```

Now we can launch the instance specified. Remember that this script will work with any Windows image. It does not require a custom AMI.

```
$Reservation = New-EC2Instance -ImageId $AMI -KeyName $KeyName -SubnetId $SubnetId
    -InstanceType $InstanceType -MinCount 1 -MaxCount 1 -UserData $UserData
```

Next, I retrieve the instance ID and IP address. I also label the instance with the name tag.

```
$Instance = $Reservation.RunningInstance[0].InstanceId
$IP = $Reservation.RunningInstance[0].PrivateIpAddress

$Tag = New-Object Amazon.EC2.Model.Tag
$Tag.Key = 'Name'
$Tag.Value = $ServerName
New-EC2Tag -ResourceId $Instance -Tag $Tag
```

Then, I wait for the administrator password to become available.

```
$LocalPassword = $null
While( $LocalPassword -eq $null) {
  Try {
    Write-Host "Waiting for password."
    $LocalPassword = Get-EC2PasswordData -InstanceId $InstanceId
      -PemFile $PemFile -ErrorAction SilentlyContinue
  }Catch{}
  Start-Sleep -s 60
}
```

In order to add the server to a domain, we need two sets of credentials. First, we need credentials to log into the new server. Second, we need credentials to log into the domain to add the server.

```
$DomainPassword = $DomainPassword | ConvertTo-SecureString -asPlainText -Force
$DomainCredential = New-Object System.Management.Automation.PSCredential($DomainUser,
    $DomainPassword)
```

```
$LocalComputer = $IP
$LocalPassword = $LocalPassword | ConvertTo-SecureString -asPlainText -Force
$LocalUsername = "administrator"
$LocalCredential = New-Object System.Management.Automation.PSCredential("administrator",
    $LocalPassword)
```

Now we can call Add-Computer, the PowerShell command to add a server to the domain.

```
Add-Computer -ComputerName $LocalComputer -LocalCredential $LocalCredential
    -NewName $ServerName -DomainName $DomainName
    -Credential $DomainCredential -Restart -Force
```

As you can see, you can either create a custom AMI with your changes baked in, or you can use an Amazon AMI and then script the customizations. Of course, you could also choose a hybrid approach. You might build a custom AMI that includes common tools like management and antivirus agents, and then use scripting to further customize the instance for a specific application.

Although it is easy to customize an Amazon AMI, it would be great if we could leverage the library of images we already have onsite. In Exercise 7.2, I will show you how to import an existing VM image from an onsite hypervisor like VMware or Hyper-V.

EXERCISE 7.2: UPLOADING A VM

Many of us already have a library of images that we have built for our VMware or Hyper-V environments. The good news is that Amazon allows you to upload an existing image into EC2. The bad news is that you cannot use PowerShell for this.

There are PowerShell commands for the import process, but they assume that your image has been uploaded to S3 in a very specific and poorly documented format. Luckily, the EC2 Command Line Interface Tools for Java support the end-to-end process including the upload.

The entire process works like this:

1. Export the VM from VMware or another hypervisor.

2. Break the VMDK into 10BM chunks and upload to S3.

3. Import the chucks into EC2 Classic as a running instance.

4. Install tools and drives on the instance.

5. Create an Amazon Machine Image from the instance.

First, let's set up the Java Tools. I assume you have Java installed on your machine already. You can download the EC2 Tools from http://aws.amazon.com/developertools/351. The tools are packaged as a zip file, not an installer. Simply unzip the package into c:\AWS.

Next, you will need an S3 bucket to upload the image to. If you don't already have one, open AWS Management Console and choose S3 from the services menu. Click the Create Bucket button on the first page to load the Create Bucket dialog box shown in Figure 7-6. Name the bucket, and choose a region, then click Create. Don't worry about the details; we will discuss S3 in detail in Chapter 10.

Figure 7-6. Create a Bucket dialog box

Before you export the image you should prepare the VM by checking the following:

1. Check that remote desktop is enabled.

2. Check that Windows Firewall allows public RDP traffic.

3. Check that all patches and virus definitions are up to date.

4. Remove any virtualization tools such as the VMware Tools.

Now, it is time to export the image from your hypervisor. Note the ec2-import-instance command only imports the OS volume. If you want to import additional volumes, use ec2-import-volume. Export the OS volume using the management tools for your hypervisor. The import process supports VMDK, VHD, and OVF file formats.

Next, we need to configure our Java environment. Open a new command prompt and set up the following environment variables. Obviously you may need to change a few paths depending on where you installed the various tools. Note that there is a complete batch file included with the example code.

```
SET JAVA_HOME=C:\Program Files\Java\jre6
SET EC2_HOME=C:\AWS\ec2-api-tools-1.6.7.2
SET CLASSPATH=%CLASSPATH%;%EC2_HOME%\lib
SET PATH=%JAVA_HOME%\bin;%PATH%;%EC2_HOME%\bin.
```

We also need to set a few default values. You will need your keys from Chapter 2 and the name of the S3 bucket you created at the beginning of this exercise. Note that you do not need to specify the region. The image will be imported into the same region you created the S3 bucket in.

```
SET AWS_ACCESS_KEY = AKIAIQPQNCQG3EYO6LIA
SET AWS_SECRET_KEY = +QYg/Uxmjs3HeMk2hNVEyjIyLeXZfY++PEGyXjMV
SET BUCKET_NAME = MyBucket
```

Now you can call `ec2-import-instance` command. For example:

```
ec2-import-instance "c:\aws\MyImage.vhd" -t t1.micro -f VHD -a i386
    -b %BUCKET_NAME% -o %AWS_ACCESS_KEY% -w %AWS_SECRET_KEY%
```

The `ec2-import-instance` command will dump a bunch of data to the screen and then display a progress bar. Note the TaskId in the format import-i-fh37272p. You will need this to check the progress later.

The progress bar you see on screen represents the upload process. Depending on the size of the image, the upload can take a long time. Luckily, if it fails, you do not need start over. You can resume an upload using the `ec2-resume-import` command. For example:

```
ec2-resume-import "c:\aws\MyImage.vhd" -t import-i-fh37272p
    -o %AWS_ACCESS_KEY% -w %AWS_SECRET_KEY%
```

Once the upload completes, Amazon will begin the conversion behind the scenes. There is no progress bar for this, but you can check on the conversion progress using `ec2-describe-conversion-tasks` command and passing your TaskId. For example:

```
ec2-describe-conversion-tasks import-i-fh37272p
```

Once the conversion completes you will have an instance running in EC2 Classic. The import command does not clean up the temporary data stored in S3. You can delete it manually, or use the `ec2-delete-disk-image` command. For example:

```
ec2-delete-disk-image -t import-i-fh37272p
    -o %AWS_ACCESS_KEY% -w %AWS_SECRET_KEY%
```

Now you can log into the new instance. Note that you use the same password you used to log into the instance on site. You cannot retrieve the password from EC2 because EC2 never knew the password. Once you log in, you need to install a couple of tools. First, install the EC2Config Service, which can be downloaded from http://aws.amazon.com/developertools/5562082477397515. Second install the Citrix PV Drivers are available from http://aws.amazon.com/developertools/2187524384750206.

At this point your instance has been fully converted. You can either use it as is or follow the instructions in this chapter to create an AMI. As you can see the ec2-import-instance command will allow you to leverage your existing image library in the cloud and ensure that you have the same bits running on site and in the cloud.

Summary

In this chapter we learned about Amazon Machine Images. We saw how to find and leverage the over 20,000 images already available. Then we discussed how to create our own custom images. We discussed how to prepare a Windows instance using SysPrep. Finally, we learned how to share our images with others.

Then, in the first exercise, we saw an alternative to rolling a custom image: scripted builds. In the second exercise, we saw how to import an existing image from VMware or Hyper-V. In the next chapter we will talk about scalability and high availability.

CHAPTER 8

■ ■ ■

Monitoring and High Availability

This chapter is about architecting your application for high availability. It is also the last chapter on Elastic Compute Cloud (EC2). We have covered almost all of the PowerShell commands for EC2, but EC2 is only one of many services that AWS offers. In this chapter we will examine a few of the services that you can use in concert with EC2 to build a highly available application. These services include Elastic Load Balancers (ELB), Simple Notification Service (SNS), CloudWatch, Auto Scaling, and Route 53.

We will start by creating a new VPC focused on high availability. This will be a great opportunity to review the material in the prior chapters. Next, we will create an ELB to balance HTTP and HTTPS web traffic across multiple instances. We will configure the ELB to automatically detect errors and remove unhealthy instances. Then, we will use SNS and CloudWatch to create an early warning system that can e-mail us when the application is under stress.

Once that detection system is running, we will use Auto Scaling to automatically scale the application by monitoring load. Auto Scaling will leverage scripted builds to launch and terminate instances throughout the day without human involvement. Finally, we will discuss how Route 53 can be used to extend our application across multiple regions, serving each user from the location nearest them.

This chapter has two exercises. In the first, we consolidate everything we learned in the chapter into one streamlined script. In the second, we create a script to scale up (or resize) an instance. Let's get started.

Architecting for High Availability

In Chapters 5 and 6 we spent a lot of time discussing VPC with a focus on security. This section focuses on availability. This is not to suggest that we must trade security for high availability. AWS gives you everything you need to achieve both.

We have also discussed regions and availability zones on multiple occasions. Remember that each region includes multiple availability zones connected by high speed, low latency links. Each availability zone is a stand-alone data center with distinct power, Internet, and resources. By designing an application to span availability zones you can build redundancy into your application.

A VPC is limited to a single region, but as shown in Figure 8-1, it can span multiple availability zones. As you already know, a VPC can contain multiple subnets, and each subnet can be in its own availability zone. By spreading our application across availability zones, we can ensure high availability. If one of the data centers was to fail, the application could continue running in the other.

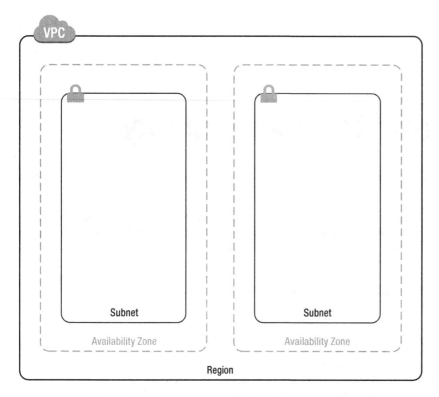

Figure 8-1. *High availability VPC*

Let's get started by creating the VPC in Figure 8-1. This will be a great opportunity to review much of what we learned in prior chapters.

Let's assume our application is a simple, single-tier web application with no database. First, we create a new VPC and pick two availability zones in the same region. For example, I am using a private 192.168.0.0 network and the Northern Virginia region. You may have to change the script to use availability zones in your region.

```
$VPC = New-EC2Vpc -CidrBlock '192.168.0.0/16'
$AvailabilityZone1 = 'us-east-1a'
$AvailabilityZone2 = 'us-east-1b'
```

Next, we create two subnets in our VPC. Notice that each subnet is using a different availability zone. (If any of this is unfamiliar, go back and review Chapter 5.)

```
$WebSubnet1 = New-EC2Subnet -VpcId $VPC.VpcId -CidrBlock '192.168.3.0/24'
    -AvailabilityZone $AvailabilityZone1
$WebSubnet2 = New-EC2Subnet -VpcId $VPC.VpcId -CidrBlock '192.168.4.0/24'
    -AvailabilityZone $AvailabilityZone2
```

We need to launch at least two instances. This is going to be a web application, so I am using the user data parameter to install and configure IIS. You could use the same method to install your application. (If you have forgotten how to do this, return to Chapter 3.)

```
$UserData = [System.Convert]::ToBase64String([System.Text.Encoding]::ASCII.GetBytes(@'
<powershell>
Install-WindowsFeature Web-Server -IncludeManagementTools -IncludeAllSubFeature
</powershell>
'@))
```

Finally, we launch the two instances being careful to specify different subnets. (We covered this in Chapter 6 if you want to review.)

```
$AMI = Get-EC2ImageByName 'WINDOWS_2012_BASE'
$Reservation1 = New-EC2Instance -ImageId $AMI[0].ImageId -KeyName 'MyKey'
    -InstanceType 't1.micro' -MinCount 1
    -MaxCount 1 -SubnetId $WebSubnet1.SubnetId -UserData $UserData
$Instance1 = $Reservation1.RunningInstance[0]
$Reservation2 = New-EC2Instance -ImageId $AMI[0].ImageId -KeyName 'MyKey'
    -InstanceType 't1.micro' -MinCount 1
    -MaxCount 1 -SubnetId $WebSubnet2.SubnetId -UserData $UserData
$Instance2 = $Reservation2.RunningInstance[0]
```

At this point we have new VPC with two subnets each in a different availability zone. In addition, we have launched two identical instances. If one of the instances fails, the other will keep running. In fact, even if the entire availability zone failed, the instance in the other zone will keep running. In the next section, we create a load balancer to distribute the load between our two instances.

Managing Elastic Load Balancers

Now that we have multiple instances deployed in multiple data centers, we need a way to distribute requests between them. This is the role of a load balancer. An Elastic Load Balancer (ELB) receives requests and forwards them to instances in our VPC. The ELB also monitors the health of the instances and automatically stops sending requests to unhealthy instances. In addition, the ELB can be configured to terminate SSL and offload the encryption/decryption from the instances acting as web servers.

Figure 8-2 shows our VPC from the prior section with an ELB added. Notice that the ELB is configured in both availability zones. Obviously we need the ELB to be highly available just like the instances we created in the last section. Luckily Amazon does a lot of the heavy lifting for us when we use an ELB. Let's create one now.

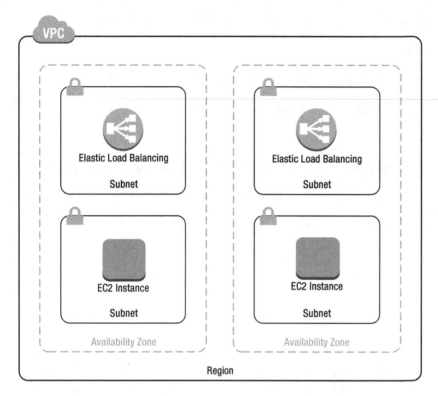

Figure 8-2. *VPC with ELB*

Preparing the VPC for an ELB

First, we need to create a subnet in each availability zone for the ELB to live in. When we configure the ELB, we tell Amazon to use these subnets. Initially, Amazon will launch an ELB into either one of the subnets. If that availability zone fails, Amazon will automatically launch another ELB in the other availability zone. In addition, if the load grows so that one ELB cannot handle the load, Amazon will launch additional ELBs to spread the load. For this reason, each subnet must have at least 20 IP addresses available. Let's create two more subnets.

```
$ElbSubnet1 = New-EC2Subnet -VpcId $VPC.VpcId -CidrBlock '192.168.1.0/24'
    -AvailabilityZone $AvailabilityZone1
$ElbSubnet2 = New-EC2Subnet -VpcId $VPC.VpcId -CidrBlock '192.168.2.0/24'
    -AvailabilityZone $AvailabilityZone2
```

This ELB is going to accept requests from the Internet; therefore, we need to add an Internet gateway to our VPC.

```
$InternetGateway = New-EC2InternetGateway
Add-EC2InternetGateway -InternetGatewayId $InternetGateway.InternetGatewayId -VpcId $VPC.VpcId
```

■ **Note**   Not all ELBs are Internet facing. You can create an internal ELB that balances traffic between tiers of your application. I'll show you how to do that when we launch the ELB in the next section.

Now that we have an Internet gateway, we are going to need to configure the route table to use it. One great side effect of using an ELB is that only the ELB needs to be exposed to the Internet. Our instances can live on the private network with no connection to the Internet. Let's configure a new route table so that only our ELB subnets are public. (If you need to review Internet gateways and route tables see Chapter 5.)

```
$PublicRouteTable = New-EC2RouteTable -VpcId $VPC.VpcId
New-EC2Route -RouteTableId $PublicRouteTable.RouteTableId -DestinationCidrBlock '0.0.0.0/0'
    -GatewayId $InternetGateway.InternetGatewayId
$NoEcho = Register-EC2RouteTable -RouteTableId $PublicRouteTable.RouteTableId
    -SubnetId $ElbSubnet1.SubnetId
$NoEcho = Register-EC2RouteTable -RouteTableId $PublicRouteTable.RouteTableId
    -SubnetId $ElbSubnet2.SubnetId
```

We also need to configure security groups. Let's create a new security group for the ELBs. The ELBs will receive HTTP requests on port 80 and HTTPS requests on port 443. This ELB is public facing; therefore, it should accept traffic from anywhere. (If you want to review security groups go back to Chapter 6.)

```
$ElbGroupId = New-EC2SecurityGroup -GroupName 'ELB' -GroupDescription "Elastic Load Balancers"
    -VpcId $VPC.VpcId
$HTTPRule = New-Object Amazon.EC2.Model.IpPermission
$HTTPRule.IpProtocol='tcp'
$HTTPRule.FromPort = 80
$HTTPRule.ToPort = 80
$HTTPRule.IpRanges = '0.0.0.0/0'
$HTTPSRule = New-Object Amazon.EC2.Model.IpPermission$HTTPSRule.IpProtocol='tcp'
$HTTPSRule.FromPort = 443
$HTTPSRule.ToPort = 443
$HTTPSRule.IpRanges = '0.0.0.0/0'
$NoEcho = Grant-EC2SecurityGroupIngress -GroupId $ElbGroupId -IpPermissions $HTTPRule,
    $HTTPSRule
```

Note that I have not configured network ACLs. You can, and should, configure ACLs for your public subnets, but for this example I am going to keep it simple and use the default ACL. In addition, note that we did not configure the security groups for the web server instances in the prior section to allow requests from the ELBs. Remember that the default security group allows communication on any port between any members of the default group. So, as long as we add both the ELB and web server instances to the default group they will be able to communicate. Before we create the ELB, let's get a reference to the default security group for our VPC.

```
$VPCFilter = New-Object Amazon.EC2.Model.Filter
$VPCFilter.Name = 'vpc-id'
$VPCFilter.Value = $VPC.VpcId
$NameFilter = New-Object Amazon.EC2.Model.Filter
$NameFilter.Name = 'group-name'
$NameFilter.Value = 'default'
$DefaultGroup = Get-EC2SecurityGroup -Filter $VPCFilter, $NameFilter
```

Now that we have our VPC configured, let's create an ELB.

Configuring an ELB for HTTP

Let's get started by configuring an ELB for HTTP. (We will configure HTTPS in the next section.) The first thing we need is a listener. The listener configures the ELB to receive traffic. We use a .Net object to describe the listener. In the following example, I create a listener that listens for HTTP traffic on port 80 and forwards it to an instance on port 80.

```
$HTTPListener = New-Object 'Amazon.ElasticLoadBalancing.Model.Listener'
$HTTPListener.Protocol = 'http'
$HTTPListener.LoadBalancerPort = 80
$HTTPListener.InstancePort = 80
```

Now that we have the listener defined, we can create an ELB using the New-ELBLoadBalancer command. In addition to the listener configuration, New-ELBLoadBalancer takes a name, a list of subnets to use, and the security groups it should be a member of.

```
New-ELBLoadBalancer -LoadBalancerName 'WebLoadBalancer'
    -Subnets $ElbSubnet1.SubnetId, $ElbSubnet2.SubnetId
    -Listeners $HTTPListener -SecurityGroups $DefaultGroup.GroupId, $ElbGroupId
```

If you want to create an internal ELB that is not accessible from the Internet, just add the scheme parameter with a value of Internal. For example:

```
New-ELBLoadBalancer -LoadBalancerName 'WebLoadBalancer'
    -Subnets $ElbSubnet1.SubnetId, $ElbSubnet2.SubnetId
    -Listeners $HTTPListner -SecurityGroups $DefaultGroup.GroupId, $ElbGroupId -Scheme Internal
```

While the ELB is launching, let's talk about health monitoring. As I mentioned, the ELB monitors the health of the instances. If an instance is unhealthy, the ELB stops forwarding traffic to it. Let's check out the configuration using Get-ELBLoadBalancer. For example:

```
(Get-ELBLoadBalancer -LoadBalancerName 'WebLoadBalancer').HealthCheck
```

The previous command returns the following results:

```
Target             : TCP:80
Interval           : 30
Timeout            : 5
UnhealthyThreshold : 2
HealthyThreshold   : 10
```

This is the default health check and it works as follows. Every 30 seconds (the interval) the ELB will attempt to create a TCP connection on port 80 (the target). If it succeeds, the instance is healthy. If the connection is not completed within 5 seconds (the time-out) the instance is unhealthy. If the instance fails on 2 (the unhealthy threshold) consecutive health checks, the ELB will stop forwarding traffic. At this point the ELB will continue to monitor the instance. If the instance again appears healthy, the ELB will continue to monitor it until the check succeeds 10 (the healthy threshold) consecutive times, at which point the ELB will begin forwarding traffic to it again.

Note that this is just checking the TCP connection. There are many other things that could go wrong. For example there may be an issue in the application configuration. It would be much better to request a specific web page and ensure that it is responding correctly. Let's change the rule to check a specific page. In the following example, I have configured the target to request the iisstart.htm page using HTTP on port 80. If the web server responds with a 200 status, the instance will be considered healthy. If not it will be marked unhealthy.

```
Set-ELBHealthCheck -LoadBalancerName 'WebLoadBalancer' -HealthCheck_Target
    'HTTP:80/iisstart.htm'
    -HealthCheck_Interval 30 -HealthCheck_Timeout 5 -HealthCheck_HealthyThreshold 2
    -HealthCheck_UnhealthyThreshold 10
```

Now that the ELB is configured, we can finally add our instances using the `Register-ELBInstanceWithLoadBalancer` command. For example:

```
Register-ELBInstanceWithLoadBalancer -LoadBalancerName 'WebLoadBalancer'
    -Instances $Instance1.InstanceId, $Instance2.InstanceId
```

The last thing we need is the DNS name of our load balancer. To get the name, use the `Get-ELBLoadBalancer` command and check the DNSName.

```
(Get-ELBLoadBalancer -LoadBalancerName 'WebLoadBalancer').DNSName
```

You will get a name similar to the following. Just copy the DNS name into your browser and it should display the IIS start page. Don't be alarmed if the first request takes a few seconds. Subsequent requests will be much faster.

```
WebLoadBalancer-62156217.us-east-1.elb.amazonaws.com
```

Obviously we don't want to share this ugly URL. You can use a DNS CNAME to create a friendly alias. For example, I created an alias for `aws.brianbeach.com`. The process will depend on your DNS provider. I use GoDaddy and the configuration looks like the one shown in Figure 8-3.

CName (Alias) 🔒		
Host	Points To	TTL
aws	webloadbalancer-62156217.us-east-1.elb.amazonaws.com	1 Hour

Figure 8-3. *Creating a DNS CName in GoDaddy.com*

If the ELB is not working, you can check the health of the instances using `Get-ELBInstanceHealth`. It will list each of the instances, if they are healthy, and the reason. If you are debugging an ELB, remember that it is configured for 10 consecutive healthy checks before it considers an instance healthy, which will take 5 minutes. To check the health of our ELB use the following command:

```
Get-ELBInstanceHealth -LoadBalancerName 'WebLoadBalancer'
```

At this point our ELB is running and forwarding HTTP requests to our instances. In the next section we add support for HTTPS.

Configuring an ELB for HTTPS

Most applications today require SSL for at least some portion of the site. As I mentioned earlier, an ELB can be configured to terminate HTTPS. Note that the ELB can also receive an HTTPS request and forward it to the instance without decrypting it, but I did not include an example. Let's add a new listener to our ELB that terminates HTTPS.

The first step is to import the SSL certificate. If you don't have an SSL certificate, see the sidebar for instructions to create a self-signed certificate for testing. To import the certificate, use the `Publish-IAMServerCertificate` command. Note that this command is from the Identity and Access Management (IAM) service. (We will look at

IAM in detail in Chapter 11). The Publish-IAMServerCertificate command takes as parameters the certificate and private key as well as a name.

```
$Cert = [IO.File]::ReadAllText('C:\AWS\MyCert.cer')
$PrivateKey = [IO.File]::ReadAllText('C:\AWS\MyCert.pem')
$ServerCert = Publish-IAMServerCertificate -ServerCertificateName 'MyCert'
    -CertificateBody $Cert -PrivateKey $PrivateKey
```

GENERATING A SELF-SIGNED CERTIFICATE WITH OPENSSL

Once you become accustomed to paying two cents an hour for a server, an SSL certificate from VeriSign seems very expensive. You can use OpenSSL, available from www.openssl.org, to create a self-signed certificate for testing. Obviously no one is going to trust your certificate, but it will suffice for testing.

First, generate a new private key. The following example creates a 2048 bit RSA key and saves it in a file called MyCert.pem.

```
openssl.exe genrsa 2048 > MyCert.pem
```

Next, we create a certificate request and save it as MyCert.csr.

```
openssl.exe req -new -key MyCert.pem -out MyCert.csr
```

When you run the prior command you will be asked a bunch of questions. You can leave them all blank (just press Enter) except for the common name. When asked for the common name, enter the fully qualified domain name of your server. For example, to create a certificate for https://aws.brianbeach.com I responded:

```
Country Name (2 letter code) [AU]:
State or Province Name (full name) [Some-State]:
Locality Name (eg, city) []:
Organization Name (eg, company) [Internet Widgits Pty Ltd]:
Organizational Unit Name (eg, section) []:
Common Name (e.g. server FQDN or YOUR name) []:aws.brianbeach.com
Email Address []:
Please enter the following 'extra' attributes to be sent with your certificate request
A challenge password []:
An optional company name []:
```

Usually you would send your certificate request to a certificate authority like VeriSign. We will use OpenSSL again to sign the request with our private key and generate a certificate in the file MyCert.cer.

```
bin\openssl x509 -req -days 365 -in MyCert.csr -signkey MyCert.pem -out MyCert.cer
```

You can use this certificate in the remaining examples.

Now that we have imported our certificate, we can create a new listener that uses HTTPS. Notice in the following example that the ELB is listening on port 443 and forwarding the decrypted request to the instance on port 80.

```
$HTTPSListener = New-Object 'Amazon.ElasticLoadBalancing.Model.Listener'
$HTTPSListener.Protocol = 'https'
$HTTPSListener.LoadBalancerPort = 443
$HTTPSListener.InstancePort = 80
$HTTPSListener.SSLCertificateId = $ServerCert.Arn
```

We can add the new listener to our existing ELB using the New-ELBLoadBalancer command as follows:

```
New-ELBLoadBalancerListener -LoadBalancerName 'WebLoadBalancer' -Listeners $HTTPSListener
```

The ELB is now listening for both HTTP traffic on port 80 and HTTPS traffic on port 443. The instance does not care which protocol is being used. It only sees decrypted traffic on port 80.

Before we move on let's spend a minute discussing stickiness.

Managing Stickiness Policies

By default the ELB will balance each request independently. This means that each request from a user may be sent to a different instance. Often the application maintains state on the instance and subsequent requests must be sent to the same instance. Sending all traffic from a specific user to the same server is called stickiness.

For example, most ASP.Net applications use a cookie to maintain session state. The ELB can be configured to use this cookie to maintain stickiness. To configure a stickiness policy that uses the ASP.Net session cookie, we use New-ELBAppCookieStickinessPolicy and specify the name of the cookie. For example:

```
New-ELBAppCookieStickinessPolicy -LoadBalancerName 'WebLoadBalancer'
    -PolicyName 'ASPNETSession' -CookieName 'ASP.NET_SessionId'
```

Each listener can use a different policy to maintain stickiness. Therefore, we must assign the policy to a specific listener using the Set-ELBLoadBalancerPolicyOfListener command. For example:

```
Set-ELBLoadBalancerPolicyOfListener -LoadBalancerName 'WebLoadBalancer'
    -LoadBalancerPort 80
    -PolicyNames 'ASPNETSession'
```

Some applications do not use a cookie to maintain state. If the application does not have a cookie you can have the ELB add one using the New-ELBLBCookieStickinessPolicy command. For example, the following command will add a cookie to each request with a 15-minute expiration. Note that the cookie the ELB adds is called "AWSELB."

```
New-ELBLBCookieStickinessPolicy -LoadBalancerName 'WebLoadBalancer'
    -PolicyName 'ELB-15M'
    -CookieExpirationPeriod (60*15)
```

Again we have to associate the policy with a listener using Set-ELBLoadBalancerPolicyOfListener. For example:

```
Set-ELBLoadBalancerPolicyOfListener -LoadBalancerName 'WebLoadBalancer' -LoadBalancerPort 443
    -PolicyNames 'ELB-15M'
```

At this point our ELB is fully configured. It is listening for both HTTP and HTTPS requests. In addition, we have configured both the health policy and stickiness policy. In the next section we will use CloudWatch to monitor our instances and notify us when something goes wrong.

Monitoring with CloudWatch

Our application is now highly available and will failover automatically. While automatic issue resolution is desirable, we still want to know what is happening with our application in the cloud. We need monitoring to alert us when something goes wrong. In this section we will use CloudWatch to create an alert that will e-mail us when CPU utilization exceeds 75% for an extended period of time.

CloudWatch is Amazon's monitoring solution. CloudWatch can be used to monitor any of the AWS services. Appendix E lists the metrics that can be monitored for all of the services we discussed in this book. In addition, you can create custom metrics using the CloudWatch API. You can configure CloudWatch to take multiple actions when it detects an issue, including the following: sending an e-mail, terminating the instance, launching additional instances, and many other actions.

The first step in creating an e-mail alert is to create a topic with Simple Notification Service (SNS). SNS is a generic service for sending notifications. It uses a publish-subscriber architecture where many receivers subscribe to notifications that are published using the SNS API. Let's begin by creating a new topic using the New-SNSTopic command.

```
$Topic = New-SNSTopic -Name 'MyTopic'
```

Now that our topic is defined we want to subscribe to it using e-mail. To create a subscription, use the Connect-SNSNotification command. You will get an e-mail asking you to confirm your e-mail address, and you must accept it before you can receive notifications.

```
Connect-SNSNotification -TopicArn $Topic -Protocol 'email' -Endpoint 'alerts@brianbeach.com'
```

Now that our notification is configured, let's test it. Remember that SNS is a generic notification service. CloudWatch uses it to send alerts, but you can also use it to send custom notifications. To publish a new message, use the Publish-SNSMessage command. You should receive an e-mail notification with the custom message. For example:

```
Publish-SNSMessage -TopicArn $Topic -Message "This is a test!"
```

Now that our notification is configured we can create an alert. We want to monitor our two instances and receive a notification when CPU utilization exceeds 75% for an extended period of time. The first thing we need to do is define the CloudWatch dimension. A dimension is used to group alerts. In this case we want to group our alerts by instance. Without this dimension we would be measuring the average CPU utilization of all instances in our account. We use a .Net object to create a dimension for the first instance.

```
$Dimension = New-Object 'Amazon.CloudWatch.Model.Dimension'
$Dimension.Name = 'InstanceId'
$Dimension.Value = $Instance1.InstanceId
```

Now we can create the alarm using the Write-CWMetricAlarm command. This command has a ton of parameters. Here is a description of each:

- AlarmName is just a name unique within the account.

- AlarmDescription is anything that will help you remember what the alarm does.

- Namespace defines which AWS service is being monitored (see Appendix E for a list).

- MetricName is what we want to monitor. For example CPU Utilization (see Appendix E for a list).

- Statistic describes how to aggregate the metric. For example average, minimum, maximum, etc.

- Threshold is the value to compare the metric to.

- Unit is the units the metric is measured in. For example, MB, GB, etc.

- ComparisonOperator can be greater than, less than, etc.

- EvaluationPeriods is the number of periods the condition must be true before the alarm is raised.

- Period is the length of the evaluation period. In my example we are waiting for two five-minute periods before raising the alarm.

- Dimensions are the dimensions we created earlier.

- AlarmActions is the action to take when the alarm is raised. In my example, send a notification.

The following example will create an alarm when the average CPU utilization exceeds 75% for two consecutive five-minute monitoring periods.

```
Write-CWMetricAlarm -AlarmName 'CPU75' -AlarmDescription 'Alarm when CPU exceeds 75%'
    -Namespace 'AWS/EC2' -MetricName 'CPUUtilization' -Statistic 'Average'  -Threshold 75
    -Unit 'Percent'
    -ComparisonOperator 'GreaterThanThreshold' -EvaluationPeriods 2 -Period (60*5)
    -Dimensions $Dimension -AlarmActions $Topic
```

CloudWatch is now monitoring our instance. You could create another alarm to monitor the other instance if you want, but I will show an easier way to monitor an entire group of instances in the next section. It will take at least 10 minutes (2 periods of 5 minutes) to gather enough data to determine the current state. In the meantime, let's test our notification by explicitly setting the alarm using the Set-CWAlarmState command.

```
Set-CWAlarmState -AlarmName 'CPU75' -StateValue 'ALARM' -StateReason 'Testing'
```

You should receive an e-mail alarm just like the one you would receive if an instance were in distress. This section has hardly scratched the surface of SNS and CloudWatch. Appendix E includes a list of metrics and dimensions available for each AWS service. In the next section, we will use Auto Scaling to automatically add and remove instances depending on load.

Using Auto Scaling

Notifications are a great start, but depending on an administrator to respond to alarms is slow. The cloud brings infinite elasticity and with it a whole new way of thinking. Auto Scaling allows us to build an application that automatically responds to changes in demand. Our application can scale out when demand is high and scale in when demand is low. In addition, Auto Scaling can detect issues and replace unhealthy instances.

Figure 8-4 shows the same web application we have been working on throughout this chapter, but the two web instances have been replaced by an Auto Scaling group. The Auto Scaling group is responsible for measuring current load and launching the appropriate number of instances to serve our users.

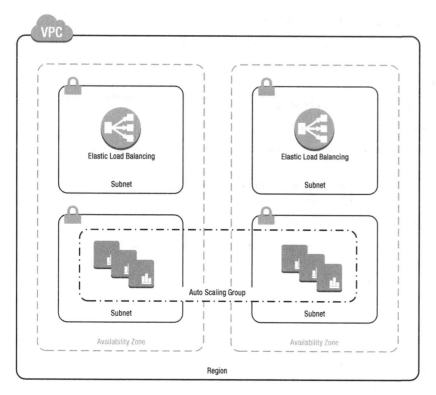

Figure 8-4. *Auto Scaling*

The first thing we need to do is terminate the two instances we launched earlier. Going forward, we are going to let the Auto Scaling group launch all of our instances. We don't want to confuse things by launching instances manually.

```
Stop-EC2Instance -Instance $Instance1.InstanceId -Terminate
Stop-EC2Instance -Instance $Instance2.InstanceId -Terminate
```

Rather than launching instances one at a time, we are going to define a launch configuration and save it for later. The launch configuration is simply a template that the Auto Scaling group will use whenever it needs to launch an instance. Creating a launch configuration is very similar to launching an instance. First, we define the user data script.

```
$UserData = [System.Convert]::ToBase64String([System.Text.Encoding]::ASCII.GetBytes(@'
<powershell>
Install-WindowsFeature Web-Server -IncludeManagementTools -IncludeAllSubFeature
</powershell>
'@))
```

Then, we call the `New-ASLaunchConfiguration` command. `New-ASLaunchConfiguration` takes all the same parameters as `New-EC2Instance` and a name used to save the configuration.

```
$AMI = Get-EC2ImageByName 'WINDOWS_2012_BASE'
New-ASLaunchConfiguration -LaunchConfigurationName 'MyLaunchConfig' -ImageId $AMI[0].ImageId
    -KeyName 'MyKey' -SecurityGroups $DefaultGroup.GroupId -UserData $UserData
    -InstanceType 't1.micro'
```

With our launch configuration defined, we can create an Auto Scaling group using `New-ASAutoScalingGroup`. The Auto Scaling group defines how many instances can be launched. `DesiredCapacity` is the number of instances we think we need, but we also define a min and max that Auto Scaling can work within depending on load. Auto Scaling will ensure that we always have at least the minimum number of instances, but not more than the max.

In addition, we tell the group what subnets to launch instances into, and optionally, which load balancer to register with when they start. Note that not all applications will require a load balancer. Some applications will get work from a queue or database table. If you are using a load balancer, you can use `HealthCheckType=ELB`. By default, Auto Scaling will use instance health (essentially a ping) to ensure the instance is healthy. The ELB health check will rely on the rules defined in ELB to determine health. Remember that we defined a rule that checks a specific web page every 30 seconds.

Finally, we can define a `HealthCheckGracePeriod` and `DefaultCoolDown`. These last two parameters are really important. `HealthCheckGracePeriod` defines how long, in seconds, to wait before evaluating the health of a new instance. The default value is 5 minutes, but it can take 10-15 minutes for a Windows instance to launch and configure itself. If we do not override the defaults, the Auto Scaling group will think the instance is unhealthy and replace it before it finishes configuration. Similarly, `DefaultCoolDown` defines how long to wait between each Auto Scaling action. Again the default is 5 minutes. If we don't change this, Auto Scaling will keep launching more and more instances while it waits for the first instance to boot up.

```
$VPCZoneIdentifier = $WebSubnet1.SubnetId + "," + $WebSubnet2.SubnetId
New-ASAutoScalingGroup -AutoScalingGroupName 'MyAutoScalingGroup'
    -LaunchConfigurationName 'MyLaunchConfig'
    -MinSize 2 -MaxSize 8 -DesiredCapacity 2
    -LoadBalancerNames 'WebLoadBalancer' -VPCZoneIdentifier $VPCZoneIdentifier
    -HealthCheckType 'ELB' -HealthCheckGracePeriod (15*60) -DefaultCooldown (30*60)
```

As soon as we run `New-ASAutoScalingGroup`, the group will begin to launch new instances. You can use the `Get-ELBInstanceHealth` command to monitor the instances that the group is managing and determine the status of each. You will use this command often while you tune your Auto Scaling rules.

```
Get-ELBInstanceHealth -LoadBalancerName 'WebLoadBalancer'
```

At this point, the Auto Scaling group will launch the desired number of instances and monitor health. If an instance fails, it will be replaced, but we have not defined any Auto Scaling rules so it will not yet respond to changes in load. We use CloudWatch to define the rules just like we did before, but rather than sending a notification, the rule will trigger an Auto Scaling policy.

The first thing we need to do is define a new CloudWatch dimension. In the previous example, we measured the load of an individual instance. In this example, we want to measure the average load of our Auto Scaling group. The following dimension will calculate the aggregate over the entire group:

```
$Dimension = New-Object 'Amazon.CloudWatch.Model.Dimension'
$Dimension.Name = 'AutoScalingGroupName'
$Dimension.Value = 'MyAutoScalingGroup'
```

Now we can define a policy to scale up using `Write-ASScalingPolicy`. This policy simply says to increase the capacity by two instances. Note that you can also override the default cooldown to ensure the instance has time to boot before the next scaling occurs.

```
$ScaleUpArn = Write-ASScalingPolicy -PolicyName 'MyScaleOutPolicy'
    -AutoScalingGroupName 'MyAutoScalingGroup'
    -ScalingAdjustment 2 -AdjustmentType 'ChangeInCapacity' -Cooldown (30*60)
```

You can also define a percentage change rather than a specific count.

```
$ScaleUpArn = Write-ASScalingPolicy -PolicyName 'MyScaleOutPolicy'
    -AutoScalingGroupName 'MyAutoScalingGroup'
    -ScalingAdjustment 20 -AdjustmentType 'PercentChangeInCapacity' -Cooldown (30*60)
```

With the scaling policy defined, we can create a CloudWatch alarm to trigger it. This is almost identical to the alarm we created for notification except that the action invokes the scaling policy rather than sending an e-mail.

```
Write-CWMetricAlarm -AlarmName 'AS75'
    -AlarmDescription 'Add capacity when average CPU within the auto scaling group is
    more than 75%'
    -MetricName 'CPUUtilization' -Namespace 'AWS/EC2' -Statistic 'Average' -Period (60*5)
    -Threshold 75
    -ComparisonOperator 'GreaterThanThreshold' -EvaluationPeriods 2 -AlarmActions $ScaleUpArn
    -Unit 'Percent' -Dimensions $Dimension
```

Of course, we also need a policy to remove instances when load diminishes. Otherwise our application will grow and never contract. The policy and alarm are almost identical with a few exceptions. First, the ScalingAdjustment is a negative number to indicate we are removing instances. Second, our alarm is defined as less than 25%.

```
$ScaleInArn = Write-ASScalingPolicy -PolicyName 'MyScaleInPolicy'
    -AutoScalingGroupName 'MyAutoScalingGroup'
    -ScalingAdjustment -2 -AdjustmentType 'ChangeInCapacity' -Cooldown (30*60)
```

```
Write-CWMetricAlarm -AlarmName 'AS25'
    -AlarmDescription 'Remove capacity when average CPU within the auto scaling group
    is less than 25%'
    -MetricName 'CPUUtilization' -Namespace 'AWS/EC2' -Statistic 'Average' -Period (60*5)
    -Threshold 25
    -ComparisonOperator 'LessThanThreshold' -EvaluationPeriods 2 -AlarmActions $ScaleInArn
    -Unit 'Percent' -Dimensions $Dimension
```

Once your Auto Scaling group is running, it will work continuously to keep the application running. In fact, if you manually terminate an instance, it will be replaced within a few minutes. So, as we approach the end of this chapter, how do we stop this monster we created? You can use the Remove-ASAutoScalingGroup command to delete the group. Add the ForceDelete flag, if you want the instances deleted and the traditional force flag to suppress the confirmation.

```
Remove-ASAutoScalingGroup -AutoScalingGroupName 'MyAutoScalingGroup' -ForceDelete $true -Force
```

At this point, we have created a self-healing, Auto Scaling application that can serve countless users. The only limitation we face is network latency. In the next section we will look at how Route 53 can solve the latency issue.

Using Route 53

Our application is now designed to serve unlimited users, but we still have latency issues. My application is located in Northern Virginia. If my user is in China, the application is going to feel slow regardless of how large we scale. The only way to fix this is to get the application closer to the user. This is where Route 53 comes in.

As seen in Figure 8-5, Route 53 can be used to balance traffic between regions, similar to how an ELB routes traffic between instances. Route 53 is a DNS service and requires that you make AWS your DNS provider. This is a significant commitment you are not likely willing to make to run a few samples from a book. As a result, I have not included any examples in this section, but I wanted you to be aware of Route 53 and how it can help you scale.

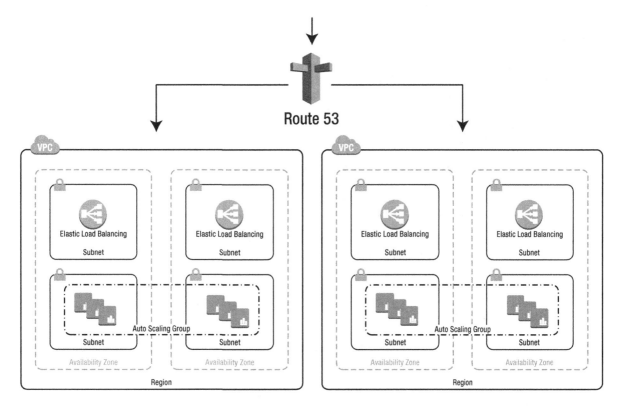

***Figure 8-5.** Route 53*

As you know, AWS offers multiple regions around the world. If we deploy our application in each region, we can serve users from the region closest to them, minimizing latency. In addition, we add another layer of redundancy. Now, even if all of the availability zones in Northern Virginia fail, our application will continue running in the other regions.

The advantage of using Amazon's DNS service is that it offers latency-based routing. Latency-based routing uses geolocation to determine which region is closest to the user, and will therefore give them the best experience. In addition, Route 53 can monitor the health of each region and will not route users to a region that is unhealthy.

As we have seen throughout this chapter, AWS offers many services that can be used to monitor and scale an application. In the first exercise we will pull together everything we learned in this chapter into a single script.

EXERCISE 8.1: SCALING OUT

In this chapter we learned how to use EC2, VPC, SNS, CloudWatch, Auto Scaling, and Route 53 to create a self-healing application that automatically responds to changes in load. In the process, we took a roundabout approach focused more on exploring each technology than the final solution. In this exercise, we will pull together everything we learned into a single provisioning script that will add an Auto Scaling group to an existing VPC.

First, we need to define the input parameters. This script will add to an existing VPC; therefore, we expect the VPC, subnets (two for the ELBs and two for the application instances), and security groups, to be defined already. In addition, the script takes the instance type, AMI, and user data configuration script.

```
param
(
    [string][parameter(mandatory=$true)]$VpcId,
    [string][parameter(mandatory=$true)]$ElbSubnet1Id,
    [string][parameter(mandatory=$true)]$ElbSubnet2Id,
    [string][parameter(mandatory=$true)]$WebSubnet1Id,
    [string][parameter(mandatory=$true)]$WebSubnet2Id,
    [string][parameter(mandatory=$true)]$ElbSecurityGroupId,
    [string][parameter(mandatory=$true)]$DefaultSecurityGroupId,
    [string][parameter(mandatory=$false)]$InstanceType = 't1.micro',
    [string][parameter(mandatory=$false)]$AmiId,
    [string][parameter(mandatory=$true)]$UserData,
    [string][parameter(mandatory=$false)]$KeyName = 'MyKey'
)
```

Note that the instance type and AMI are optional. If the AMI is missing we will look up the 2012 Base image for the current region.

```
If([System.String]::IsNullOrEmpty($AmiId)){ $AmiId = (Get-EC2ImageByName -Name
    'WINDOWS_2012_BASE')[0].ImageId}
```

Next, we launch the new load balancer for our application. In this exercise I am only configuring HTTP, but you could easily adapt the script to support HTTPS as described in the chapter.

```
$HTTPListener = New-Object 'Amazon.ElasticLoadBalancing.Model.Listener'
$HTTPListener.Protocol = 'http'
$HTTPListener.LoadBalancerPort = 80
$HTTPListener.InstancePort = 80

New-ELBLoadBalancer -LoadBalancerName 'WebLoadBalancer' -Subnets $ElbSubnet1Id,
    $ElbSubnet2Id
    -Listeners $HTTPListener -SecurityGroups $DefaultSecurityGroupId,
    $ElbSecurityGroupId
```

Note that I did not configure a health policy. Since we don't know anything about the application, we don't know what page to monitor. Remember that the default rule simply establishes a TCP connection on the specified port (in this case, port 80). You should update the rule to be specific to your application.

Now, we create a launch configuration based on the instance type, AMI and user data passed in.

```
$UserData = [System.Convert]::ToBase64String([System.Text.Encoding]::ASCII.
GetBytes($UserData))
    New-ASLaunchConfiguration -LaunchConfigurationName 'MyLaunchConfig'
    -ImageId $AmiId -KeyName $KeyName
    -SecurityGroups $DefaultSecurityGroupId -UserData $UserData
    -InstanceType $InstanceType
```

Then, we create the Auto Scaling group. Here I am specifying 2-8 instances with a 30-minute grace period and cooldown. This is probably too high, but again we don't know what the application is; therefore, it is better to err on the high side. If the instance is not up and running within the cooldown period, it will be killed and replaced. This will result in thrashing, where the Auto Scaling continuously kills and replaces instances without giving them time to become effective.

```
New-ASAutoScalingGroup -AutoScalingGroupName 'MyAutoScalingGroup'
    -LaunchConfigurationName 'MyLaunchConfig'
    -MinSize 2 -MaxSize 8 -DesiredCapacity 2 -LoadBalancerNames 'WebLoadBalancer'
    -VPCZoneIdentifier "$WebSubnet1Id, $WebSubnet2Id" -HealthCheckType 'ELB'
    -HealthCheckGracePeriod (30*60) -DefaultCooldown (30*60)
```

Now we can configure CloudWatch to monitor our application. First, we create a new dimension that aggregates metrics across the entire Auto Scaling group.

```
$Dimension = New-Object 'Amazon.CloudWatch.Model.Dimension'
$Dimension.Name = 'AutoScalingGroupName'
$Dimension.Value = 'MyAutoScalingGroup'
```

Next, we create a policy and alarm to add two instances when CPU utilization exceeds 75%.

```
$ScaleUpArn = Write-ASScalingPolicy -PolicyName 'MyScaleOutPolicy'
    -AutoScalingGroupName 'MyAutoScalingGroup'
    -ScalingAdjustment 2 -AdjustmentType 'ChangeInCapacity' -Cooldown (30*60)
Write-CWMetricAlarm -AlarmName 'AS75'
    -AlarmDescription 'Add capacity when average CPU within the auto scaling group is
    more than 75%'
    -MetricName 'CPUUtilization' -Namespace 'AWS/EC2' -Statistic 'Average'
    -Period (60*5) -Threshold 75
    -ComparisonOperator 'GreaterThanThreshold' -EvaluationPeriods 2
    -AlarmActions $ScaleUpArn
    -Unit 'Percent' -Dimensions $Dimension
```

Finally, we create a policy and alarm to remove two instances when CPU utilization is below 25%.

```
$ScaleInArn = Write-ASScalingPolicy -PolicyName 'MyScaleInPolicy'
    -AutoScalingGroupName 'MyAutoScalingGroup'
    -ScalingAdjustment -2 -AdjustmentType 'ChangeInCapacity' -Cooldown (30*60)
Write-CWMetricAlarm -AlarmName 'AS25'
    -AlarmDescription 'Remove capacity when average CPU within the auto scaling group
    is less than 25%'
    -MetricName 'CPUUtilization' -Namespace 'AWS/EC2' -Statistic 'Average'
    -Period (60*5) -Threshold 25
    -ComparisonOperator 'LessThanThreshold' -EvaluationPeriods 2
    -AlarmActions $ScaleInArn
    -Unit 'Percent' -Dimensions $Dimension
```

That's all you need to build a self-healing application that automatically responds to changes in load. Auto Scaling is a great solution, but the application must be built with scaling in mind. Some applications are simply not built to scale out. For these applications you must scale up. In the next section we create a script to scale up, or move from one instance type to another.

EXERCISE 8.2: SCALING UP

In this chapter we created a solution to scale out in respond to load. Scaling out refers to adding additional instances in response to demand. Another option is to scale up, or increase the size of an instance. Some systems, such as relational databases, do not scale out easily. These applications must be scaled up.

Luckily AWS has a command for this named Edit-EC2InstanceAttribute. Edit-EC2InstanceAttribute allows you to change many of an instance's attributes including:

- BlockDeviceMappings
- DisableApiTermination
- EbsOptimized
- Groups
- InstanceInitiatedShutdownBehavior
- InstanceType
- Kernel
- Ramdisk
- SourceDestCheck
- UserData

We are interested in changing the InstanceType. Let's create a quick script to resize an instance. Our script will take two simple parameters: the instance id you want to modify and the new instance type.

```
Param(
    [string][Parameter(Mandatory=$false)] $InstanceId,
    [string][Parameter(Mandatory=$false)] $NewInstanceType
)
```

Now all we need to do is call Edit-EC2Instance specifying the InstanceType attribute.

```
Edit-EC2InstanceAttribute -InstanceId $InstanceId -InstanceType $NewInstanceType
```

That's all there is to it. Once again AWS makes it easy to do something that would be really hard with physical servers in a traditional data center.

Before we wrap up, I want to point out a few limitations of this script:

1. Your instance must be stopped before you can resize it.

2. Be really careful with ephemeral storage. Ephemeral disk configurations depend on the instance type and are not always compatible across systems. For example, a t1.micro has no ephemeral storage. If you move from a larger instance with ephemeral storage to a t1.micro, the ephemeral disks will not exist. Table 8-1 lists the ephemeral storage available in each instance type.

Table 8-1. *Available Ephemeral Storage for Various Instance Types*

Instance Type	Ephemeral Storage
cc2.8xlarge	4 x 840 GiB
c1.xlarge	4 x 420 GiB
c1.medium	1 x 340 GiB
cr1.8xlarge	2 x 120 GiB SSD
c3.large	2 X 16 Gib SSD
c3.xlarge	2 X 40 Gib SSD
c3.2xlarge	2 X 80 Gib SSD
c3.4xlarge	2 X 160 Gib SSD
c3.8xlarge	2 X 320 Gib SSD
cg1.4xlarge	2 x 840 GiB
Cg2.2xlarge	2 X 60 Gib SSD
hi1.4xlarge	2 x 1024 GiB SSD
m2.2xlarge	1 x 840 GiB
m2.xlarge	1 x 410 GiB
m2.4xlarge	2 x 840 GiB
hs1.8xlarge	24 x 2048 GiB
m1.xlarge	4 x 420 GiB
m1.large	2 x 420 GiB
m1.medium	1 x 400 GiB
m1.small	1 x 150 GiB
m3.2xlarge	None
m3.xlarge	None
t1.micro	None

3. Be really careful with Elastic Network Interfaces (ENI) and secondary IP addresses. Again, ENIs and secondary IP configurations differ among instance types. Table 8-2 lists the number of ENIs and IPs for each instance type.

Table 8-2. *ENIs and IPs for Various Instance Types*

Instance Type	Maximum ENIs	IP Addresses per ENI
cc2.8xlarge	8	30
cg1.4xlarge	8	30
c1.xlarge	4	15
c1.medium	2	6
hi1.4xlarge	8	30
m2.2xlarge	4	30
m2.xlarge	4	15
m2.4xlarge	8	30
cr1.8xlarge	8	30
hs1.8xlarge	8	30
m1.xlarge	4	15
m1.large	3	10
m1.medium	2	6
m1.small	2	4
m3.2xlarge	4	30
m3.xlarge	4	15
t1.micro	2	2

4. Be careful with marketplace instances. Marketplace instances cannot be resized as you are licensed for a specific size.

In this exercise we created a script that can be used to resize an instance. In general, scaling out is preferred, but when the application does not support it, we can always scale up.

Summary

In this chapter we saw the true power of the Cloud and AWS. We used VPC to build a highly available application served from two or more active-active data centers. We developed a notification system using SNS and CloudWatch to provide an early warning system that informs the administrator before the application fails.

We also used an ELB to balance traffic across multiple instances and monitor the health of the individual instances. In addition, we used Auto Scaling to monitor load in real time to dynamically resize the application by launching and terminating instances in response to load. Finally, we deployed our application in multiple regions and used Route 53 to automatically route users to the nearest region, minimizing latency.

In the exercises we created scripts to scale out and scale up depending on the application.

It is very easy to overlook the power of what we just did. What we accomplished in this chapter, only a handful of companies can do. Very few traditional enterprises can achieve Web Scale using their own data centers and enterprise solution. But, using the cloud, a single person can build a world-class application from his or her favorite coffee shop.

This chapter wraps up our discussion on Elastic Compute Cloud (EC2). In the remaining three chapters we will examine Relational Database Service (RDS), Simple Storage Service (S3), and Identity and Access Management (IAM).

■ ■ ■

CHAPTER 9

Relational Database Service

Relational Database Service (RDS) is a service that makes it easy to create and manage a database in the cloud. And while EC2 is classified as Infrastructure as a Service (IaaS), RDS is classified as Platform as a Service (PaaS). This means RDS instances are managed by AWS, eliminating time-consuming activities, such as patching and backups, and allowing you to focus on your application. The tradeoff is that you have limited access to the database and no access to the underlying operating system.

In this chapter we discuss the RDS architecture and learn to launch an SQL Server RDS instance. Next, we will learn to configure an RDS instance using parameters and options. Then, we will learn to manage backups and restores using both snapshots and point-in-time restores.

RDS also supports highly available configurations spread across multiple availability zones. Unfortunately this is not yet supported with SQL Server; therefore, we will use MySQL to learn how to configure high availability and read replicas.

In the exercises we will focus on securing a RDS instance running SQL Server. In the first exercise, we will enable SSL to encrypt the connection to SQL Server. In the second exercise, we will enable Transparent Database Encryption (TDE) to encrypt data and back up files stored on disk.

RDS Architecture

RDS is designed to be deployed in multiple availability zones for high availability. Therefore, your VPC must have subnets in at least two availability zones. Even if you choose to launch only a single stand-alone instance, you must have two subnets in different availability zones to use RDS.

AWS uses a DB Subnet Group to identify which subnets are reserved for RDS. You simply create two or more subnets in multiple availability zones and add them to the Subnet Group. In addition, we use VPC ACL and Security Groups to control access to the RDS instances.

Figure 9-1 shows the basic configuration for the first half of this chapter. Let's assume we have two web servers running on EC2 instances, and they will use an RDS SQL Server instance to store data. The RDS instance will be launched into one of the two subnets that make up the DB Subnet Group. Let's first configure the VPC.

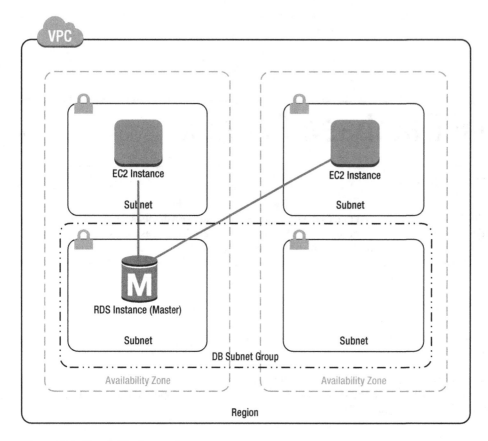

Figure 9-1. *Simple Deployment*

Creating a VPC

Before we can create a database instance, we need to configure a VPC for it to live in. Let's begin by creating a new VPC. If you prefer, you can add two new subnets to an existing VPC (for example, the VPC created in Chapter 8). First, I create a new VPC using the 192.168.0.0 private IP range.

```
$VPC = New-EC2Vpc -CidrBlock '192.168.0.0/16'
```

Next, I create two subnets in our VPC. These are the subnets that the database instance will live in. Because we want to be able to support a multi-AZ deployment, I am using two different availability zones. (This should all be familiar by now, but if you need to review, go back to Chapter 5.)

```
$AvailabilityZone1 = 'us-east-1a'
$AvailabilityZone2 = 'us-east-1b'
$PrimarySubnet = New-EC2Subnet -VpcId $VPC.VpcId -CidrBlock '192.168.5.0/24'
    -AvailabilityZone $AvailabilityZone1
$StandbySubnet = New-EC2Subnet -VpcId $VPC.VpcId -CidrBlock '192.168.6.0/24'
    -AvailabilityZone $AvailabilityZone2
```

Creating a Subnet Group

Now that we have our VPC configured, we need to describe how we plan to use it. We need to tell RDS which subnets to use for database instances. We do this using a subnet group. To create a subnet group, use the New-RDSSubnetGroup command. New-RDSSubnetGroup requires a name and description, along with a list of subnets to use. You will use the name rather than an id to refer to this subnet group later. For example:

```
New-RDSDBSubnetGroup -DBSubnetGroupName 'MySubnetGroup' -DBSubnetGroupDescription 'Pair of
    subnets for RDS'
    -SubnetIds $PrimarySubnet.SubnetId, $StandbySubnet.SubnetId
```

Despite the fact that RDS does not support multi-AZ instances of SQL Server, you must specify at least two subnets when creating a subnet group. In addition, the subnets must be in different availability zones.

Configuring Security Groups

The last thing we need is a security group. This security group is used to define which EC2 instances can connect to the RDS database instance. First, we create a new security group for the RDS instance.

```
$RDSGroupId = New-EC2SecurityGroup –VpcId $VPC.VpcId -GroupName 'RDS' -GroupDescription "RDS Instances"
```

Next, we get a reference to the default group. In this example I am going to allow any instance in the default group to access to our database instance. I am using filters to find the default group. (If you need to review, see Chapter 6.)

```
$VPCFilter = New-Object Amazon.EC2.Model.Filter
$VPCFilter.Name = 'vpc-id'
$VPCFilter.Value = $VPC.VpcId
$GroupFilter = New-Object Amazon.EC2.Model.Filter
$GroupFilter.Name = 'group-name'
$GroupFilter.Value = 'default'
$DefaultGroup = Get-EC2SecurityGroup -Filter $VPCFilter, $GroupFilter
$DefaultGroupPair = New-Object Amazon.EC2.Model.UserIdGroupPair
$DefaultGroupPair.GroupId = $DefaultGroup.GroupId
```

Then, we create a new rule allowing access on the default SQL Server port 1433, and specify the default group as the source.

```
$SQLServerRule = New-Object Amazon.EC2.Model.IpPermission
$SQLServerRule.IpProtocol='tcp'
$SQLServerRule.FromPort = 1433
$SQLServerRule.ToPort = 1433
$SQLServerRule.UserIdGroupPair = DefaultGroupPair

Grant-EC2SecurityGroupIngress -GroupId $RDSGroupId -IpPermissions $SQLServerRule
```

In addition, we are going to use MySQL in the High Availability example later in this chapter, so let's configure rules for MySQL as well.

```
$MySQLRule = New-Object Amazon.EC2.Model.IpPermission
$MySQLRule.IpProtocol='tcp'
$MySQLRule.FromPort = 3306
$MySQLRule.ToPort = 3306
$MySQLRule.UserIdGroupPair = DefaultGroupPair

Grant-EC2SecurityGroupIngress -GroupId $RDSGroupId -IpPermissions $MySQLRule
```

■ **Note**   I am describing how to configure security groups for VPC instances. EC2 classic instances use a completely different security group configuration. If you are reading the RDS help files, don't be confused by references to RDS Security Groups. RDS Security Groups are not used with VPC.

Now that we have our VPC configured, we are ready to launch a database instance. In the next section, we will create an SQL Server instance. Remember that SQL Server instances do not support multi-AZ deployments. Later in the chapter we will examine a multi-AZ configuration using My SQL.

Managing RDS Instances

Now that we have our VPC configured, we can begin working with RDS instances. Let's get started by launching a new SQL Server database on RDS.

Launching an Instance

To launch a new instance, we use the New-RDSDBInstance command. It takes a few minutes for a new instance to launch – especially using the micro instances – so let's jump right in and launch one. This is another one of those commands with a ton of options. While the new instance is launching, we can examine all of the optional parameters available.

Since you're reading a book on PowerShell, I assume you are most interested in SQL Server. Remember that RDS does not support multi-AZ instances of SQL Server. Therefore, we are going to create a stand-alone instance. To create a new stand-alone SQL Server instance, enter the following command:

```
New-RDSDBInstance -DBInstanceIdentifier 'SQLServer01' -Engine 'sqlserver-ex' -AllocatedStorage 20
    -DBInstanceClass 'db.t1.micro' -MasterUsername 'sa' -MasterUserPassword 'password'
    -DBSubnetGroupName 'MySubnetGroup' -VpcSecurityGroupIds $GroupId
```

■ **Note**   Never use "password" as a password. Please choose something more complex and novel.

The previous command includes the minimum set of the parameters required to launch a database instance into a VPC, which are:

- **DBInstanceIdentifier** is simply a unique name you will use to refer to the database instance later. Unlike the EC2 and VPC commands we have been using, RDS uses a name, called an identifier, rather than an id.

- **Engine** defines which type of database you want to use. RDS supports multiple versions of MySQL, Oracle, and SQL Server. If you are not familiar with the various versions of each database, see the vendor's web site for details. The specific engine types are:

  - **mysql** – There is only one version of MySQL that includes all options

  - **oracle-se1** – Oracle Standard Edition One

  - **oracle-se** – Oracle Standard Edition

  - **oracle-ee** – Oracle Enterprise Edition

  - **sqlserver-ex** – SQL Server Express

  - **sqlserver-web** – SQL Server Web Express

  - **sqlserver-se** – SQL Server Standard Edition

  - **sqlserver-ee** – SQL Server Enterprise Edition

- **AllocatedStorage** describes how much storage to allocate to the database. The maximum storage is 1024GB, and each engine type has a different minimum. See Table 9-1 for details of each database engine. Note that you cannot resize an SQL Server instance after creating it, so I recommend you err on the high side.

Table 9-1. *Storage by Engine Type*

Engine	Min Storage	Max Storage
MySQL	5GB	1024GB
oracle-se1	10GB	1024GB
oracle-se	10GB	1024GB
oracle-ee	10GB	1024GB
sqlserver-ee	200GB	1024GB
sqlserver-se	200GB	1024GB
sqlserver-ex	30GB	1024GB
sqlserver-web	30GB	1024GB

- **DBInstanceClass** describes the hardware your database instance will use. This is similar to the EC2 instance types. See Table 9-2 for a list of instance classes and the SQL Server Engines supported on each.

Table 9-2. *Supported Instance Classes by Engine Type*

Engine	Enterprise Edition	Standard Edition	Web Edition	Express Edition
db.t1.micro				X
db.m1.small	X	X	X	X
db.m1.large	X	X	X	
db.m1.xlarge				
db.m2.xlarge	X	X	X	
db.m2.2xlarge	X	X	X	
db.m2.4xlarge	X	X	X	

- **MasterUsername** and **MasterUserPassword** are used to log into the database. Note that the master user does not have sys admin rights to the database. Remember that you do not have access to the underlying operating system when using RDS. Therefore, the master user has limited access. In addition, note that SQL Server only supports database accounts. You cannot use Windows Integrated Security and you cannot join the database instance to an Active Directory domain. Of course you can create additional database accounts after logging in.

- **DBSubnetGroupName** is the name of the subnet group we created earlier. RDS will launch the instance into one of the subnets in this group. If you want to specify which subnet to use, see the optional AvailabilityGroup parameter described later.

- **VpcSecurityGroupIds** is a list of security groups the RDS instance should be placed into.

In addition to the required parameters, New-RDSDBInstance also supports a bunch of optional parameters, which include:

- **LicenseModel** allows you to choose from multiple software licensing models. Depending on the engine you are using, you can choose to bring your own license, or have the cost of license included in with the hourly cost of the instance. The licensing models available for each engine are described in Table 9-3.

Table 9-3. *License by Engine Type*

Engine	General Public License	Bring Your Own	Included
MySQL	X		
oracle-se1		X	X
oracle-se		X	
oracle-ee		X	
sqlserver-ee		X	
sqlserver-se		X	X
sqlserver-ex			X
sqlserver-web			X

- **EngineVersion** defines the specific version of each database type. For example, RDS supports SQL Server 2008 R2 and 2012. If you omit this parameter, RDS will use the latest version. At the time I am writing this, the latest version of SQL Server is SQL Server 2012 version 11.00.2100.60.v1. If you want to list all of the supported engine versions, use the command: Get-RDSDBEngineVersion | Format-Table.

- **AutoMinorVersionUpgrade** tells RDS to automatically apply minor updates. Updates are applied during the maintenance windows defined later. Major upgrades (e.g., SQL 2008R2 to SQL 2012) are not supported. This option is enabled by default.

- **MultiAZ** specifies that you want to create both a primary and standby instance. The primary and standby will be launched into subnets in different availability zones as defined in the subnet group. (See the section on multi-AZ configuration later in this chapter.) Note that SQL Server is not supported in a multi-AZ configuration.

- **AvailabilityZone** specifies which availability zone to launch the instance into. In a VPC, RDS will use the subnet in the specified availability zone. You cannot specify availability zone if you are using the MultiAZ option.

- **Iops** specifies the I/O operations per second (IOPS) desired from the disk. This is similar to provisioned Iops in EC2, and you pay a premium for this option just like EC2. RDS uses striping and can support 1,000–30,000 IOPS.

- **PreferredMaintenanceWindow** defines a weekly outage window when Amazon can apply patches to the RDS instance. For example, you might specify sat:22:00-sat:23:00. If you omit this option, AWS will choose a random 30-minute window from an 8-hour block defined for each region. AWS will choose a time that is generally considered "off hours" for the region, but it is best to specify your own window.

- **PreferredBackupWindow** defines when the daily full backup is taken. For example, you might specify 23:00-24:00. The backup windows cannot overlap the maintenance window and must be a minimum of 30 minutes. (There is more detail on backup and recovery later in this chapter.)

- **BackupRetentionPeriod** defines how long to save backups. You can specify 0-8 days. The default is 1 day and specifying 0 days disables backup.

- **PubliclyAccessible** specifies that the instance will be assigned a public IP address and can be accessed from the Internet. In general this is a bad idea; I prefer to have a micro instance on the VPC that I can use for administration. In the default VPC this option is enabled by default, but in a custom VPC it is disabled.

- **Port** allows you to change the default port for your database. Table 9-4 lists the default ports for each engine.

Table 9-4. *Default Port by Engine Type*

Engine	Default Port
MySQL	3306
Oracle	1521
SQL Server	1433

- **DBParameterGroupName** allows you to alter engine parameters. For example, I will show you how to enable the Common Language Runtime (CLR) in the next section. Note that Appendix F includes a list of SQL Server parameters that you can alter.

- **DBOptionGroupName** allows you to alter engine options. For example, I will show you how to enable Transparent Data Encryption (TDE) in the next section.

Wow, that was a lot of options to discuss. By now our instance should be running. You can use the Get-RDSDBInstance command to check on it. Check the DBInstanceStatus attribute. For example:

```
(Get-RDSDBInstance -DBInstanceIdentifier 'SQLServer01').DBInstanceStatus
```

It will take a while for the instance to start. Once it is running you can get the endpoint address needed to connect to SQL Server. For example:

```
(Get-RDSDBInstance -DBInstanceIdentifier 'SQLServer01').Endpoint.Address
```

In my case this returned:

```
sqlserver01.cz8cihropmwk.us-east-1.rds.amazonaws.com
```

You can now enter the address into SQL Server Management Studio to connect. Figure 9-2 shows an example.

Figure 9-2. *Logging into an RDS Instance*

Modifying an Instance

No sooner do you a launch a new instance than you realize you need to change something. Many of the options we discussed in the last section can be modified after the RDS instance has been launched by using Edit-RDSDBInstance.

For example, the following command will change the security groups the instance is a member of:

```
Edit-RDSDBInstance -DBInstanceIdentifier 'SQLServer01' -VpcSecurityGroupIds $NewGroupId
```

The following options can be altered using Edit-RDSDBInstance. Some options take effect immediately, while others are applied during the next maintenance window.

- AllocatedStorage
- AllowMajorVersionUpgrade
- ApplyImmediately

- AutoMinorVersionUpgrade

- BackupRetentionPeriod

- DBInstanceClass

- DBParameterGroupName

- DBSecurityGroups

- EngineVersion

- Iops

- MasterUserPassword

- MultiAZ

- NewDBInstanceIdentifier

- OptionGroupName

- PreferredBackupWindow

- PreferredMaintenanceWindow

- VpcSecurityGroupIds

■ **Note**   SQL Server does not support resizing the disk. Therefore you must create a new instance and copy the data manually.

Deleting an Instance

When you no longer need an instance, you can delete it using the `Remove-RDSDBInstance` command. If you want to take a snapshot of the database before deleting it, you can simply specify the identifier when you call remove. (I will explain RDS snapshots later in the chapter.) The following command will delete the database we created:

```
Remove-RDSDBInstance -DBInstanceIdentifier 'SQLServer01' -FinalDBSnapshotIdentifier
    'SQLServer01-Final-Snapshot' -Force
```

If you don't need a backup of the instance, you can use the `SkipFinalSnapshot` parameter to tell RDS not to back up the instance.

```
Remove-RDSDBInstance -DBInstanceIdentifier 'SQLServer01' -SkipFinalSnapshot $true -Force
```

As you can see, RDS makes launching and managing a database instance really easy. In the next section we will discuss how to configure options specific to SQL Server.

Configuring a Database Engine

So far, all of the parameters we have configured are common to all of the database engines. Obviously there are also engine specific configuration options to choose from. RDS breaks these into two categories: parameters and options. Let's spend a minute looking at parameters and options specific to SQL Server.

Modifying Parameters

Parameters allow you to configure your database engine. RDS organizes parameters into parameter groups for each engine type. For example, the default parameter group for SQL Server Express is default.sqlserver-ex-11.0. You can get a list of parameter groups using the Get-RDSDBParameterGroup command.

There are numerous parameters available for SQL Server. I have included a list in Appendix F, but not all parameters are available on all SQL Server editions. For example, some options are only available on the enterprise edition. To list the parameters available, use the Get-RDSDBParameter command. For example, the following code will list the parameters specific to SQL Server Express.

```
Get-RDSDBParameter -DBParameterGroupName default.sqlserver-ex-11.0 |
    Format-Table ParameterName, Description, ParameterValue -AutoSize
```

If you want to customize the parameters, you can create your own parameter group using the New-RDSDBParameterGroup command. For example, let's assume you want to enable the Common Language Runtime (CLR).

```
New-RDSDBParameterGroup -DBParameterGroupName 'SQL2012' -DBParameterGroupFamily
    'sqlserver-ex-11.0'
    -Description "SQL2012 with CLR enabled"
```

Now you can configure the individual parameters in the group. Once again, we use a .Net object to describe the change and pass it to the EditRDSDBParameterGroup command. For example:

```
$Parameter = New-Object Amazon.RDS.Model.Parameter
$Parameter.ParameterName = 'clr enabled'
$Parameter.ParameterValue = 1
$Parameter.ApplyMethod = 'immediate'
Edit-RDSDBParameterGroup -DBParameterGroupName 'SQL2012' -Parameters $Parameter
```

Note the ApplyMethod parameter. Some parameter changes can be applied immediately while others require a reboot. You can check if a reboot is required by checking the apply type column in Appendix F. If the apply type is static, then a reboot is required. If the apply type is dynamic, you can choose to apply the change immediately or after a reboot. To apply the change immediately, set the ApplyMethod parameter to immediate. To wait for the next reboot, set the ApplyMethod parameter to pending-reboot. You can force the reboot using the Restart-RDSDBInstance method.

Use the DBParameterGroupName of the New-RDSDBInstance or Edit-RDSDBInstance command to associate the new parameter group with an instance.

Modifying Options

Some database engines offer optional features that you can choose to enable. For example, SQL Server Enterprise Edition offers Transparent Data Encryption (TDE). Actually, this is the only option available for SQL Server at the moment. RDS refers to these features as options and allows you to configure them using option groups.

Option groups work a lot like parameter groups. First, you create a custom option group, and then you associate your instance with the custom group. Let's get started by creating a custom option group to enable SQL TDE on 2012. To create a new group, use the New-RDSOptionGroup command and specify the database engine and version. For example:

```
New-RDSOptionGroup -OptionGroupName 'SQL2012TDE' -OptionGroupDescription
    "SQL2012 Enterprise Edition with TDE"
    -EngineName sqlserver-ee -MajorEngineVersion '11.00'
```

■ **Note**   TDE is only available with the enterprise edition; therefore, you must use the bring-your-own license model when you launch an instance.

Now, we need to describe the option we want to enable using a .Net object. TDE has no configuration parameters so we simply specify a name.

```
$Option = New-Object Amazon.RDS.Model.OptionConfiguration
$Option.OptionName = 'TDE'
```

Then, we pass the option description to the EditRDSOptionGroup command.

```
Edit-RDSOptionGroup -OptionGroupName 'SQL2012' -OptionsToInclude $Option
    -ApplyImmediately $true
```

Now you can launch a new SQL Server instance and specify the option group. See Exercise 9-2 for a complete example.

Working with Snapshots

RDS supports two types of backup: snapshots and point-in-time recovery. The backup windows and retention period we discussed earlier are related to point-in-time recovery and will be discussed in the next section. This section is about RDS snapshots, which are similar to EC2 snapshots.

A RDS snapshot creates a copy of the database just like an EC2 snapshot creates a copy of a volume. They are created manually using either the AWS management console or the API. You can create as many snapshots as you want, any time you want. Snapshots are retained until you manually delete them and are not effected by the retention period specified when you create the instance.

When you restore a RDS snapshot, AWS always creates a new instance. You cannot overwrite an existing database using a snapshot. This is just like restoring an EC2 snapshot, which, we already know, always creates a new volume rather than overwriting an existing one.

You can create a new snapshot using the New-RDSDBSnapshot command. This command simply takes the name of the instance you want to back up and a name to identify the snapshot.

```
New-RDSDBSnapshot -DBSnapshotIdentifier 'MySnapshot' -DBInstanceIdentifier 'SQLServer01'
```

It will take a few minutes to create the snapshot. You can check on the status of the snapshot using the Get-RDSDBSnapshot command. For example, to check on the snapshot we just created, use the following command:

```
Get-RDSDBSnapshot -DBSnapshotIdentifier 'MySnapshot'
```

The Get-RDSDBSnapshot command can also be used to list all the snapshots taken for a given database instance. The following command will list all snapshots taken of the SQLServer01 instance:

```
Get-RDSDBSnapshot -DBInstanceIdentifier 'SQLServer01'
```

You can restore a snapshot using the Restore-RDSDBInstanceFromDBSnapshot command. Remember that restoring a snapshot always creates a new instance. Therefore, we need to include a new identifier. In addition, we can change many of the parameters we specified when we created the database instance.

The following command will restore a RDS snapshot creating a new RDS instance called SQLServer02. The new instance will have a new DNS name and you must update your application to use the new name.

```
Restore-RDSDBInstanceFromDBSnapshot -DBSnapshotIdentifier 'MySnapshot' -DBInstanceIdentifier
    'SQLServer02' -DBSubnetGroupName 'MySubnetGroup'
```

Note that I had to specify the subnet group in the preceding command. In addition, I could have changed any of the following options. If you leave these options blank, RDS will use the settings that were present on the original instance rather than the defaults defined for New-RDSDBInstance.

- DBInstanceClass

- Port

- AvailabilityZone

- MultiAZ

- PubliclyAccessible

- AutoMinorVersionUpgrade

- LicenseModel

- Engine – Note that the engine must be compatible. You cannot restore an SQL Server snapshot to an Oracle database, but you can move from standard edition to enterprise edition.

- Iops

■ **Note**   Once again, you cannot change the disk size. If you want to increase disk size, you must create a new instance and copy the data.

Just like EC2, RDS snapshots can be copied to another region for an additional level of redundancy. You can copy a snapshot using Copy-RDSDBSnapshot. The copy is always initiated from the target region. Rather than specifying the source region as we did with EC2 snapshots, you must use the fully qualified Amazon Resource Name (ARN) for the source snapshot. The ARN uses the format:

```
arn:aws:rds:<region>:<account number>:<type>:<identifier>
```

For example, the following command will copy our snapshot from the Northern Virginia region to the Northern California region:

```
Copy-RDSDBSnapshot -SourceDBSnapshotIdentifier 'arn:aws:rds:us-east-
1:486469900423:snapshot:MySnapshot'
    -TargetDBSnapshotIdentifier 'MySnapshot' -Region us-west-1
```

Obviously you are charged for the storage required to keep the snapshot. When you no longer need a snapshot, you can delete it using the Remove-RDSDBSnapshot command.

```
Remove-RDSDBSnapshot -DBSnapshotIdentifier 'MySnapshot' -Force
```

Snapshots are a great way to back up a database when you can plan for a specific risk. For example, you might take a snapshot before upgrading the application code. But, snapshots are not well suited for unexpected issues. For example, if a disk failed, you might not have taken a snapshot recently. For unexpected issues we need to take regularly scheduled database backups. In the next section we will examine how to do this.

Using Point-in-Time Restores

In addition to snapshots, RDS also supports database and transaction log backups. Using these backups we can restore a database to within a second of any point in time within the retention period. The best part is that AWS takes care of all the work required to create and maintain the backups.

When we launched the RDS instance at the beginning of this chapter, we accepted the default backup windows and retention period. Remember that the default retention period is one day. As long as the retention period is greater than zero, database backups are enabled. If backups are enabled, RDS will take a full backup of the database once a day during the backup window. In addition, it will back up the transaction log every five minutes.

These backups can be used to create a point-in-time restore. Point-in-time restores allow you to specify a specific time you want to restore, and since transaction log backups are taken every five minutes, you will never lose more than five minutes.

Now, I want to mention a few details specific to SQL Server. First, if your SQL Server has multiple databases, the individual databases will be restored to within one second of one another. Second, RDS does not support multi-AZ SQL Server instances. As a result, you should expect a momentary outage when the full backup is taken. This does not occur with multi-AZ databases because the backup is taken on the secondary instance.

Similar to snapshots, RDS point-in-time restores always create a new RDS instance. You cannot overwrite an existing instance. Before restoring an instance, you should check when the last transaction log backup was taken and how many days the backups are retained. You can restore to any point within this period. For example, to check the time of the last transaction log backup and retention period of our SQL database, use the following code.

```
$DBInstance = Get-RDSDBInstance -DBInstanceIdentifier 'SQLServer01'
$DBInstance.LatestRestorableTime
$DBInstance.BackupRetentionPeriod
```

The output of this command, shown as follows, indicates that you can restore to any point within a one-day window between November 4 at 5:22 p.m. and November 5 at 5:22 p.m.

```
Tuesday, November 5, 2013 5:22:42 PM
1
```

We can use the Restore-RDSDBInstanceToPointInTime command to create a new RDS instance restored to any point within this range. For example, to restore to November 5th 2013, at 11:15 a.m., use the following command. This is almost identical to the Restore-RDSDBInstanceFromDBSnapshot command except that I am specifying a time and day to restore to. Note that RDS expects the time in UTC.

```
Restore-RDSDBInstanceToPointInTime -SourceDBInstanceIdentifier 'SQLServer01'
    -TargetDBInstanceIdentifier 'SQLServer03' -DBSubnetGroupName 'MySubnetGroup'
    -RestoreTime (Get-date('2013-11-05T11:15:00')).ToUniversalTime()
```

If you omit the RestoreTime parameter, RDS will restore to the latest time possible. For example:

```
Restore-RDSDBInstanceToPointInTime -SourceDBInstanceIdentifier 'SQLServer01'
    -TargetDBInstanceIdentifier 'SQLServer04'
    -DBSubnetGroupName 'MySubnetGroup' -UseLatestRestorableTime $true
```

Just like when restoring a snapshot, you are creating a new instance, and you can specify many of the options that were available when we created the original instance, including:

- `DBInstanceClass`
- `Port`
- `DBSubnetGroupName`
- `AvailabilityZone`
- `MultiAZ`
- `PubliclyAccessible`
- `AutoMinorVersionUpgrade`
- `LicenseModel`
- `Engine`
- `Iops`

Unlike snapshots, there is no need to delete database backup files. They are automatically deleted after the retention period. This is the benefit of the RDS platform. AWS takes care of the maintenance for you. In addition, you cannot copy backups to another region.

In the next section we discuss how to keep track of our RDS instances using tags, and how to monitor our instances using events and logs.

Working with Tags, Events, and Logs

As your inventory of servers grows, it will become more and more difficult to keep track of everything. It is really important that you have a strategy for organizing and monitoring your resources. RDS offers tags to help categorize everything and events and logs for monitoring. Let's look at each.

Tags

We saw the power of tags with EC2. The same holds true for RDS. You can use tags to include metadata describing your RDS resources. For example, you might want to tag an instance with the department that owns it so you can create a chargeback report and know whom to contact if something goes wrong.

Creating a tag is similar to EC2. You begin by creating a .Net object used to describe the tag. Then you add a key and value. For example, the following code will create a tag specifying the department=marketing.

```
$Tag = New-Object('Amazon.RDS.Model.Tag')
$Tag.Key = 'Department'
$Tag.Value = 'Marketing'
```

To add the tag to a RDS resource, you use the `Add-RDSTagsToResource` command. Remember that RDS uses names rather than ids to identify resources. Different resource types can have the same name. For example, I can name both an instance and snapshot "database1." As a result, we have to use the fully qualified Amazon Resource Name (ARN) to uniquely identify a resource. Remember that ARNs follow the format:

```
arn:aws:rds:<region>:<account number>:<type>:<identifier>
```

Therefore, to add the department=marketing tag to our instance, use:

```
Add-RDSTagsToResource -ResourceName 'arn:aws:rds:us-east-1:486469900423:db:SQLServer01'
    -Tags $Tag
```

And, to add the department=marketing tag to our snapshot, use:

```
Add-RDSTagsToResource -ResourceName 'arn:aws:rds:us-east-1:486469900423:snapshot:MySnapshot'
    -Tags $Tag
```

You can retrieve the tags using the `Get-RDSTagForResoure` command. For example:

```
Get-RDSTagForResource -ResourceName 'arn:aws:rds:us-east-1:486469900423:db:SQLServer01'
```

You can also remove a tag using the `Remove-RDSTagsFromResource` command. For example:

```
Remove-RDSTagFromResource -ResourceName 'arn:aws:rds:us-east-1:486469900423:db:SQLServer01'
    -TagKeys 'Name' -Force
```

Tags are a great way to organize RDS resources. In the next section, we will look at using RDS events to monitor our instances.

Events

It is important that you always know what is going on in the cloud. Events allow us to monitor our RDS instances and receive notifications from SNS when specific events occur. For example, you might want to be notified when the disk is filling up.

To get a list of all events, we use the `Get-RDSEvent` command. For example:

```
Get-RDSEvent
```

You can control how many events are returned using the `Duration` and `MaxRecords` parameters. For example, the following command will return the first 25 events that occurred in the last 15 minutes.

```
Get-RDSEvent -Duration 15 -MaxRecords 25
```

You can also specify a specific range using `StartTime` and `EndTime`, but events are only stored for 15 days. For example:

```
Get-RDSEvent -StartTime '2013-11-01' -EndTime '2013-11-15'
```

RDS captures many event types. Events are organized into source types that correspond to the RDS resource types and include: `db-instance`, `db-security-group`, `db-parameter-group`, and `db-snapshot`. Events are further organized into categories. To get a list of categories, use the `Get-RDSEventCategories` command. For example, to get the categories available for an RDS instance:

```
(Get-RDSEventCategories -SourceType 'db-instance').EventCategories
```

You can use the parameters of the Get-RDSEvent command to limit the events returned. For example, to only retrieve events for the SQL instances we created earlier, use the following command:

```
Get-RDSEvent -SourceType 'db-instance' -SourceIdentifier 'SQLServer01'
```

Similarly you can filter for specific event categories. For example, the following command will return all information about the backup of any RDS instance.

```
Get-RDSEvent -SourceType 'db-instance' -EventCategories 'backup'
```

Of course, you can combine these in various combinations to return the events you want. The following command will return all of the backup events for a specific instance.

```
Get-RDSEvent -SourceType 'db-instance' -SourceIdentifier 'SQLServer01' -EventCategories 'backup'
```

Being able to query events is great, but we cannot expect someone to sit in front of PowerShell all day looking for issues. We really want a more proactive solution. Luckily RDS allows us to subscribe to events using Simple Notification Service (SNS) with the New-RDSEventSubscription command.

For example, let's assume we want to know whenever a failure occurs or the disk space is getting low. More specifically, we want to receive a notification via e-mail so we can respond quickly. First we need to create an SNS topic and e-mail notification. This is exactly what we did in Chapter 8, for example:

```
$Topic = New-SNSTopic -Name 'RDSTopic'
Connect-SNSNotification -TopicArn $Topic -Protocol 'email' -Endpoint 'alerts@brianbeach.com'
```

Now we can create a RDS subscription. The RDS subscription will publish a notification to the SNS topic we just created whenever a new RDS event occurs that matches the criteria we specify. To create the subscription, we use the New-RDSEventSubscription command. For example, the following command will subscribe to all failure and low-storage events and send a notification to our SNS topic.

```
New-RDSEventSubscription -SubscriptionName 'MyRDSSubscription'
    -SnsTopicArn 'arn:aws:sns:us-east-1:486469900423:RDSTopic'
    -SourceType 'db-instance' -EventCategories 'failure', 'low storage'
```

We can also subscribe to events from specific sources. For example, you might have both development and production RDS instances in the same account. You don't want to get a notification in the middle of the night if a development instance fails, so you only set up notifications for the production instances. The following example creates a subscription for a specific instance, SQLServer01.

```
New-RDSEventSubscription -SubscriptionName 'MyRDSSubscription2'
    -SnsTopicArn 'arn:aws:sns:us-east-1:486469900423:RDSTopic'
    -SourceType 'db-instance' -SourceIds 'sqlserver01'
```

■ **Caution**   The source id in the following example is all lowercase. Your source id must be lowercase or you will get an error.

As our application changes over time, you may want to add or remove instances from the subscription. You can do this using the Add-RDSSourceIdentifierToSubscription and Remove-RDSSourceIdentifierFromSubscription commands. The following two examples add and then remove an instance from the subscription.

```
Add-RDSSourceIdentifierToSubscription -SubscriptionName 'MyRDSSubscription2'
    -SourceIdentifier 'sqlserver02'
Remove-RDSSourceIdentifierFromSubscription -SubscriptionName 'MyRDSSubscription2'
    -SourceIdentifier 'sqlserver02' -Force
```

Finally, you may want to delete a subscription altogether and stop receiving notifications. You can do so using the Remove-RDSEventSubscription command. For example:

```
Remove-RDSEventSubscription  -SubscriptionName 'MyRDSSubscription' -Force
```

Events are a great way to monitor your RDS instances, but you will likely need more detail to debug a failure when it occurs. In the next section we discuss how to retrieve logs from the database engine.

Logs

With RDS you do not have access to the operating system and therefore cannot access the file system. This means that you cannot see the detailed logs produced by the database engine. In order to access the logs you need to use an API call.

To list the log files available on the instance, you use the Get-RDSDBLogFiles command. This command will list the logs files available on the server. For example:

```
Get-RDSDBLogFiles -DBInstanceIdentifier 'SQLServer01'
```

You can also use the FilenameContains parameter to find specific files. For example, to find the error log on an SQL Server use the following command. Note that the file name is case sensitive.

```
Get-RDSDBLogFiles -DBInstanceIdentifier 'SQLServer01' -FilenameContains 'ERROR'
```

Once you know which file you are looking for you can download the contents using the Get-RDSDBLogFilePortion command. For example, to read the error log on our SQL instance, use the following command.

```
$Log = Get-RDSDBLogFilePortion -DBInstanceIdentifier 'SQLServer01' -LogFileName 'log/ERROR'
$Log.LogFileData
```

As you can see, RDS gives us all the tools we need to manage and monitor our database instance. In the next section we will discuss building high availability databases using multi-AZ instances.

Multi-AZ Instances

RDS supports multi-AZ instances for high availability and durability. When you deploy a multi-AZ database, AWS deploys a primary instance in one AZ and a synchronous replica in another AZ (see Figure 9-3). All of the complexity is hidden from you, and the database appears to be one logical instance. If the primary database were to fail, RDS automatically fails over and updates the DNS entry so your application begins using the secondary without manual intervention.

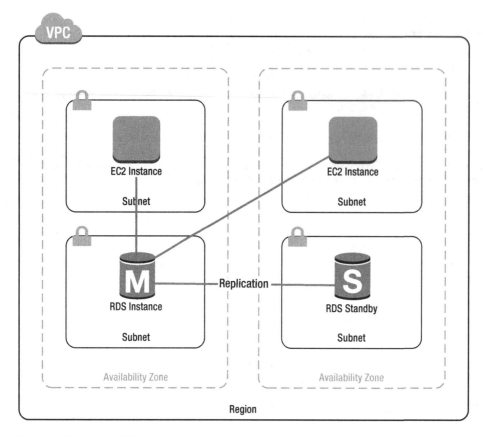

Figure 9-3. Multi-AZ Deployment

Sounds great, right? Now for the bad news: RDS does not support multi-AZ deployments of SQL Server yet. SQL Server 2012 introduced the technology, called Always On, needed to implement a multi-AZ deployment, but RDS does not support it yet. In the meantime, I will use MySQL to explain how multi-AZ deployment works.

Launching a multi-AZ instance is just like launching a stand-alone instance, except that we add the `MultiAZ` option. For example:

```
New-RDSDBInstance -DBInstanceIdentifier 'MySQL01' -Engine 'MySQL' -AllocatedStorage 20
    -DBInstanceClass 'db.t1.micro' -MasterUsername 'sa' -MasterUserPassword 'password'
    -DBSubnetGroupName 'MySubnetGroup' -VpcSecurityGroupIds $SecurityGroup.GroupId
    -MultiAZ $true
```

That is all there is to it! RDS takes care of the heavy lifting. All of the options we discussed above are supported, except for the `AvailabilityZone` parameter on any of the commands that have it. You cannot choose which AZ the primary database runs in. RDS manages that behind the scenes.

In addition to replicating to a standby instance, RDS can also replicate to additional read replicas. Let's take a look in the next section.

Read Replicas

A read replica is similar to a standby instance in that changes are automatically replicated from the primary instance to the replica. The difference is that a read replica is read only and uses asynchronous replication. Asynchronous replication can lag the primary instance by a few seconds, and therefore, the read replica is not used for failover. Each RDS instance can have up to five read replicas.

A read replica is not intended for high availability. A read replica is designed to enable scaling by offloading some work from the primary instance. A common, and easy to implement, use of read replicas is to offload reporting tasks from the primary database. If you design your application with read replicas in mind you can send all of the read tasks to the replica and only use the primary for writes (see Figure 9-4). This can greatly reduce the load on the primary instance and allow you to scale your application dramatically.

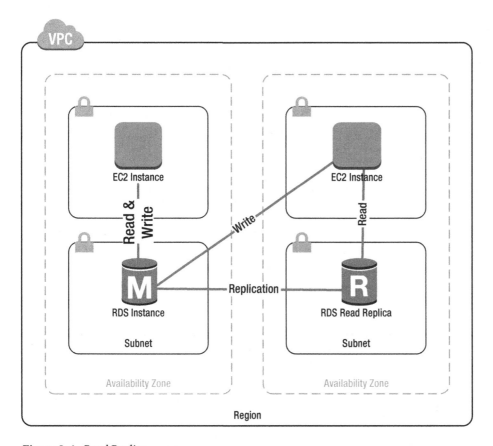

Figure 9-4. *Read Replica*

To create a read replica, you use the New-RDSDBInstanceReadReplica command and specify the source instance for replication. For example, the following command will create a read replica of the MySQL database we created in the last section called MySQLRR.

```
New-RDSDBInstanceReadReplica -DBInstanceIdentifier 'MySQL01RR'
    -SourceDBInstanceIdentifier 'MySQL01'
```

The `New-RDSDBInstanceReadReplica` command supports some of the options you have when creating a new database, including:

- **DBInstanceClass** - A read replica does not have to be the same instance type as the primary. You may have a large primary with a small replica for reporting or vice versa.

- **AvailabilityZone** - You can specify which availability zone you want to deploy the replica in. If running in a VPC, there must be at least one subnet in this AZ specified in the subnet group.

- **Iops** - Possibly your reporting database has much higher I/O requirements than the primary transactional store.

- **AutoMinorVersionUpgrade** - I recommend you keep this the same as the primary, but you can change it.

- **OptionGroupName** - I recommend you keep this the same as the primary, but you can change it.

- **PubliclyAccessible** - An interesting use case might be keeping the primary instance private, but allow end users to connect to a read replica to do business analysis using Excel or something similar.

Once your read replica is up and running, you may choose to convert it to a stand-alone instance. You can do so using the `Convert-RDSReadReplicaToStandalone` command. For example:

```
Convert-RDSReadReplicaToStandalone -DBInstanceIdentifier 'MySQL01RR'
```

Note that read replicas are not backed up, because the primary instance already is. Therefore, when you convert to stand-alone, you have the option to specify a `BackupRetentionPeriod` and `PreferredBackupWindow`.

■ **Note**   I happen to be writing this chapter while attending re:Invent 2013, and AWS just announced that RDS will soon support asynchronous read replicas across regions allowing you to replicate data around the globe. The details are not out yet, but this exciting new feature should be available by the time this book publishes.

As you can see, RDS offers everything you need to build a robust database platform without having to worry about the day-to-day details of system administration and backup. Let's wrap up this chapter with two exercises focused on securing SQL Server. The first will enable SSL to protect your connection and the second will enable Transparent Data Encryption.

EXERCISE 9.1: SQL SERVER AND SSL ENCRYPTION

It always a good practice to encrypt the connection between your client and server. It is common to do so between the user and a web server, but less common between the web server and database. SQL Server supports encrypting the connection using SSL.

You can enable SSL when using an SQL Server RDS instance. All RDS instances include a self-signed certificate. Of course your client machine will not trust the self-signed certificate until we import the public key into the trusted store. Let's build a script to do so.

You can download the public key from `https://rds.amazonaws.com/doc/rds-ssl-ca-cert.pem`. Let's use PowerShell to save a copy of the key on our client machine. This command must be run on the client machine.

```
Invoke-WebRequest 'https://rds.amazonaws.com/doc/rds-ssl-ca-cert.pem'
    -OutFile "$env:TEMP\rds-ssl-ca-cert.pem"
```

Next, we can use PowerShell to import the certificate into our trusted store. Note that you must run PowerShell as an administrator on our client machine to complete this step.

```
Import-Certificate -FilePath "$env:TEMP\rds-ssl-ca-cert.pem"
    -CertStoreLocation 'Cert:\LocalMachine\authRoot' -Confirm:$false
```

Finally, we should clean up the temporary copy of the certificate.

```
Remove-Item "$env:TEMP\rds-ssl-ca-cert.pem"
```

That's all there is to it. All you have to do to enable encryption is add two parameters to the connection string: `encrypt=true` and `TrustServerCertificate=true`. For example:

```
Server=sqlserver01.cz8cihropmwk.us-east-1.rds.amazonaws.com;Database=myDataBase;
    User Id=sa;Password=password;encrypt=true;TrustServerCertificate=true"
```

Encrypting your database connection is a simple way to add an extra layer of security. In the next example, I will show you how to encrypt the data that is stored on disk using TDE.

EXERCISE 9.2: SQL SERVER TOTAL DATABASE ENCRYPTION

Earlier in this chapter we talked about option groups, and I showed you how to create an option group that enables SQL Server Transparent Data Encryption (TDE). In this exercise, we build on that example to fully configure SQL TDE in a new instance. We will create an option group that enables TDE, launch a RDS instance that uses the new option group, create a new database on the RDS instance, and encrypt the new database.

First, we need to accept a few parameters as input to our script. These should all look familiar; they are all the parameters that will be passed to `New-RDSDBInstance`. Notice that the default engine is SQL Server Enterprise Edition. Remember that TDE is only supported on the enterprise edition of SQL Server. In addition, notice that the default instance class is small and I have allocated 200GB of disk. These are the minimum values for SQL Server Enterprise Edition.

```
param(
    [parameter(mandatory=$true)][string]$DBInstanceIdentifier,
    [parameter(mandatory=$false)][string]$DBInstanceClass = 'db.m1.small',
    [parameter(mandatory=$false)][string]$Engine = 'sqlserver-ee',
    [parameter(mandatory=$false)][string]$AllocatedStorage = 200,
    [parameter(mandatory=$true)][string]$MasterUsername,
    [parameter(mandatory=$true)][string]$MasterUserPassword,
    [parameter(mandatory=$true)][string]$DBSubnetGroupName,
    [parameter(mandatory=$true)][string]$VpcSecurityGroupIds
)
```

Next, we create the new option group just like I did earlier in this chapter. In the example below I first check to if the option group already exists, and if not, create a new group.

```
Try {
    $OptionGroup = Get-RDSOptionGroup -OptionGroupName 'SQL2012TDE'
}
Catch [Amazon.RDS.Model.OptionGroupNotFoundException]{
    $OptionGroup = New-RDSOptionGroup -OptionGroupName 'SQL2012TDE'
    -OptionGroupDescription "SQL2012 with TDE"
        -EngineName sqlserver-ee -MajorEngineVersion '11.00'
    $Option = New-Object Amazon.RDS.Model.OptionConfiguration
    $Option.OptionName = 'TDE'
    Edit-RDSOptionGroup -OptionGroupName 'SQL2012TDE' -OptionsToInclude $Option
    -ApplyImmediately $true
}
```

Now that the option group has been created, we can launch a new instance using the parameters passed into the script.

```
New-RDSDBInstance -DBInstanceIdentifier $DBInstanceIdentifier -Engine $Engine
    -AllocatedStorage $AllocatedStorage
    -DBInstanceClass $DBInstanceClass -MasterUsername $MasterUsername
    -MasterUserPassword $MasterUserPassword
    -DBSubnetGroupName $DBSubnetGroupName -VpcSecurityGroupIds $VpcSecurityGroupIds
    -OptionGroupName 'SQL2012TDE'
```

It will take a while for the instance to start. Let's add a while loop that will wait for it.

```
While ($Instance.DBInstanceStatus -ne 'available') {$Instance = Get-RDSDBInstance
$DBInstanceIdentifier; Write-Host "Waiting for RDS instance to launch.";
    Start-Sleep -s 60}
```

Once it's done we can get the address and report it back to the user so he or she can log into SQL Server and finish the configuration.

```
$Instance = (Get-RDSDBInstance -DBInstanceIdentifier 'SQLServer01').Endpoint.Address
Write-Host "The RDS instance $DBInstanceIdentifier is ready. The address is $Address."
```

At this point TDE is enabled on the instance, but the individual databases are not encrypted. TDE allows you to selectively encrypt individual databases on an instance. Each database has its own encryption keys, and the individual encryption keys are protected by the server's certificate, which was created by Amazon when we enabled TDE.

We can use SQL scripts to create and encrypt a database. The remaining scripts in this exercise are SQL scripts that should be run in SQL Management Studio against the RDS instance.

Let's begin getting the name of the server certificate. Make reference of the name that is returned; you will need it later.

```
USE [master]
SELECT TOP 1 Name FROM sys.certificates WHERE name LIKE 'RDSTDECertificate%'
```

Next, we create a new database that we will encrypt. If you already have a database on the instance, you can just skip this step.

```
USE [master]
CREATE DATABASE MyDatabase
```

Then, we create a new encryption key for our database. Replace <<PUT_NAME_HERE>> with the name of the certificate you found earlier.

```
Use [MyDatabase]
CREATE DATABASE ENCRYPTION KEY WITH ALGORITHM = AES_128 ENCRYPTION BY SERVER CERTIFICATE
    <<PUT_NAME_HERE>>
```

Finally, you can alter the database to enable encryption.

```
ALTER DATABASE MyDatabase SET ENCRYPTION ON
```

That's all there is to it. With TDE enabled, everything SQL writes to disk is encrypted including data files and backups.

Summary

RDS provides a developer everything that he or she needs to launch a database server without the burden of managing it. AWS will take care of the maintenance, backups, replication, and monitoring, so you can concentrate on your application.

We have seen how to launch and configure SQL Server instances. We learned how to restore instances from snapshots and perform point-in-time recovery from database backups. We also learned to create scalable, highly available architectures using multi-AZ instances and read replicas. Finally, we learned how to secure SQL Server using SSL to encrypt the connection and TDE to encrypt files on disk.

In the next chapter, we will focus on Simple Storage Service (S3). S3 is a highly resilient data solution for storing files. This is the data store AWS uses to keep snapshots and RDS backups, but you can use it to store anything you want.

CHAPTER 10

Simple Storage Service

Simple Storage Service (S3) is used to store objects in the cloud. S3 can scale to enormous size. You can store an unlimited number of objects and access them from anywhere. You access S3 over HTTP or HTTPS using a REST API. This is the same service Amazon uses to store data for its web site!

S3 provides an unprecedented 99.999999999% (that's 11 nines) durability by storing data multiple times across multiple availability zones within a region. A single object can be anywhere from 1 byte to 5 terabytes and you can store an unlimited number of objects.

Unlike Elastic Block Storage you cannot attach S3 storage to an instance. All access is through the REST API. In this chapter, I will show you how to create and manage buckets, which are used to store data. I will also show you how to upload and download objects and manage storage options.

Next, we will discuss versioning and object life cycle. I will go on to show you how to save money by using reduced redundancy and Glacier cold storage. Finally we will talk about security, including encryption at rest and enabling public access to objects in your bucket.

This chapter has two exercises. The first will show you how to host a static web site in S3. We will deploy and configure a web site using PowerShell. The second will discuss how to create pre-signed URLs that allow a user to access data for a specific period of time. At the end of that period the URL expires, and the user can no longer access the content. Let's get started.

Managing Buckets

S3 stores objects in buckets. It may help to think of a bucket as a drive in a file system. Like a drive, a bucket contains files and the files can be organized into a hierarchy of folders. But that is where the analogy ends. Unlike a drive, a bucket is infinitely large and can store an unlimited number of objects. Buckets are also accessible anywhere in the world using HTTP or HTTPS.

Each account can have up to 100 buckets, and each bucket must have a name that is unique across all accounts and regions. To create a bucket, use the New-S3Bucket command. I always create a bucket with the same name as the account alias for administrative storage such as logging and activity reports. For example, to create a bucket named brianbeach (the name I picked for the account alias in Chapter 2), I call New-S3Bucket and supply the name.

```
New-S3Bucket -BucketName 'brianbeach'
```

As you might expect, there is a Get-S3Bucket command that can be used to list the buckets in your account. When called without any parameters, it lists all the buckets in your account.

```
Get-S3Bucket
```

If you want to get information about a specific bucket, you can call Get-S3Bucket with the BucketName parameter.

```
Get-S3Bucket -BucketName 'brianbeach'
```

If you just want to verify that a bucket exists, there is a separate command, Test-S3Bucket, that will return true if the bucket exists and false if it does not. Of course you can always use Get-S3Bucket and compare the result to null, but Test-S3Bucket is more convenient.

```
Test-S3Bucket -BucketName 'brianbeach'
```

The Get-S3Bucket command returns very little information. It only includes the name and creation date of the bucket. If you want to know where the bucket is located, use the Get-S3BucketLocation command.

```
Get-S3BucketLocation -BucketName 'brianbeach'
```

■ **Note**   The Northern Virginia region is special. Unlike the other regions, buckets created in the Northern Virginia region can store data in both the east and west region. The Northern Virginia region was the first, and since then AWS has standardized the design. Buckets created in all other regions store data in only one region. As a result, Get-S3BucketLocation will return "US" for buckets created in Northern Virginia. Buckets in all other regions will return the region name (e.g., us-west-1).

Finally, if you want to delete a bucket, you can use the Remove-S3Bucket command. The bucket must be empty before you can delete it or you can add the –DeleteObjects parameter to delete the contents of a bucket. Of course, you also need to include the Force option to avoid being prompted for confirmation.

```
Remove-S3Bucket -BucketName 'brianbeach' -Force
```

Enough about buckets. Let's put some data in there already. In the next section we learn how to read and write objects.

Managing Objects

Now that we have a bucket created, we can start to upload files using the Write-S3Object command. For example, the following command uploads the local file C:\AWS\HelloWorld.txt to the brianbeach bucket and saves it as HelloWorld.txt.

```
Write-S3Object -BucketName 'brianbeach' -Key 'HelloWorld.txt'
    -File 'C:\aws\HelloWorld.txt'
```

You can also use the Content parameter to upload data without storing it on the local file system first. For example:

```
Write-S3Object -BucketName 'brianbeach' -Key 'HelloWorld.txt'
    -Content "Hello World!!!"
```

If you want to list the objects in a bucket, you use the `Get-S3Object` command. `Get-S3Object` does not return the objects, but rather lists the objects and a few attributes.

```
Get-S3Object -BucketName 'brianbeach'
```

You can also use `Get-S3Object` to discover information about a specific object. For example, the following command will list information about the HelloWorld.txt file we uploaded earlier.

```
Get-S3Object -BucketName 'brianbeach' -Key 'HelloWorld.txt'
```

When you are ready to download a file, you use the `Read-S3Object` command. Unlike `Write-S3Object`, `Read-S3Object` does not support the content parameter and must be used to write to a file on the local file system. For example, the following command will download the HelloWorld.txt file and overwrite the original copy.

```
Read-S3Object -BucketName 'brianbeach' -Key 'HelloWorld.txt'
    -File 'C:\AWS\HelloWorld.txt'
```

Obviously we can create a copy of an object by downloading and uploading it with a different name. But, remember that we pay for the bandwidth used. Therefore, it is more efficient to use the `Copy-S3Object` to create a copy on the server without transferring the data. For example:

```
Copy-S3Object -BucketName 'brianbeach' -Key 'HelloWorld.txt'
     -DestinationKey 'HelloWorldCopy.txt'
```

We can also use `Copy-S3Object` to copy an object from one bucket to another. These buckets can even be in different regions allowing you to move data directly from one region to another without making a local copy.

```
Copy-S3Object -BucketName 'brianbeach' -Key 'HelloWorld.txt'
     -DestinationBucket brianbeach2'
     -DestinationKey 'HelloWorldCopy.txt'
```

When you no longer need an object, you can delete it using the `Remove-S3Object` command. Remember to use the `Force` option to avoid the confirmation prompt.

```
Remove-S3Object -BucketName 'brianbeach' -Key 'HelloWorld.txt' -Force
```

Now that we know how to create and use objects, let's look at how we can use folders to organize them.

Managing Folders

In the previous examples we copied objects into the root of the bucket. As you add more objects you will end up with a confusing mess. We use folders to organize objects. For example, we could have uploaded the HelloWorld.txt file into a folder called MyFolder by modifying the Key.

```
Write-S3Object -BucketName 'brianbeach' -Key 'MyFolder/HelloWorld.txt'
     -File 'C:\AWS\HelloWorld.txt'
```

If you want to list the files in a folder, use the `KeyPrefix` parameter with `Get-S3Object`.

```
Get-S3Object -BucketName 'brianbeach' -KeyPrefix 'MyFolder'
```

■ **Note**   Before we go any further, I want to say that folders don't really exist in S3. At least they do not exist like they do in a traditional file system. There is no folder object. The previous example is simply listing all files that begin with 'MyFolder.' I could just have easily uploaded a file called 'MyFolder_HelloWorld.txt.' AWS would not have cared, and `Get-S3Object` would still have listed the file because it begins with 'MyFolder.'

Folders are just a conversion used by the AWS Management Console. When the Console sees a forward slash, it creates a folder icon and groups the files under it. With that said, you will likely find the folders in the Console very convenient.

You may find that on occasion you want to make an empty folder appear in the AWS Management Console. To create an empty folder, just create a dummy object that has a key that ends with a slash.

```
Write-S3Object -BucketName 'brianbeach' -Key 'EmptyFolder/'
    -Content "Dummy Content"
```

The `KeyPrefix` (or folder) can be really useful. One great feature is the ability to upload an entire directory of files with a single command. For example, the following command will upload all the files in the C:\AWS folder and prefix all the files with "utils/."

```
Write-S3Object -BucketName 'brianbeach' -KeyPrefix 'utils' -Folder 'c:\aws'
```

The previous command will ignore subfolders, but there is also an option to recursively upload all files in all of the subfolders.

```
Write-S3Object -BucketName 'brianbeach' -KeyPrefix 'utils'
    -Folder 'c:\aws' -Recurse
```

When you read files you can use the `KeyPrefix` parameter to download all files that begin with a certain string. Rather than using the `File` parameter as we did in a previous command, you use the `Folder` parameter. The `Folder` parameter specifies where to put the files on the local file system. Note that `Read-S3Object` is always recursive.

```
Read-S3Object -BucketName 'brianbeach' -KeyPrefix 'utils' -Folder 'c:\aws'
```

On occasion you may find that you want to upload files that match a certain pattern. For example, you can upload all executables in the c:\aws folder by using the `SearchPattern` parameter.

```
Write-S3Object -BucketName 'brianbeach' -KeyPrefix 'utils' -Folder 'c:\aws'
    -SearchPattern '*.exe'
```

Unfortunately, there is no `SearchPattern` attribute on `Read-S3Object`. We can use a combination of `Get-S3Object` and `Read-S3Object` to produce a little PowerShell magic. For example:

```
Get-S3Object -BucketName 'brianbeach' -KeyPrefix 'utils' |
    Where-Object {$_.Key -like '*.exe'} | % {
        Read-S3Object -BucketName $_.BucketName -Key $_.Key
            -File ('C:\' + $_.Key.Replace('/','\'))
    }
```

As you can see, folders are a really powerful way to act on multiple objects at once. Next, we will look at how to deal with large numbers of files.

Managing Public Access

Many buckets require public or anonymous access. For example, we might be using S3 to store images for a web site or the installer for our latest application. In both cases we want the objects to be available to the general public. To create a bucket that holds objects that can be read by the general public, add the `PublicReadOnly` attribute to `New-S3Bucket`. For example:

```
New-S3Bucket -BucketName 'brianbeach' -PublicReadOnly
```

Marking the bucket as public does not make all the objects in the bucket public. It only means that you *can* store public objects. You still have to mark the individual objects as public when you upload them. For example:

```
Write-S3Object -BucketName 'brianbeach' -Key 'HelloWorld.txt'
    -Content "Hello World!!!" -PublicReadOnly
```

You can also configure a bucket to allow anonymous users to write to a bucket. For example, you might allow customers to upload log files to your server so you can help debug an issue they are having. In general it is dangerous to allow unauthenticated user to upload files. Not only could the individual files be dangerous, but you are also charged for files they upload. If you allow anonymous uploads there is nothing stopping a nefarious user from uploading large amounts of data, costing you thousands of dollars. If you still want to create a bucket with anonymous read/write access, you can use the `PublicReadWrite` attribute with `New-S3Bucket`. For example:

```
New-S3Bucket -BucketName 'brianbeach' -PublicReadWrite
```

We will discuss identity and access management in detail in the next chapter.

Managing Versions

Often you want to store multiple versions of a document as you make changes. You may have regulatory requirements that demand it, or you may just want the option to roll back. S3 supports this through bucket versioning.

When you enable versioning, S3 stores every version of every document in the bucket. If you overwrite an object, AWS keeps the original. If you delete a document, AWS simply marks the document as deleted, but keeps all the prior versions. When you read a document, AWS returns the latest version, but you can always request a specific version.

Before we enable versioning, let's overwrite the HelloWorld document we created earlier so we have a clean starting point. When you do, the old copy is replaced by this new copy.

```
Write-S3Object -BucketName 'brianbeach' -Key 'HelloWorld.txt'
    -Content "Hello World Version 1!!!"
```

Now, let's enable versioning. Versioning is always enabled at the bucket. You cannot enable versioning within a specific folder. To enable versioning, use the `Write-S3BucketVersioning` command.

```
Write-S3BucketVersioning -BucketName 'brianbeach'
    -VersioningConfig_Status 'Enabled'
```

Now that versioning is enabled, let's overwrite the HelloWorld document. You do not have to do anything special to create a version. Just write the new object and S3 will create a new version and retain the original.

```
Write-S3Object -BucketName 'brianbeach' -Key 'HelloWorld.txt'
    -Content "Hello Version 2!!!"
```

If you were to call Get-S3Object, you would not see any difference. In fact, all of the commands we have used so far are unaffected by versioning. The command below will return the latest version, which you can verify by checking the date.

```
Get-S3Object -BucketName 'brianbeach' -Key 'HelloWorld.txt'
```

To list the versions of all the objects in a bucket use the Get-S3Version command. Note that Get-S3Version returns a complicated structure. You can ignore most of it and use the Versions property to list the versions. For example:

```
(Get-S3Version -BucketName 'brianbeach').Versions
```

Unfortunately, this command is a bit primitive. There is no way to specify a specific object, only a prefix. Often this is enough. For example, you could get the versions of our HellowWorld.txt document like this:

```
(Get-S3Version -BucketName 'brianbeach' -Prefix 'HelloWorld.txt').Versions
```

But, there are times when the prefix is not unique. For example, if we had both HelloWorld.doc and HelloWorld. docx in a folder, it is impossible to list the versions of HelloWorld.doc without getting HelloWorld.docx. Therefore, it is best to check the versions you get back by piping it to Where-Object.

```
(Get-S3Version -BucketName 'brianbeach' -Prefix 'HelloWorld.doc').Versions |
    Where-Object {$_Key -eq 'HelloWorld.doc'}
```

If you want to download a specific version of a document, the Read-S3Object accepts a version parameter. First, you have to get the version using Get-S3Version. Note that Get-S3Version returns an array and the array is sorted in reverse order so that the latest version is position 0. Once you find the version you want, you can pass the id to Read-S3Object. For example:

```
$Versions = (Get-S3Version -BucketName 'brianbeach'
    -Prefix 'HelloWorld.txt').Versions
Read-S3Object -BucketName 'brianbeach' -Key 'HelloWorld.txt'
    -Version $Versions[1].VersionId -File 'c:\aws\versiontest.txt'
```

You can delete a version the same way:

```
Remove-S3Object -BucketName 'brianbeach' -Key 'HelloWorld.txt'
    -Version $Versions[1].VersionId
```

When you delete a version it is physically removed from the bucket. But, when you call Remove-S3Object, S3 simply marks the object as deleted. If you delete an object and list the versions, you will see that there is a new version called a delete marker.

```
Remove-S3Object -BucketName 'brianbeach' -Key 'HelloWorld.txt' -Force
(Get-S3Version -BucketName 'brianbeach' -Prefix 'HelloWorld.txt').Versions
```

Note that the delete marker has the attribute IsDeleteMaker=True and a size of 0. You can still access the old versions by specifying a version id. For example:

```
$Versions = (Get-S3Version -BucketName 'brianbeach'
    -Prefix 'HelloWorld.txt').Versions
Read-S3Object -BucketName 'brianbeach' -Key 'HelloWorld.txt'
    -Version $Versions[1].VersionId -File 'c:\aws\versiontest.txt'
```

You can also undelete an object by removing the delete marker. Just find the version with `IsDeleteMaker=True` and use `Remove-S3Object` to remove it.

```
$Marker = (Get-S3Version -BucketName 'brianbeach'
    -Prefix 'HelloWorld.txt').Versions |
    Where-Object {$_.IsDeleteMaker -eq $true}
Remove-S3Object -BucketName 'brianbeach' -Key 'HelloWorld.txt'
    -Version $Marker.VersionId -Force
```

Once you have versioning enabled, you cannot disable it, but you can choose to suspend versioning. When versioning is suspended, the existing versions are maintained but new versions are not created. To suspend versioning, call `Write-S3BucketVersioning` and set the status to `Enabled`.

```
Write-S3BucketVersioning -BucketName 'brianbeach'
    -VersioningConfig_Status 'Suspended'
```

As you can imagine, versioning, combined with 99.99999999 durability, will ensure that you never lose a document again. Of course storing objects forever can get expensive. In the next section we will explore life-cycle policies to manage aging objects.

Using Life-Cycle Management and Glacier

Over time you will accumulate a vast collection of objects. Sometimes you want to save these forever, but usually you do not. You may need to keep to certain documents for a specified period of time. For example, the Sarbanes-Oxley act, enacted after the Enron collapse, recommends that you keep ledgers for seven years and invoices for three.

Obviously you have the tools to create a PowerShell script to delete objects older than a certain date. But, S3 also has a built in life-cycle policy that can manage retention for you. In addition, life-cycle management can be used to copy objects to a cold storage solution called Glacier.

Glacier provides the same high durability as S3 for about 10% of the price. The tradeoff is that objects stored in Glacier are not immediately available. You have to request that objects be restored, which takes about four hours.

One limitation of life-cycle policy is that you cannot apply policies to a bucket that has versioning enabled. Therefore, I am going to delete and re-create my bucket.

```
Remove-S3Bucket -BucketName 'brianbeach' -DeleteObjects -Force
New-S3Bucket -BucketName 'brianbeach'
```

Now that we have a new bucket we can configure the life-cycle policy. We describe the policy using a series of .Net objects. Let's assume our bucket holds log files from a web server running on EC2. The development team often refers to the logs to diagnose errors, but this almost always happens within a few hours of the error occurring. In addition, the security team requires that we maintain logs for one year. Therefore, we decide to keep the logs online, in S3, for one week. After one week, the logs are moved to cold storage, in Glacier, for one year. After one year the logs can be deleted.

First, we define a life-cycle transition. The transition defines how long the logs are maintained in S3 and where to move them after. The policy is always defined in days. The transition also defines the storage class to move the document to. In the following example, I am moving the object to Glacier. You can also move an object to reduced redundancy storage. (I will discuss reduced redundancy storage later in this chapter.)

```
$Transition = New-Object Amazon.S3.Model.LifecycleTransition
$Transition.Days = 7
$Transition.StorageClass = "Glacier"
```

Next, we define the expiration policy. The expiration policy defines how long to keep the object before it is deleted. In this case, I am keeping the object for 365 days. Note that the expiration is defined from the day the object was first uploaded to S3, not the day it was transitioned to Glacier.

```
$Expiration = New-Object Amazon.S3.Model.LifecycleRuleExpiration
$Expiration.Days = 365
```

Now that we have both the transition and expiration defined, we can combine them into a single rule and apply it to the bucket. Note that you do not need to define both the transition and expiration. Some rules only define a transition and the object is maintained in Glacier until you manually delete it. Other rules only define an expiration and the document is deleted from S3 without being transitioned.

```
$Rule = New-Object Amazon.S3.Model.LifecycleRule
$Rule.Transition = $Transition
$Rule.Expiration = $Expiration
Write-S3LifecycleConfiguration -BucketName 'brianbeach'
    -Configuration_Rules $Rule
```

Sometimes you want to have different rules applied to each folder in a bucket. You can define a folder level rule by adding a prefix. For example:

```
$Rule = New-Object Amazon.S3.Model.LifecycleRule
$Rule.Transition = $Transition
$Rule.Expiration = $Expiration
$Rule.Prefix = "logs/"
Write-S3LifecycleConfiguration -BucketName 'brianbeach'
    -Configuration_Rules $Rule
```

Now, let's assume a user of our web site claims his data was deleted a few months ago and we need to understand why. We need to pull the log files from July 22 to diagnose the cause. First we check if the object exists and where it is by using Get-S3Object. For example:

```
Get-S3Object -BucketName 'brianbeach' -Key 'logs/2013-07-22.log'
```

This command returns the following output. Note that the log files have been moved to Glacier, but have not yet been deleted.

```
Key          : logs/2013-07-22.log
BucketName   : brianbeach
LastModified : Mon, 22 July 2013 23:59:39 GMT
ETag         : "793466320ce145cb672e69265409ffeb"
Size         : 1147
Owner        : Amazon.S3.Model.Owner
StorageClass : GLACIER
```

To restore the object, we use the Restore-S3Object command. Restore-S3Object requires the bucket and key. In addition, the Days parameter defines how long to keep the object in S3. In the following example I request that object be restored for seven days. This should be plenty of time to figure out what happened to our user's data. After seven days, the object is automatically deleted from S3, but is still stored in Glacier until the expiration date.

```
Restore-S3Object -BucketName 'brianbeach' -Key '/logs/2013-07-22.log' -Days 7
```

If you want to remove the life-cycle policy from a bucket, you can use the `Remove-S3LifecycleConfiguration` command. For example:

```
Remove-S3LifecycleConfiguration -BucketName 'brianbeach'
```

As you can see, S3 gives you the tools to automate data retention. This is a great way to keep data sprawl in check and manage costs. In the next section we will look at a few miscellaneous commands and then move on to the exercises.

Miscellaneous S3 Options

In this section we will look at a few miscellaneous options, none of which are big enough to warrant their own section.

Tagging

We have seen the power of tagging in EC2. S3 also supports tagging at the bucket level. To tag a bucket, create a tag you use the `Write-S3BucketTagging` command and a few .Net helper classes. For example:

```
$Tag = New-Object Amazon.S3.Model.Tag
$Tag.Key = 'Owner'
$Tag.Value = 'bbeach'
$TagSet = New-Object Amazon.S3.Model.TagSet
$TagSet. Tags = $Tag
Write-S3BucketTagging -BucketName brianbeach -TagSets $TagSet
```

You can also get the tags using the `Get-S3BucketTagging` command:

```
Get-S3BucketTagging -BucketName brianbeach
```

And, you can remove all tags using the `Remove-S3BucketTagging` command

```
Remove-S3BucketTagging -BucketName brianbeach -Force
```

Pagination

As you add more and more objects to S3 it can become very difficult to sort through them all. AWS gives you the ability to list files in batches. This is really convenient if you are trying to display the objects on a web page or other user interface.

Imagine you have hundreds of files in a bucket and you need to browse through them all. The following example will return the first 10 objects in the bucket.

```
$Objects = Get-S3Object -BucketName 'brianbeach'  -MaxKeys 10
```

After you browse through these first 10, you want to get 10 more. You can use the `MaxKeys` parameter to tell the S3 to return the next 10 objects. For example:

```
$Objects = Get-S3Object -BucketName 'brianbeach'
    -MaxKeys 10 -Marker $Objects[9].Key
```

Encryption

When you upload an object to S3 you can have S3 encrypt the file before saving it. To enable encryption, use the ServerSideEncryption parameter. At the moment, AES256 is the only supported encryption option. Note that in this scenario AWS manages the encryption key.

```
Write-S3Object -BucketName 'brianbeach' -Key 'HelloWorld.txt'
    -Content "Hello World!!!" -ServerSideEncryption AES256
```

Reduced Redundancy

There are times when 99.999999999% durability is not required. For example, if you storing log files you probably don't want to pay for such high assurances. S3 supports reduced redundancy, which guarantees 99.99% durability. As the name implies, reduced redundancy stores fewer copies of an object at a reduced price. To store an object with reduced redundancy, include the ReducedRedundancyStorage parameter during upload. For example:

```
Write-S3Object -BucketName 'brianbeach' -Key 'HelloWorld.txt'
    -Content "Hello World!!!" -ReducedRedundancyStorage
```

Content Type

When you upload an object the content type is set to "application/octet-stream." You can optionally include the content type to tell the client what type of file it is. For example, your browser will always download files of type "application/octet-stream". If you want the browser to display the file, change the type to "text/plain."

```
Write-S3Object -BucketName 'brianbeach' -Key 'HelloWorld.txt'
    -Content "Hello World!!!" -ContentType 'text\plain'
```

We will see an example of content type used in Exercise 1 where we create a static web site.

EXERCISE 10.1: STATIC HOSTING ON S3

You may have noticed that S3 feels a lot like a web server. We use HTTP or HTTPS to get objects using a URL. In fact, you can use S3 to host a static web site with a few minor alterations. First, we are going to want a vanity URL that does not reference S3. Second, we are going to want to support a default and custom error page. S3 supports all of this and more.

Let's create a simple web site with only two pages. I am going to use the domain name aws.brianbeach.com, but you can use anything you want. The first thing we need to do is create a bucket. The bucket must be named with the domain name of our web site and we must enable public read-only access. For example:

```
New-S3Bucket -BucketName 'aws.brianbeach.com' -PublicReadOnly
```

Next we need to create a page. A page is just an S3 object with the content type set to "text/html." Remember that if you do not set the content type, it will be set to "application/octet-stream" and your browser will download the file rather than displaying it. You can upload images and other resources, but you have to set the content type correctly for each. We also need to the enable public read-only access to each file. The following example creates a new page called index.htm:

```
$Content = @"
<HTML>
  <HEAD>
    <TITLE>Hello World</TITLE>
  </HEAD>
  <BODY>
    <H1>Hello World</H1>
    <P>Hello from my Amazon Web Services site.</P>
  </BODY>
</HTML>
"@

Write-S3Object -BucketName 'aws.brianbeach.com' -Key 'index.htm' -Content $Content
    -ContentType 'text/html' -PublicReadOnly
```

Next, we need to create an error page. This page will be displayed whenever an error occurs. Once again, remember the content type and public read-only flag.

```
$Content = @"
<HTML>
  <HEAD>
    <TITLE>Oops</TITLE>
  </HEAD>
  <BODY>
    <H1>Oops</H1>
    <P>Something seems to have gone wrong.</P>
  </BODY>
</HTML>
"@

Write-S3Object -BucketName 'aws.brianbeach.com' -Key 'error.htm' -Content $Content
    -ContentType 'text/html' -PublicReadOnly
```

Now that our bucket is all set up, we can enable the WebSite feature. Write-S3BucketWebsite allows us to identify the default and error documents in the site. The default document will be shown if the user requests http://aws.brainbeach.com without including the path to a document. The error page will be displayed whenever something goes wrong.

```
Write-S3BucketWebsite -BucketName 'aws.brianbeach.com'
    -WebsiteConfiguration_IndexDocumentSuffix 'index.htm'
    -WebsiteConfiguration_ErrorDocument 'error.htm'
```

You're almost there. At this point the site is up and running on the URL: http://BUCKET.s3-website-REGION. amazonaws.com. For example my site is running on aws.brianbeach.com.s3-website-us-east-1.amazonaws.com. AWS does not own the domain brianbeach.com, and, therefore, cannot configure DNS to point to our bucket. You must do that yourself by creating a CNAME record that points your domain name to the AWS bucket URL. The process will depend on your provider. I use GoDaddy and the configuration looks like the one shown in Figure 10-1.

CName (Alias) 🔲		
Host	**Points To**	**TTL**
aws	webloadbalancer-62156217.us-east-1.elb.amazonaws.com	1 Hour

Figure 10-1. *Creating a DNS CName in GoDaddy.com*

Once the CNAME is done we can test:

- If you navigate to `http://aws.brianbeach.com/index.htm`, you should see the welcome page we uploaded.

- If you navigate to `http://aws.brianbeach.com`, you should again see the welcome page.

- If you navigate to `http://aws.brianbeach.com/DoesNotExist`, you should see our custom error page.

As you can see, S3 is a reliable and inexpensive way to host a static web site. In the next exercise, we will use pre-signed URLs to grant temporary access to a customer without requiring them to log in.

EXERCISE 10.2: USING PRE-SIGNED URLS

At the beginning of this chapter, we discussed enabling anonymous access to a bucket, and I mentioned there is a better way: pre-signed URLs. This is a really simple command to use and does not warrant an exercise of its own, but it is a great opportunity to describe how AWS authentications works using access keys.

Imagine that you run a help desk and you often need to make tools and patches available to customers. You want these tools available only to customers who call the help desk. Furthermore, customers should not be able to download the tools later or share the link with friends. You could create a username and password for the user, but then you have to manage another user. This is a great use case for a pre-signed URL.

A pre-signed URL has been signed with a secret key. In addition, the URL includes an expiration date after which it can no longer be used. Note that the URL has been signed with the secret key, but does not include the secret key. This allows AWS to prove the authenticity of the URL without exposing the secret key to the customer.

In fact, this is how all AWS web service calls work. Your secret key is never sent to AWS. Whenever we use a PowerShell method, PowerShell creates the request and includes a digital signature to prove that the user knows the secret.

Let's get back to the help desk. You want to create a pre-signed URL. PowerShell has a command for this called `Get-S3PresignedURL`. You need to pass in your access key and secret key as well as the HTTP verb, bucket, key, and expiration date.

■ **Note**   You should use StoredCredentials rather than passing the access keys explicitly. (See Chapter 2 for details.) I am including them here only to help explain how the encryption works.

```
#Authentication Keys
$AccessKey = 'AKIAJ5N3RMX5LGUMP6FQ'
$SecretKey = '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'

#Web Query
$Verb = "GET"
$ExpirationDate = [DateTime]::Parse('2014-01-01')
$Bucket = 'MyBucket'
$Key = 'MyPath/MyFile.txt'

Get-S3PreSignedURL -Verb $Verb -Expires $ExpirationDate -Bucket $Bucket -Key $Key
    -AccessKey $AccessKey -SecretKey $SecretKey
```

The preceding code will return the following URL, which you can share with your customer. Notice that the URL includes the access key and expiration date we supplied. The expiration date has been converted to seconds from January 1, 1970. In addition, the URL incudes a signature created by the PowerShell command. Also notice that your secret key is not included in the URL.

```
https://s3.amazonaws.com/MyBucket/MyPath/MyFile.txt?AWSAccessKeyId=
AKIAIQPQNCQG3EYO6LIA&Expires=1388552400&Signature=wBUgYztEdlE%2Btw9argXicUKvftw%3D
```

You can share this URL with your customer and they can download a single file. They do not have the secret key and therefore cannot use it for anything else. In addition, AWS will refuse it after the expiration date. If the customer changes anything in the URL, he or she will invalidate the signature and AWS will refuse it. What a simple solution to a difficult problem.

While the Get-PreSignedURL method is really simple to use, this is a great opportunity to see how AWS signatures work. Let's write our own code to create a signature so we better understand how it works. If you're not interested, feel free to skip the rest of this example, but remember the Get-S3PreSignedURL method.

First, we will accept the same parameters as the Get-PreSignedURL command. My method only works for GET requests, but you could easily add support for other HTTP verbs.

```
Param
(
    [string][parameter(mandatory=$true)]$AccessKey,
    [string][parameter(mandatory=$true)]$SecretKey,
    [string][parameter(mandatory=$false)]$Verb = 'GET',
    [DateTime][parameter(mandatory=$true)]$Expires,
    [string][parameter(mandatory=$true)]$Bucket,
    [string][parameter(mandatory=$true)]$Key
)
```

Next, we must calculate the expiration. Remember that the expiration is expressed in seconds since January 1, 1970. Also note that I am converting the time to UTC because the AWS servers may be in a different time zone than our client.

```
$EpochTime = [DateTime]::Parse('1970-01-01')
$ExpiresSeconds = ($Expires.ToUniversalTime() - $EpochTime).TotalSeconds
```

Then, we need to canonicalize the input parameters to be signed. Before we can sign the data we must agree on how the data will formatted. If both sides don't agree on a common format, the signatures will not match. This process is called canonicalization.

For AWS, we include the following data separated by a newline character.

- HTTP Verb

- MD5 Hash of the Content

- Content Type

- Expiration Date

- Optional HTTP Headers

- URL Encoded Path

In our case, we are only supporting GET; therefore, the content and content type will always be blank. In addition, I am not supporting any HTTP headers.

```
$Path = [Amazon.S3.Util.AmazonS3Util]::UrlEncode("/$Bucket/$Key", $true)
$Data = "$Verb`n`n`n$ExpiresSeconds`n$Path"
```

Now that we have the canonicalized data we can use the .Net crypto libraries to sign it with our secret key. Here I am using the SHA1 algorithm to generate the signature. Note that you must be very careful with how data is encoded. The secret key must be UTF8 encoded and the resulting signature must be URL encoded.

```
$HMAC = New-Object System.Security.Cryptography.HMACSHA1
$HMAC.key = [System.Text.Encoding]::UTF8.GetBytes($SecretKey);
$signature = $HMAC.ComputeHash(
    [System.Text.Encoding]::UTF8.GetBytes($Data.ToCharArray()))
$signature_encoded = [Amazon.S3.Util.AmazonS3Util]::UrlEncode(
    [System.Convert]::ToBase64String($signature), $true)
```

Finally, we can build the URL. The result should be identical to what Get-PreSignedURL returned earlier.

```
"https://s3.amazonaws.com/$Bucket/$Key" + "?AWSAccessKeyId=$AccessKey&Expires=$ExpiresSeconds
&Signature=$signature_encoded"
```

That may have been a bit more than you wanted to know, but now that you know how to sign a request, you can call the S3 Web Service methods directly in any language.

Summary

In this chapter we reviewed Simple Storage Service (S3). S3 allows you to store a seemingly limitless number of objects in the cloud. We learned to create and manage buckets and folders and we learned to upload and download objects.

We learned how versioning can be used to store multiple versions of a document as it changes over time. We also learned to use life-cycle policies to create retention rules and how to use Glacier cold storage to reduce costs for long-term storage.

In the exercises, we created a static web site hosted entirely in S3 and then learned to create a pre-signed URL that can be shared without needing AWS credentials. We also learned how AWS uses digital signatures in authentication. In the next chapter we will learn how to use PowerShell to automate Identity and Access Management.

CHAPTER 11

■ ■ ■

Identity and Access Management

As is too often the case, I have saved security for last. If you have been following along from the beginning, we have completed all of the examples in this book while signed in as a user with administrator privileges. While this is a convenient way to learn a new technology, you should never run a production system with administrator privileges. If part of the system were compromised, you want to ensure you limit access as much as possible.

This chapter is all about Identity and Access Management (IAM). IAM is how you manage users, groups, and permissions. In this chapter, I show you how to create users and groups. I also explain how IAM policies work and how to create them. IAM policies describe which resources a user can access and the operations they can perform on those resources. You will see that IAM gives you unprecedented control over access.

Finally, in the two exercises at the end of the chapter, we will create a framework for least privileged access and grant access to billing and support. Let's get started.

Managing Users

Let's begin by adding a few users to our AWS account. We added a single user back in Chapter 2 using the AWS Management Console. Now let's add a few using PowerShell.

To add users you use the New-IAMUser command. The following script will add six users.

```
New-IAMUser -UserName 'alice'
New-IAMUser -UserName 'bob'
New-IAMUser -UserName 'chris'
New-IAMUser -UserName 'dan'
New-IAMUser -UserName 'eve'
New-IAMUser -UserName 'frank'
```

As you might expect there is also a Get-IAMUser command that can be used to get information about a user, such as the username and date the account was created.

```
Get-IAMUser -UserName 'alice'
```

Get-IAMUser works a bit differently from other commands. Most get methods return a list of all objects when you call them without parameters. If you call Get-IAMUser without the UserName parameter, it returns the currently logged-in user. This is useful when writing a generic script that needs to discover who is currently logged in. For example, you might want to tag an instance with the name of the current user.

```
$User = Get-IAMUser
$AMI = Get-EC2ImageByName -Name 'WINDOWS_2012_BASE'
$Reservation = New-EC2Instance -ImageId $AMI[0].ImageId -KeyName 'MyKey'
    -InstanceType 't1.micro' -MinCount 1 -MaxCount 1
```

```
$InstanceId = $Reservation.RunningInstance[0].InstanceId
$Tag = New-Object Amazon.EC2.Model.Tag
$Tag.Key ='Owner'
$Tag.Value = $User.UserName
New-EC2Tag -ResourceId $Instance.InstanceId -Tag $Tag
```

If you want to list all of the users in the account, use the `Get-IAMUsers` command.

```
Get-IAMUsers | Format-Table
```

You may remember from Chapter 2 that there are multiple types of credentials. We discussed that users need a password to access the AWS Management Console, and access keys to use the REST API and PowerShell. But not all users require both types of credentials. To allow a user to access the AWS Management Console, you must assign a password using the `New-IAMLoginProfile` command.

```
New-IAMLoginProfile -UserName 'alice' -Password 'PASSWORD'
```

Conversely, if you want to remove a login profile and deny access to the AWS Management Console, use the `Remove-IAMLoginProfile` command.

```
Remove-IAMLoginProfile -UserName 'alice' -Force
```

If you want the user to able to use the REST API, you must create an access key using the `New-IAMAccessKey` command. Remember that we are using the REST API with PowerShell. Therefore, a user needs an access key to use PowerShell for AWS. The `New-IAMAccessKey` command returns an object that includes both the `AccessKeyId` and `SecretAccessKey`.

```
$Keys = New-IAMAccessKey -UserName 'alice'
$Keys.AccessKeyId
$Keys.SecretAccessKey
```

Remember to save the secret key because you cannot get it again. To store a copy in your PowerShell session, you can use the `Set-AWSCredentials` command discussed in Chapter 2. For example:

```
$Keys = New-IAMAccessKey -UserName 'alice'
Set-AWSCredentials -AccessKey $Keys.AccessKeyId -SecretKey $Keys.SecretAccessKey
    -StoreAs 'alice'
```

If you want to delete a user's access keys you can use `Remove-IAMAccessKey`.

```
Remove-IAMAccessKey -User Name 'alice' -AccessKeyId 'AKIAJV64XS4XLRAJIBAQ' -Force
```

You may find that you need to check if a user has either a password or access keys. You can use `Get-IAMLoginProfile` and `Get-IAMAccessKey` to check if they exist.

```
Get-IAMLoginProfile -UserName 'alice'
Get-IAMAccessKey -UserName 'alice'
```

Each user can have two sets of access keys. The truly security conscious will rotate these keys on a regular basis. For example, you might replace the older set of keys every 30 days. The following script will find the oldest set of keys for a user, delete them, and create a new set.

```
$Key = Get-IAMAccessKey -UserName 'alice' | Sort-Object CreateDate
    -Descending | Select AccessKeyId -First 1
Remove-IAMAccessKey -UserName 'alice' -AccessKeyId $Key.AccessKeyId-Force
$Keys = New-IAMAccessKey -UserName 'alice'
$Keys.AccessKeyId
$Keys.SecretAccessKey
```

Now that we have a user created we need to assign the user permissions. Before we do, let's look at groups. Groups allow you to group related users together and assign them permissions as a unit. This process is usually less time consuming and less error prone.

Managing Groups

When you apply permissions to individual users, it is very difficult to keep track of who has access to which resources. Grouping related users makes managing permissions much easier. Groups reduce the number of unique permissions sets you need to keep track of. (In the first exercise at the end of this chapter we build a set of common groups as a starting point.)

To create a new group, use the New-IAMGroup command and assign a name.

```
New-IAMGroup -GroupName 'AWS_USERS'
```

Initially the group is empty. To add a user to a group, use the Add-IAMUserToGroup command and pass the name of the user and the group to add him or her to.

```
Add-IAMUserToGroup -UserName 'alice' -GroupName 'AWS_USERS'
```

If you want to remove a user from a group, use the Remove-IAMUserFromGroup command passing the name of the user and the group to remove him or her from.

```
Remove-IAMUserFromGroup -UserName 'alice' -GroupName 'AWS_USERS' -Force
```

Listing groups is similar to listing users. You use the Get-AIMGroups (plural) command to list all the groups in your account.

```
Get-IAMGroups
```

You use the Get-IAMGroup (singular) command to get a specific group.

```
Get-IAMGroup -GroupName 'AWS_USERS'
```

Note that these two commands return different information. The Get-IAMGroups (plural) command returns a group object that does not include the group members. The Get-IAMGroup (singular) command returns a GetGroupResult object that includes the group and a collection of users.

Therefore, to list the members of a group, use Get-IAMGroup and then read the users property.

```
(Get-IAMGroup -GroupName 'AWS_USERS').Users
```

To get the opposite – a list of groups a user is a member of – you can use the Get-IAMGroupForUser command. For example:

```
Get-IAMGroupForUser 'alice'
```

Unlike the Get-IAMUser command, Get-IAMGroupForUser cannot be called without a group parameter. It would be nice if calling Get-IAMGroupForUser would list the groups the current user is a member of. We can use a little PowerShell magic to combine Get-IAMUser and Get-IAMGroupForUser to get the list. For example:

```
Get-IAMUser | Get-IAMGroupForUser
```

At this point we have created a few users and groups and have added users to groups. But, our users still don't have permission to do anything. In the next section, we will grant permission to our users.

Managing Policies

We use policies to grant permissions to users and groups. Policies are JSON statements that describe what API calls a user or group is allowed to call. You can grant or deny access to just about every API call. Before we get started, let's do a quick review of JSON.

JSON PRIMER

JavaScript Object Notation (JSON) was first used to send objects from a web server to a browser. JSON uses key/value pairs to represent attributes. Here are a few examples of attributes in JSON:

```
"Name": "Joe"
"Age": 35
"Male": true
```

An array can be represented by a single key and multiple values in square brackets. For example:

```
"Children": ["Mary", "Charles", "Sam"]
```

An object is simply a list of key/value pairs separated by commas and enclosed in curly braces. For example, we might represent a person as:

```
{
    "Name": "Joe",
    "Age": 35,
    "Male": true,
    "Children": ["Mary", "Charles", "Sam"]
}
```

We can also nest objects inside other objects. For example:

```
{
    "Name": "Joe",
    "Age": 35,
    "Male": true,
    "Children": [
        {
            "Name": "Mary",
            "Age": 3,
            "Male": false
        },
```

```
    {
        "Name": "Charles",
        "Age": 5,
        "Male": true
    },
    {

        "Name": "Sam",
        "Age": 7,
        "Male": true
    }
  ]
}
```

This is a very brief introduction, but you can see that JSON can be used to represent very complex structures. I could write a whole book on JSON – and others have – but this is all we need to understand IAM policy statements.

Policy statements are written in JSON. The statement must include three sections: effect, action, and resource. The effect of the statement is to either allow access or deny access. The action is a list of API calls that are allowed. The resource is the objects the user is allowed to act on. For example, the following statement will allow a user to call any method on any object. In other words, this is an administrator policy.

```
{
  "Statement": [
    {
      "Effect": "Allow",
      "Action": "*",
      "Resource": "*"
    }
  ]
}
```

Policy Actions

Actions determine which API calls are allowed or denied by a policy. The actions are the web service methods that are allowed. Remember that PowerShell commands call API WebMethods. In other words, you can grant or deny access to just about every PowerShell command.

Before we can write a policy, we need to know the API method name. As you can see in the following example, the PowerShell help files often tell you what API method a command will call. Unfortunately this is not always true. (I have included a mapping of PowerShell to API methods in Appendix D.)

```
PS C:\aws> help Get-IAMUsers

NAME
    Get-IAMUsers
```

SYNOPSIS
    Invokes the **ListUsers** operation against AWS Identity and Access Management.

...

Now that we know the method names, let's write a custom policy. We use an array to list multiple methods in a single policy. Note that the method name is preceded by the service type (i.e., "iam:") The following example allows access to all the read methods in IAM. In other words, this policy grants read only access to IAM.

```
{
  "Statement": [
    {
      "Effect": "Allow",
      "Action": [
        "iam:GetAccountPasswordPolicy",
        "iam:GetAccountSummary",
        "iam:GetGroup",
        "iam:GetGroupPolicy",
        "iam:GetInstanceProfile",
        "iam:GetLoginProfile",
        "iam:GetRole",
        "iam:GetRolePolicy",
        "iam:GetServerCertificate",
        "iam:GetUser",
        "iam:GetUserPolicy",
        "iam:ListAccessKeys",
        "iam:ListAccountAliases",
        "iam:ListGroupPolicies",
        "iam:ListGroups",
        "iam:ListGroupsForUser",
        "iam:ListInstanceProfiles",
        "iam:ListInstanceProfilesForRole",
        "iam:ListMFADevices",
        "iam:ListRolePolicies",
        "iam:ListRoles",
        "iam:ListServerCertificates",
        "iam:ListSigningCertificates",
        "iam:ListUserPolicies",
        "iam:ListUsers",
        "iam:ListVirtualMFADevices"
      ],
      "Resource": "*"
    }
  ]
}
```

Often you want to grant access to an entire service such as EC2. In the administrator example, we used a wildcard ("*") to allow all actions. We can also scope a wildcard to grant access to a specific service. The following example will grant access to EC2 and S3.

```
{
  "Statement": [
    {
      "Effect": "Allow",
      "Action": [
        "ec2:*",
        "s3:*"
        ],
      "Resource": "*"
    }
  ]
}
```

As you can see, IAM policies allow fine-grained control over access. In Exercise 11.1 we will develop a set of least privileged roles for EC2. Now let's look at resources.

Policy Resources

So far, the policies we have written apply to all resources. When we granted access to S3 in the following example, we allowed the user to act on all objects in all buckets. Some services allow you to scope the access. In S3, we might want to allow access to a specific bucket or folder.

For example, to scope access to the "MyBucket" bucket:

```
{
  "Statement": [
    {
      "Effect": "Allow",
      "Action": *,
      "Resource": "arn:aws:s3:::MyBucket"
    }
  ]
}
```

The resource statement is always written using an Amazon Resource Name (ARN). An ARN is used to uniquely identify an AWS resource across accounts and regions. The ARN format is as follows.

```
arn:aws:service:region:account:resource
```

Note that S3 is a special case. The bucket name is already unique; therefore, the ARN does not include the account and region and follows the format:

```
arn:aws:s3:::BUCKET/KEY
```

The following example will scope access to the MyFolder folder in the MyBucket bucket:

```
{
  "Statement": [
    {
      "Effect": "Allow",
      "Action": *,
```

```
        "Resource": "arn:aws:s3:::MyBucket/MyFolder"
    }
  ]
}
```

You could also scope access to a specific object in S3:

```
{
  "Statement": [
    {
      "Effect": "Allow",
      "Action": *,
      "Resource": "arn:aws:s3:::MyBucket/MyFolder/MyFile.txt"
    }
  ]
}
```

IAM also allows a few variables in the policy statements. (See the sidebar for a list of supported variables.) Variables make it easier to create a generic policy . For example, let's assume that every user has a personal folder in S3 that is named with the user's username. You can write a generic policy that grants each user access to his or her own folder as follows:

```
{
  "Statement": [
    {
      "Effect": "Allow",
      "Action": *,
      "Resource": ["arn:aws:s3:::MyBucket/${aws:username}/*"]
    }
  ]
}
```

POLICY VARIABLES

Here is a list of variables supported in IAM policy statements.

Name	Description
aws:CurrentTime	Date and time of the request
aws:principaltype	A value that indicates whether the principal is an account, user, federated, or assumed role (see the explanation that follows)
aws:SecureTransport	Boolean representing whether the request was sent using SSL
aws:SourceIp	The requester's IP address, for use with IP address conditions
aws:UserAgent	Information about the requester's client application, for use with string conditions
aws:userid	Unique ID for the current user

(continued)

Name	Description
aws:username	Username of the current user
s3:prefix	Prefix passed in some S3 commands
s3:max-keys	Max-Keys information passed in some S3 commands
sns:Endpoint	Endpoint passed in some SNS calls
sns:Protocol	Protocol passed in some SNS calls

Unfortunately, not all services support resources. For example, S3 and IAM do, but EC2 does not. Luckily we can use conditions to control access to EC2 objects by tag. But, before we talk about conditions, let's look at policy actions.

Policy Actions

All of the policy statements we have written so far allow access to a resource. You can also deny access to a resource by using the deny action. For example, I could keep a user from terminating instances by denying access to the ec2:TerminateInstances action.

```
{
  "Statement": [
    {
      "Effect": "Deny",
      "Action": "ec2:TerminateInstances",
      "Resource": "*"
    }
  ]
}
```

Effect, resource, and action are required components of every policy statement. There are also numerous optional components. I'm not going to cover all of the options here, but I do want to discuss conditions. AWS recently added conditions, which are very useful for controlling access to EC2. Let's have a look.

Policy Conditions

Conditions allow you to write custom logic to determine if an action is allowed. This is a complex topic that could easily fill a chapter. I am only going to show you how to write conditions based on EC2 tags. You can read more about conditions in the IAM user guide.

Building on the prior example, imagine you want to allow users to terminate instances considered DEV but not those considered QA or PROD. You could grant access to the terminate action, but use a condition to limit access to those instances that have a tag called "environment" with the value "dev".

```
  "Version": "2012-10-17",
  "Statement": [{
    "Effect": "Allow",
    "Action": "ec2:TerminateInstances",
    "Resource": "arn:aws:ec2:us-east-1:123456789012:instance/*",
```

```
      "Condition": {
        "StringEquals": {
          "ec2:ResourceTag/environment": "dev"
        }
      }
    }
  ]
}
```

Notice that I have included the optional version to tell AWS this policy requires the latest version of the policy language. Also notice the format of the resource ARN. Remember to replace the 123456789012 with your account number.

Now that we know how to write a policy, let's associate it with a user and group using PowerShell.

Creating Policies with PowerShell.

Creating an IAM policy in PowerShell is really easy. You simply create the JSON statement as a string and then associate it with a user or group. For example, to grant Alice full control, use the `Write-IAMUserPolicy` command.

```
$Policy = @"
{
  "Statement": [
    {
      "Effect": "Allow",
      "Action": "*",
      "Resource": "*"
    }
  ]
}
"@

Write-IAMUserPolicy -UserName "alice" -PolicyName "alice-FullControl" -PolicyDocument $Policy
```

Assigning a policy to a group is just as easy. For example, to grant full control to the ADMINS group, use the `Write-IAMGroupPolicy` command.

```
Write-IAMGroupPolicy -GroupName "ADMINS" -PolicyName "ADMINS-FullControl"
    -PolicyDocument $Policy
```

As you can see, IAM policies give you fine-grained control over access to AWS. You can be very specific about who has access to which resources. The details are all contained in the policy statement. In Exercise 11.1 we will create a common set of groups with least privileged policy defined. But before we do that, let's talk about IAM roles.

Managing Roles

Remember from Chapter 2 that an IAM role can be used to associate a policy with an instance, rather than a user. This way scripts running on that instance do not need to include credentials.

To list the roles defined in your account use the `Get-IAMRoles` command. If you run this command, you should see the "AdminRole" we created using the AWS Management Console in Chapter 2.

```
Get-IAMRoles
```

You can also get a specific role using the Get-IAMRole command.

```
Get-IAMRole -Rolename AdminRole
```

Creating a new role is similar to the process we used to create a group, but we also need a second policy that defines what resources can assume the role. There are two policies required: the first describes who can use the role; the second describes what the role can do.

Let's begin by defining who can use this role. The policy shown here allows the EC2 service to assume this role. In other words, this policy can be used by EC2 instances, but not RDS instances.

```
$AssumeRolePolicy = @"
{
  "Version":"2008-10-17",
  "Statement":[
    {
      "Sid":"",
      "Effect":"Allow",
      "Principal":{"Service":"ec2.amazonaws.com"},
      "Action":"sts:AssumeRole"
    }
  ]
}
"@
```

Next, we create an access policy just like we did in the prior section. This policy gives the role admin access to all services.

```
$AccessPolicy = @"
{
  "Statement": [
    {
      "Effect": "Allow",
      "Action": "*",
      "Resource": "*"
    }
  ]
}
"@
```

Now we can create the role using the New-IAMRole command, passing in the access policy.

```
New-IAMRole -RoleName 'MyAdminRole' -AssumeRolePolicyDocument $AssumeRolePolicy
```

Next, we use Write-IAMRolePolicy to associate the access policy to the role, just like users and groups.

```
Write-IAMRolePolicy -RoleName 'MyAdminRole'
    -PolicyName 'MyAdminRole-FullControl' -PolicyDocument $AccessPolicy
```

Finally, we need to create a new instance profile and add the new role to it.

```
New-IAMInstanceProfile -InstanceProfileName 'MyAdminRoleInstanceProfile'
Add-IAMRoleToInstanceProfile -RoleName 'MyAdminRole'
    -InstanceProfileName  'MyAdminRoleInstanceProfile'
```

Remember from Chapter 3 that roles are assigned to an instance when they are launched. At this point you know how to manage permissions for user, groups, and roles. Before we close this chapter, I want to discuss a few miscellaneous IAM commands.

Miscellaneous IAM Commands

I want to discuss a few miscellaneous IAM commands that did not warrant their own section. Therefore, I included them all here.

Managing Password Policy

Users that have access to the AWS Management Console need to have a password. Many organizations require a specific password policy. You can control the IAM password policy using the Update-IAMAccountPasswordPolicy command.

```
Update-IAMAccountPasswordPolicy
    -MinimumPasswordLength 8
    -RequireSymbols $false
    -RequireNumbers $true
    -RequireUppercaseCharacters $true
    -RequireLowercaseCharacters $true
    -AllowUsersToChangePassword $true
```

You can also get the current policy using Get-IAMAccountPasswordPolicy and remove the policy using Remove-IAMAccountPasswordPolicy.

Using the Account Summary

You can use the Get-IAMAccountSummary command to generate a report. The report includes the total number of users, groups, and roles; how many users have Multi Factor Auth (MFA) enabled; and other interesting details.

Setting the Account Alias

Finally, you can get and set the account alias. Remember from Chapter 2 that the account alias is used to create an easy-to-remember sign-in URL.

You can set the account alias using the New-IAMAccountAlias command.

```
New-IAMAccountAlias -AccountAlias 'brianbeach'
```

You can also get the current alias using Get-IAMAccountAlias and remove the alias using Remove-IAMAccountAlias.

That brings us to the exercises. As you have seen, IAM gives you fine-grained control over access to AWS resources. You can be very specific about who has access to which resources. In Exercise 11.1 we create a set of common groups that provide least privileged access. In Exercise 11.2 we will learn how to permit access to billing and support.

EXERCISE 11.1: CREATING LEAST PRIVILEGED GROUPS

Throughout this book we have been using a single account that has administrator access to all services. Obviously this is a bad idea in production. We only want to allow those permissions that each user needs. Let's create a few common groups as a starting point.

Let's assume that our company is using AWS for development. The main users are software developers. We have a team of AWS experts who support the developers. In addition, the developers are supported by the traditional system administrators and network administrators. The system administrators support the operating system, and the network administrators are responsible for routing, load balancers, and network security.

First, all users require a few common permissions. At a minimum they all need the ability to change their own password. Let's start by creating a group that allows a user to see the password policy change his or her own password. All users should be a member of this group. Note that all of these examples are included with the source code for this chapter.

```
$Policy = @"
{
  "Statement": [
    {
      "Effect": "Allow",
      "Action": [
        "iam:ChangePassword",
        "iam:GetAccountPasswordPolicy"
        ],
      "Resource": "*"
    }
  ]
}
"@

New-IAMGroup -GroupName "USERS"
Write-IAMGroupPolicy -GroupName "USERS" -PolicyName "USERS-ChangePassword"
     -PolicyDocument $Policy
```

Second, the AWS administrators require full access. Let's create a group that has full control of all services. This should be a very small group of people.

```
$Policy = @"
{
  "Statement": [
    {
      "Effect": "Allow",
      "Action": "*",
      "Resource": "*"
    }
  ]
}
```

```
"@
New-IAMGroup -GroupName "ADMINS"
Write-IAMGroupPolicy -GroupName "ADMINS" -PolicyName "ADMINS-FullControl"
      -PolicyDocument $Policy
```

Third, the developers are using continuous development. They need to be able to create, start, stop, and terminate instances. Let's create a group for the developers.

```
$Policy = @"
{
  "Statement": [
    {
      "Effect": "Allow",
      "Action": [
        "ec2:AttachVolume",
        "ec2:CopySnapshot",
        "ec2:CreateKeyPair",
        "ec2:CreateSnapshot",
        "ec2:CreateTags",
        "ec2:CreateVolume",
        "ec2:DeleteKeyPair",
        "ec2:DeleteSnapshot",
        "ec2:DeleteTags",
        "ec2:DeleteVolume",
        "ec2:DescribeAddresses",
        "ec2:DescribeAvailabilityZones",
        "ec2:DescribeBundleTasks",
        "ec2:DescribeConversionTasks",
        "ec2:DescribeCustomerGateways",
        "ec2:DescribeDhcpOptions",
        "ec2:DescribeExportTasks",
        "ec2:DescribeImageAttribute",
        "ec2:DescribeImages",
        "ec2:DescribeInstanceAttribute",
        "ec2:DescribeInstances",
        "ec2:DescribeInstanceStatus",
        "ec2:DescribeInternetGateways",
        "ec2:DescribeKeyPairs",
        "ec2:DescribeLicenses",
        "ec2:DescribeNetworkAcls",
        "ec2:DescribeNetworkInterfaceAttribute",
        "ec2:DescribeNetworkInterfaces",
        "ec2:DescribePlacementGroups",
        "ec2:DescribeRegions",
        "ec2:DescribeReservedInstances",
        "ec2:DescribeReservedInstancesOfferings",
        "ec2:DescribeRouteTables",
        "ec2:DescribeSecurityGroups",
        "ec2:DescribeSnapshotAttribute",
        "ec2:DescribeSnapshots",
        "ec2:DescribeSpotDatafeedSubscription",
```

```
        "ec2:DescribeSpotInstanceRequests",
        "ec2:DescribeSpotPriceHistory",
        "ec2:DescribeSubnets",
        "ec2:DescribeTags",
        "ec2:DescribeVolumeAttribute",
        "ec2:DescribeVolumes",
        "ec2:DescribeVolumeStatus",
        "ec2:DescribeVpcs",
        "ec2:DescribeVpnConnections",
        "ec2:DescribeVpnGateways",
        "ec2:DetachVolume",
        "ec2:EnableVolumeIO",
        "ec2:GetConsoleOutput",
        "ec2:GetPasswordData",
        "ec2:ImportKeyPair",
        "ec2:ModifyInstanceAttribute",
        "ec2:ModifySnapshotAttribute",
        "ec2:ModifyVolumeAttribute",
        "ec2:MonitorInstances",
        "ec2:RebootInstances",
        "ec2:ReportInstanceStatus",
        "ec2:ResetInstanceAttribute",
        "ec2:ResetSnapshotAttribute",
        "ec2:RunInstances",
        "ec2:StartInstances",
        "ec2:StopInstances",
        "ec2:TerminateInstances",
        "ec2:UnmonitorInstances",
        "elasticloadbalancing:RegisterInstancesWithLoadBalancer"
      ],
      "Resource": "*"
    }
  ]
}
"@
New-IAMGroup -GroupName "DEVELOPERS"
Write-IAMGroupPolicy -GroupName "DEVELOPERS" -PolicyName "DEVELOPERS-ManageInstances"
    -PolicyDocument $Policy
```

Fourth, the network administrators need full control over the VPC features. They also create and configure load balancers and manage security groups. On the other hand, network administrators do not need to create and destroy instances. Let's create a group for the network administrators.

```
$Policy = @"
{
  "Statement": [
    {
      "Effect": "Allow",
      "Action": [
        "directconnect:*",
        "ec2:AllocateAddress",
```

```
"ec2:AssociateAddress",
"ec2:AssociateDhcpOptions",
"ec2:AssociateRouteTable",
"ec2:AttachInternetGateway",
"ec2:AttachNetworkInterface",
"ec2:AttachVpnGateway",
"ec2:AuthorizeSecurityGroupEgress",
"ec2:AuthorizeSecurityGroupIngress",
"ec2:CreateCustomerGateway",
"ec2:CreateDhcpOptions",
"ec2:CreateInternetGateway",
"ec2:CreateNetworkAcl",
"ec2:CreateNetworkAclEntry",
"ec2:CreateNetworkInterface",
"ec2:CreateRoute",
"ec2:CreateRouteTable",
"ec2:CreateSecurityGroup",
"ec2:CreateSubnet",
"ec2:CreateTags",
"ec2:CreateVpc",
"ec2:CreateVpnConnection",
"ec2:CreateVpnGateway",
"ec2:DeleteCustomerGateway",
"ec2:DeleteDhcpOptions",
"ec2:DeleteInternetGateway",
"ec2:DeleteNetworkAcl",
"ec2:DeleteNetworkAclEntry",
"ec2:DeleteNetworkInterface",
"ec2:DeleteRoute",
"ec2:DeleteRouteTable",
"ec2:DeleteSecurityGroup",
"ec2:DeleteSubnet",
"ec2:DeleteTags",
"ec2:DeleteVpc", •
"ec2:DeleteVpnConnection",
"ec2:DeleteVpnGateway",
"ec2:DescribeAddresses",
"ec2:DescribeAvailabilityZones",
"ec2:DescribeBundleTasks",
"ec2:DescribeConversionTasks",
"ec2:DescribeCustomerGateways",
"ec2:DescribeDhcpOptions",
"ec2:DescribeExportTasks",
"ec2:DescribeImageAttribute",
"ec2:DescribeImages",
"ec2:DescribeInstanceAttribute",
"ec2:DescribeInstances",
"ec2:DescribeInstanceStatus",
"ec2:DescribeInternetGateways",
"ec2:DescribeKeyPairs",
"ec2:DescribeLicenses",
```

```
    "ec2:DescribeNetworkAcls",
    "ec2:DescribeNetworkInterfaceAttribute",
    "ec2:DescribeNetworkInterfaces",
    "ec2:DescribePlacementGroups",
    "ec2:DescribeRegions",
    "ec2:DescribeReservedInstances",
    "ec2:DescribeReservedInstancesOfferings",
    "ec2:DescribeRouteTables",
    "ec2:DescribeSecurityGroups",
    "ec2:DescribeSnapshotAttribute",
    "ec2:DescribeSnapshots",
    "ec2:DescribeSpotDatafeedSubscription",
    "ec2:DescribeSpotInstanceRequests",
    "ec2:DescribeSpotPriceHistory",
    "ec2:DescribeSubnets",
    "ec2:DescribeTags",
    "ec2:DescribeVolumeAttribute",
    "ec2:DescribeVolumes",
    "ec2:DescribeVolumeStatus",
    "ec2:DescribeVpcs",
    "ec2:DescribeVpnConnections",
    "ec2:DescribeVpnGateways",
    "ec2:DetachInternetGateway",
    "ec2:DetachNetworkInterface",
    "ec2:DetachVpnGateway",
    "ec2:DisassociateAddress",
    "ec2:DisassociateRouteTable",
    "ec2:GetConsoleOutput",
    "ec2:GetPasswordData",
    "ec2:ModifyNetworkInterfaceAttribute",
    "ec2:MonitorInstances",
    "ec2:ReleaseAddress",
    "ec2:ReplaceNetworkAclAssociation",
    "ec2:ReplaceNetworkAclEntry",
    "ec2:ReplaceRoute",
    "ec2:ReplaceRouteTableAssociation",
    "ec2:ResetNetworkInterfaceAttribute",
    "ec2:RevokeSecurityGroupEgress",
    "ec2:RevokeSecurityGroupIngress",
    "ec2:UnmonitorInstances",
    "elasticloadbalancing:ConfigureHealthCheck",
    "elasticloadbalancing:CreateAppCookieStickinessPolicy",
    "elasticloadbalancing:CreateLBCookieStickinessPolicy",
    "elasticloadbalancing:CreateLoadBalancer",
    "elasticloadbalancing:CreateLoadBalancerListeners",
    "elasticloadbalancing:DeleteLoadBalancer",
    "elasticloadbalancing:DeleteLoadBalancerListeners",
    "elasticloadbalancing:DeleteLoadBalancerPolicy",
    "elasticloadbalancing:DeregisterInstancesFromLoadBalancer",
    "elasticloadbalancing:DescribeInstanceHealth",
    "elasticloadbalancing:DescribeLoadBalancers",
```

```
            "elasticloadbalancing:DisableAvailabilityZonesForLoadBalancer",
            "elasticloadbalancing:EnableAvailabilityZonesForLoadBalancer",
            "elasticloadbalancing:RegisterInstancesWithLoadBalancer",
            "elasticloadbalancing:SetLoadBalancerListenerSSLCertificate",
            "elasticloadbalancing:SetLoadBalancerPoliciesOfListener"
        ],
        "Resource": "*"
      }
    ]
}
"@
New-IAMGroup -GroupName "NETWORK_ADMINS"
Write-IAMGroupPolicy -GroupName "NETWORK_ADMINS" -PolicyName
     "NETWORK_ADMINS-ManageNetwork" -PolicyDocument $Policy
```

Fifth, system administrators need full control over the instances. They need all the access a developer has so they can support the developers. In addition they need to be able to create new Amazon Machine Images (AMIs). They do not need access to the networking features that are being supported by the network administrators. Let's create a group for the system administrators.

```
$Policy = @"
{
  "Statement": [
    {
      "Effect": "Allow",
      "Action": [
        "ec2:AttachVolume",
        "ec2:CancelConversionTask",
        "ec2:CancelExportTask",
        "ec2:CancelSpotInstanceRequests",
        "ec2:CopySnapshot",
        "ec2:CreateImage",
        "ec2:CreateInstanceExportTask",
        "ec2:CreateKeyPair",
        "ec2:CreatePlacementGroup",
        "ec2:CreateSnapshot",
        "ec2:CreateSpotDatafeedSubscription",
        "ec2:CreateTags",
        "ec2:CreateVolume",
        "ec2:DeleteKeyPair",
        "ec2:DeletePlacementGroup",
        "ec2:DeleteSnapshot",
        "ec2:DeleteSpotDatafeedSubscription",
        "ec2:DeleteTags",
        "ec2:DeleteVolume",
        "ec2:DeregisterImage",
        "ec2:DescribeAddresses",
        "ec2:DescribeAvailabilityZones",
        "ec2:DescribeBundleTasks",
        "ec2:DescribeConversionTasks",
        "ec2:DescribeCustomerGateways",
```

```
"ec2:DescribeDhcpOptions",
"ec2:DescribeExportTasks",
"ec2:DescribeImageAttribute",
"ec2:DescribeImages",
"ec2:DescribeInstanceAttribute",
"ec2:DescribeInstances",
"ec2:DescribeInstanceStatus",
"ec2:DescribeInternetGateways",
"ec2:DescribeKeyPairs",
"ec2:DescribeLicenses",
"ec2:DescribeNetworkAcls",
"ec2:DescribeNetworkInterfaceAttribute",
"ec2:DescribeNetworkInterfaces",
"ec2:DescribePlacementGroups",
"ec2:DescribeRegions",
"ec2:DescribeReservedInstances",
"ec2:DescribeReservedInstancesOfferings",
"ec2:DescribeRouteTables",
"ec2:DescribeSecurityGroups",
"ec2:DescribeSnapshotAttribute",
"ec2:DescribeSnapshots",
"ec2:DescribeSpotDatafeedSubscription",
"ec2:DescribeSpotInstanceRequests",
"ec2:DescribeSpotPriceHistory",
"ec2:DescribeSubnets",
"ec2:DescribeTags",
"ec2:DescribeVolumeAttribute",
"ec2:DescribeVolumes",
"ec2:DescribeVolumeStatus",
"ec2:DescribeVpcs",
"ec2:DescribeVpnConnections",
"ec2:DescribeVpnGateways",
"ec2:DetachVolume",
"ec2:EnableVolumeIO",
"ec2:GetConsoleOutput",
"ec2:GetPasswordData",
"ec2:ImportInstance",
"ec2:ImportKeyPair",
"ec2:ImportVolume",
"ec2:ModifyImageAttribute",
"ec2:ModifyInstanceAttribute",
"ec2:ModifySnapshotAttribute",
"ec2:ModifyVolumeAttribute",
"ec2:MonitorInstances",
"ec2:PurchaseReservedInstancesOffering",
"ec2:RebootInstances",
"ec2:RegisterImage",
"ec2:ReportInstanceStatus",
"ec2:RequestSpotInstances",
"ec2:ResetImageAttribute",
"ec2:ResetInstanceAttribute",
```

```
            "ec2:ResetSnapshotAttribute",
            "ec2:RunInstances",
            "ec2:StartInstances",
            "ec2:StopInstances",
            "ec2:TerminateInstances",
            "ec2:UnmonitorInstances"
        ],
        "Resource": "*"
    }
  ]
}
"@
New-IAMGroup -GroupName "SYS_ADMINS"
Write-IAMGroupPolicy -GroupName "SYS_ADMINS" -PolicyName "SYS_ADMINS-ManageImages"
    -PolicyDocument $Policy
```

In this exercise we created a group for each of the teams that uses AWS at our fictitious company. Obviously you will need to tweak these groups to fit your company's needs, but I hope this will create a good framework to get you started. In the next exercise, we will grant access to billing and support to IAM users.

EXERCISE 11.2: DELEGATING ACCOUNT ACCESS TO IAM USERS

Back in Chapter 2 we discussed the difference between AWS account credentials and IAM users. Remember that the AWS account is the e-mail address you used to create your account. You almost never use this account, but there are a few times you need it. Two of these reasons are accessing your bill and getting support.

By default, you must log in using your AWS account credentials to see your bill or access support, but you can also grant access to IAM users. And, as you might expect, you can control exactly which users can access the billing and support features. Note that you have to pay extra for support.

You cannot enable IAM access to billing using PowerShell. You must sign into the AWS Management Console using your account credentials to enable it. The following steps show you how:

1. Sign into the Console using the e-mail address and password you used to create your account.

2. Click on your name on the menu bar at the top right of the screen.

3. Click My Account from the drop-down menu.

4. Scroll down until you see the section shown in Figure 11-1.

5. Select both the Account Activity Page check box and the Usage Reports Page check box. Click the Activate Now button.

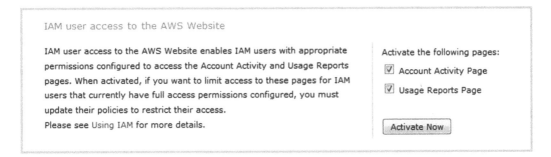

Figure 11-1. *IAM access to the AWS website*

Next we have to create an IAM policy granting access to IAM users. Interestingly, you cannot configure billing and support from the IAM wizard. You must create the policy manually. Luckily we know exactly how to do that. Let's create two groups: one for billing and one for support.

To create a group for billing you allow access to `ViewBilling` and `ViewUsage`. Billing is the summary information and usage is the raw detail. Just like the last exercise, we will associate this policy with a new group called BILLING.

```
$Policy = @"
{
  "Statement": [
    {
      "Action": [
        "aws-portal:ViewBilling",
        "aws-portal:ViewUsage"
      ],
      "Effect": "Allow",
      "Resource": "*"
    }
  ]
}
"@

New-IAMGroup -GroupName "BILLING"
Write-IAMGroupPolicy -GroupName "BILLING"
    -PolicyName "BILLING-BillingAndUsage" -PolicyDocument $Policy
```

To create a group for support we will create a policy that allows access to `support:*` and associate it with a new group called SUPPORT.

```
$Policy = @"
{
  "Statement": [
    {
      "Action": "support:*",
```

```
        "Effect": "Allow",
        "Resource": "*"
      }
    ]
  }
  "@

New-IAMGroup -GroupName "SUPPORT"
Write-IAMGroupPolicy -GroupName "SUPPORT"
        -PolicyName "SUPPORT-FullAccess" -PolicyDocument $Policy
```

Now, whenever you want to grant a user access to billing or support, you simply add the user to the appropriate group.

Summary

In this chapter we saw how IAM provides unprecedented control over access. We learned to create users and manage their passwords and access keys. Then, we learned to create groups and manage membership. We also learned to create roles for EC2 instances.

Next we learned to create policies and saw that IAM offers the granularity to enable least privileged access control over all of the AWS services. In the exercises we created a collection of groups for common IT roles and enabled access to billing and support. This is a great start for creating an enterprise access policy.

This is it! You have reached the end of the book. The remainder of this book is appendix materials. One of the appendices in particular, Appendix D, is useful for creating IAM policies. Appendix D lists the corresponding web service method for each PowerShell command. You can use this table to look up the name of the actions to include in your IAM policy for a specific PowerShell command.

APPENDIX A

Glossary of Terms

This appendix is a glossary of common terms. I have included many terms I used in the book and a description of all the AWS services, including many that were not discussed in the book.

> ■ **Note** This appendix has been adapted from documentation available on the AWS web site as of October 31, 2013. For the most current version of the AWS documentation, please visit http://aws.amazon.com/documentation/.

Access Control List (ACL): A document that defines who can access a particular object. Each object in Amazon Web Services has an ACL. The ACL defines what each type of user can do, such as write and read permissions.

Access Key: A string that AWS distributes to uniquely identify each AWS user; it is an alphanumeric token associated with your secret access key.

Amazon Machine Image (AMI): An encrypted machine image stored in Amazon Elastic Block Store or Amazon Simple Storage Service. AMIs are like a template of a computer's root drive. They contain the operating system and can also include software and layers of your application, such as database servers, middleware, web servers, and so on.

Amazon Web Services (AWS): An infrastructure web services platform in the cloud for companies of all sizes.

Auto Scaling: A web service designed to launch or terminate instances automatically based on user-defined policies, schedules, and health checks.

Availability Zone (AZ): A distinct location within a region that is insulated from failures in other Availability Zones, and provides inexpensive, low-latency network connectivity to other Availability Zones in the same region.

AWS Management Console: A graphical interface to manage compute, storage, and other cloud resources.

Bucket: A container for objects stored in Amazon S3. Every object is contained in a bucket. For example, if the object named photos/puppy.jpg is stored in the johnsmith bucket, then authorized users can access the object with the URL http://johnsmith.s3.amazonaws.com/photos/puppy.jpg.

Classless Inter-Domain Routing (CIDR): An Internet protocol address allocation and route aggregation methodology. See also http://en.wikipedia.org/wiki/CIDR_notation.

CloudFormation: A service for writing or changing templates that create and delete related AWS resources together as a unit.

CloudFront: An AWS content delivery service that helps you improve the performance, reliability, and availability of your web sites and applications.

CloudWatch: A web service that enables you to monitor and manage various metrics, and configure alarm actions based on data from those metrics. The state change may be triggered by a metric reaching the alarm threshold, or by a SetAlarmState request. Each alarm can have one or more actions assigned to each state. Actions are performed once each time the alarm changes to a state that has an action assigned, such as an Amazon Simple Notification Service notification, an Auto Scaling policy execution, or an Amazon EC2 instance stop/terminate action.

Customer Gateway: A router or software application on your side of a VPN tunnel that is managed by Amazon VPC. The internal interfaces of the customer gateway are attached to one or more devices in your home network. The external interface is attached to the VPG across the VPN tunnel.

Dedicated Instance: An instance that is physically isolated at the host hardware level and launched within a VPC.

DevPay: An easy-to-use online billing and account management service that makes it easy for you to sell an Amazon EC2 AMI or an application built on Amazon S3.

Domain Name System (DNS): A distributed naming system that associates network information with human-readable domain names on the Internet.

EC2 Compute Unit: An AWS standard for compute CPU and memory. This measure enables you to evaluate the CPU capacity of different EC2 instance types.

Elastic Block Store: A service that provides block level storage volumes for use with EC2 instances.

Elastic Compute Cloud (EC2): A web service that enables you to launch and manage Linux/UNIX and Windows server instances in Amazon's data centers.

Elastic IP Address (EIP): A fixed (static) IP address that you have allocated in Amazon EC2 or Amazon VPC and then attached to an instance. Elastic IP addresses are associated with your account, not a specific instance. They are elastic because you can easily allocate, attach, detach, and free them as your needs change. Unlike traditional static IP addresses, elastic IP addresses allow you to mask instance or Availability Zone failures by rapidly remapping your public IP addresses to another instance.

Elastic Load Balancing (ELB): A web service that improves an application's availability by distributing incoming traffic between two or more EC2 instances.

Elastic MapReduce: A web service that makes it easy to process large amounts of data efficiently. Amazon EMR uses Hadoop processing combined with several AWS products to do such tasks as web indexing, data mining, log file analysis, machine learning, scientific simulation, and data warehousing.

Elastic Network Interface (ENI): An additional network interface that can be attached to an instance. ENIs include a primary private IP address, one or more secondary private IP addresses, an elastic IP address (optional), a MAC address, membership in specified security groups, a description, and a source/destination check flag. You can create an ENI, attach it to an instance, detach it from an instance, and attach it to another instance.

HMAC: Hash-based Message Authentication Code. A specific construction for calculating a message authentication code (MAC) involving a cryptographic hash function in combination with a secret key. You can use it to verify both the data integrity and the authenticity of a message at the same time. AWS calculates the HMAC using a standard, cryptographic hash algorithm, such as SHA-256.

Identity and Access Management (IAM): A web service that enables Amazon Web Services customers to manage users and user permissions within AWS.

Instance: A copy of an Amazon Machine Image running as a virtual server in the AWS cloud.

Internet Gateway: Connects a network to the Internet. You can route traffic for IP addresses outside your VPC to the Internet gateway.

JavaScript Object Notation (JSON): A lightweight data-interchange format. For information about JSON, see http://www.json.org/.

Key: In Amazon S3, the unique identifier for an object in a bucket. Every object in a bucket has exactly one key. You can uniquely address every object in Amazon S3 through the combination of the web service endpoint, bucket name, and key, for example: http://doc.s3.amazonaws.com/2006-03-01/AmazonS3.wsdl, where doc is the name of the bucket, and 2006-03-01/AmazonS3.wsdl is the key.

Main Route Table: The default route table that any new VPC subnet uses for routing. You can associate a subnet with a different route table of your choice. You can also change which route table is the main route table.

Multi-Factor Authentication (MFA): An optional AWS account security feature. Once you enable AWS MFA, you must provide a six-digit, single-use code in addition to your sign-in credentials whenever you access secure AWS web site pages or the AWS Management Console. You get this single-use code from an authentication device that you keep in your physical possession.

NAT Instance: An instance that is configured to perform NAT in a VPC. A NAT instance enables private instances in the VPC to initiate Internet-bound traffic without being directly reachable from the Internet.

Network ACL: An optional layer of security that acts as a firewall for controlling traffic in and out of a subnet. You can associate multiple subnets with a single network ACL, but a subnet can be associated with only one network ACL at a time.

On-Demand Instance: An Amazon EC2 pricing option that charges you for compute capacity by the hour with no long-term commitment.

Pre-signed URL: A URL that uses query string authentication.

Private IP Address: All EC2 instances are assigned two IP addresses at launch, which are directly mapped to each other through Network Address Translation (NAT): a private address (following RFC 1918) and a public address. Exception: instances launched in Amazon VPC are assigned only a private IP address.

Private Subnet: A VPC subnet whose instances cannot be reached from the Internet.

Provisioned IOPS: A storage option designed to deliver fast, predictable, and consistent I/O performance. When you specify an IOPS rate while creating a DB Instance, Amazon RDS provisions that IOPS rate for the lifetime of the DB Instance.

Public AMI: An Amazon Machine Image that all AWS accounts have permission to launch.

Public Subnet: A subnet whose instances can be reached from the Internet.

Read Replica: An active copy of another RDS instance. Any updates to the data on the source DB instance are replicated to the read replica DB instance.

Region: A named set of AWS resources in the same geographical area. A region comprises at least two Availability Zones.

Relational Database Service (RDS): A web service that makes it easier to set up, operate, and scale a relational database in the cloud. It provides cost-efficient, resizable capacity for an industry-standard relational database and manages common database administration tasks.

REST: A type of HTTP-based request interface that generally uses only the GET or POST HTTP method and a query string with parameters. In some implementations of a REST interface, other HTTP verbs besides GET and POST are used.

Route 53: A web service you can use to create a new DNS service or to migrate your existing DNS service to the cloud.

Route Table: A set of routing rules that controls the traffic leaving any subnet that is associated with the route table. You can associate multiple subnets with a single route table, but a subnet can be associated with only one route table at a time.

Secret Access Key: A key that Amazon Web Services assigns to you when you sign up for an AWS account. Sometimes called simply a "secret key."

Security Group: A named set of allowed inbound network connections for an instance. (Security groups in Amazon VPC also include support for outbound connections.) Each security group consists of a list of protocols, ports, and IP address ranges. A security group can apply to multiple instances, and multiple groups can regulate a single instance.

Simple Email Service (SES): An easy-to-use, cost-effective email solution for applications.

Simple Notification Service (SNS): A web service that enables applications, end users, and devices to instantly send and receive notifications from the cloud.

Simple Queue Service (SQS): Reliable and scalable hosted queues for storing messages as they travel between computers.

Simple Storage Service (S3): Storage for the Internet. You can use it to store and retrieve any amount of data at any time, from anywhere on the Web.

Snapshot: Amazon Elastic Block Store creates snapshots or backups of your volumes and stores them in Amazon S3. You can use these snapshots as the starting point for new Amazon EBS volumes or to protect your data for long-term durability.

Source/Destination Check: A security measure to verify that an EC2 instance is the origin of all traffic that it sends and the ultimate destination of all traffic that it receives, that is, that the instance is not relaying traffic. Source/destination checking is enabled by default. For instances that function as gateways, such as VPC NAT instances, source/destination checking must be disabled.

Spot Instance: A type of EC2 instance that you can bid on to take advantage of unused Amazon EC2 capacity. If your maximum price exceeds the current price and your restrictions are met, Amazon EC2 launches instances on your behalf.

Subnet: A segment of the IP address range of a VPC that EC2 instances can be attached to. You can create subnets to group instances according to security and operational needs.

Tag: Metadata (consisting of up to 10 key/value pairs) that you can define and assign to Amazon EC2 resources.

Virtual Private Cloud (VPC): A web service that enables you to create a virtual network for your AWS resources. An elastic network populated by infrastructure, platform, and application services that share common security and interconnection.

Virtual Private Gateway (VPG): The Amazon side of a VPN connection that maintains connectivity. The internal interfaces of the virtual private gateway connect to your VPC via the VPN attachment and the external interfaces connect to the VPN connection, which leads to the customer gateway.

VPN Connection: Although VPN connection is a general term, we specifically mean the IPsec connection between a VPC and some other network, such as a corporate data center, home network, or co-location facility.

■ ■ ■

Metadata URL Structure

This appendix includes a list of metadata URL paths to access common information about an instance. We discussed the metadata URL in Chapter 3.

■ **Note** This appendix has been adapted from documentation available on the AWS web site as of October 31, 2013. For the most current version of the AWS documentation, please visit `http://aws.amazon.com/documentation/`.

Path	Description
ami-id	The AMI ID used to launch the instance.
ami-launch-index	If you started more than one instance at the same time, this value indicates the order in which the instance was launched. The value of the first instance launched is 0.
ami-manifest-path	The path to the AMI's manifest file in Amazon S3. If you used an EBS-backed AMI to launch the instance, the returned result is unknown.
ancestor-ami-ids	The AMI IDs of any instances that were rebundled to create this AMI. This value will exist only if the AMI manifest file contained an ancestor-amis key.
block-device-mapping/ami	The virtual device that contains the root/boot file system.
block-device-mapping/ebsN	The virtual devices associated with Amazon EBS volumes, if any are present. This value is available in metadata only if it is present at launch time. The N indicates the index of the Amazon EBS volume (such as ebs1 or ebs2).
block-device-mapping/ephemeralN	The virtual devices associated with ephemeral devices, if any are present. The N indicates the index of the ephemeral volume.
block-device-mapping/root	The virtual devices or partitions associated with the root devices, or partitions on the virtual device, where the root (/ or C:) file system is associated with the given instance.
block-device-mapping/swap	The virtual devices associated with swap. Not always present.

(continued)

Path	Description
hostname	The private hostname of the instance. In cases where multiple network interfaces are present, this refers to the eth0 device (the device for which the device number is 0).
iam/info	Returns information about the last time the instance profile was updated, including the instance's LastUpdated date, InstanceProfileArn, and InstanceProfileId.
iam/security-credentials/role-name	Where role-name is the name of the IAM role associated with the instance. Returns the temporary security credentials (AccessKeyId, SecretAccessKey, SessionToken, and Expiration) associated with the IAM role.
instance-action	Notifies the instance that it should reboot in preparation for bundling. Valid values: none | shutdown | bundle-pending.
instance-id	The ID of this instance.
instance-type	The type of instance.
kernel-id	The ID of the kernel launched with this instance, if applicable.
local-hostname	The private DNS hostname of the instance. In cases where multiple network interfaces are present, this refers to the eth0 device (the device for which the device number is 0).
local-ipv4	The private IP address of the instance. In cases where multiple network interfaces are present, this refers to the eth0 device (the device for which the device number is 0).
mac	The instance's media access control (MAC) address. In cases where multiple network interfaces are present, this refers to the eth0 device (the device for which the device number is 0).
network/interfaces/macs/mac/device-number	The device number associated with that interface. Each interface must have a unique device number. The device number serves as a hint to device naming in the instance: for example, device-number is 2 for the eth2 device.
network/interfaces/macs/mac/ipv4-associations/public-ip	The private IPv4 addresses that are associated with each public IP address and assigned to that interface.
network/interfaces/macs/mac/local-hostname	The interface's local hostname.
network/interfaces/macs/mac/local-ipv4s	The private IP addresses associated with the interface.
network/interfaces/macs/mac/mac	The instance's media access control (MAC) address.
network/interfaces/macs/mac/owner-id	The ID of the owner of the network interface. In multiple-interface environments, an interface can be attached by a third party, such as Elastic Load Balancing. Traffic on an interface is always billed to the interface owner.
network/interfaces/macs/mac/public-hostname	The interface's public DNS. If the instance is in a VPC, this category is returned only if the enableDnsHostnames attribute is set to true.

(*continued*)

Path	Description
`network/interfaces/macs/mac/public-ipv4s`	The elastic IP addresses associated with the interface. There may be multiple IP addresses on an instance.
`network/interfaces/macs/mac/security-groups`	Security groups to which the network interface belongs. Returned only for EC2 instances launched into a VPC.
`network/interfaces/macs/mac/security-group-ids`	IDs of the security groups to which the network interface belongs. Returned only for EC2 instances launched into a VPC.
`network/interfaces/macs/mac/subnet-id`	The ID of the subnet in which the interface resides. Returned only for EC2 instances launched into a VPC.
`network/interfaces/macs/mac/subnet-ipv4-cidr-block`	The CIDR block of the subnet in which the interface resides. Returned only for EC2 instances launched into a VPC.
`network/interfaces/macs/mac/vpc-id`	The ID of the VPC in which the interface resides. Returned only for EC2 instances launched into a VPC.
`network/interfaces/macs/mac/vpc-ipv4-cidr-block`	The CIDR block of the VPC in which the interface resides. Returned only for EC2 instances launched into a VPC.
`placement/availability-zone`	The availability zone in which the instance launched.
`product-codes`	Product codes associated with the instance, if any.
`public-hostname`	The instance's public DNS. If the instance is in a VPC, this category is returned only if the `enableDnsHostnames` attribute is set to true.
`public-ipv4`	The public IP address. If an elastic IP address is associated with the instance, the value returned is the elastic IP address.
`public-keys/0/openssh-key`	Public key. Only available if supplied at instance launch time.
`ramdisk-id`	The ID of the RAM disk specified at launch time, if applicable.
`reservation-id`	ID of the reservation.
`security-groups`	The names of the security groups applied to the instance.

■ ■ ■

List of Filters by EC2 Command

This appendix includes a list of filters for the EC2 "Get" commands. These are not included in the PowerShell help files but are really useful.

■ **Note** This appendix has been adapted from documentation available on the AWS web site as of October 31, 2013. For the most current version of the AWS documentation, please visit http://aws.amazon.com/documentation/.

Get-EC2Address

Filter	Description	Type
domain	Indicates whether the address is for use in a VPC. Valid values: standard | vpc.	String
instance-id	The instance the address is associated with (if any).	String
public-ip	The elastic IP address.	String
allocation-id	The allocation ID for the address (VPC only).	String
association-id	The association ID for the address (VPC only).	String
network-interface-id	The network interface (if any) that the address is associated with (VPC only).	String
network-interface-owner-id	The owner ID.	String
private-ip-address	The private IP address associated with the Elastic IP address (VPC only).	String

Get-EC2AvailabilityZone

Filter	Description	Type
message	Information about the availability zone.	String
region-name	The region for the availability zone (for example, us-east-1).	String
state	The state of the availability zone. Valid values: available | impaired | unavailable.	String
zone-name	The name of the zone.	String

Get-EC2BundleTask

Filter	Description	Type
bundle-id	The ID of the bundle task.	String
error-code	If the task failed, the error code returned.	String
error-message	If the task failed, the error message returned.	String
instance-id	The ID of the instance that was bundled.	String
progress	The level of task completion, as a percentage (for example, 20%).	String
s3-bucket	The Amazon S3 bucket to store the AMI.	String
s3-prefix	The beginning of the AMI name.	String
start-time	The time the task started (for example, 2008-09-15T17:15:20.000Z).	DateTime
state	The state of the task. Valid values: pending | waiting-for-shutdown | bundling | storing | cancelling | complete | failed.	String
update-time	The time of the most recent update for the task (for example, 2008-09-15T17:15:20.000Z).	DateTime

Get-EC2CustomerGateway

Filter	Description	Type
bgp-asn	The customer gateway's Border Gateway Protocol (BGP) Autonomous System Number (ASN).	String
customer-gateway-id	The ID of the customer gateway.	String
ip-address	The IP address of the customer gateway's Internet-routable external interface (for example, 12.1.2.3).	String
state	The state of the customer gateway. Valid values: pending | available | deleting | deleted.	String
type	The type of customer gateway. Currently, the only supported type is ipsec.1.	String
tag-key	The key of a tag assigned to the resource. This filter is independent of the tag-value filter. For example, if you use both the filter "tag-key=Purpose" and the filter "tag-value=X", you get any resources assigned both the tag key Purpose (regardless of what the tag's value is), and the tag value X (regardless of what the tag's key is). If you want to list only resources where Purpose is X, see the tag:key filter.	String
tag-value	The value of a tag assigned to the resource. This filter is independent of the tag-key filter.	String
tag:key	Filters the response based on a specific tag/value combination.	String

Get-EC2DhcpOption

Filter	Description	Type
dhcp-options-id	The ID of a set of DHCP options.	String
key	The key for one of the options (for example, domain-name).	String
value	The value for one of the options.	String
tag-key	The key of a tag assigned to the resource. This filter is independent of the tag-value filter. For example, if you use both the filter "tag-key=Purpose" and the filter "tag-value=X", you get any resources assigned both the tag key Purpose (regardless of what the tag's value is), and the tag value X (regardless of what the tag's key is). If you want to list only resources where Purpose is X, see the tag:key filter.	String
tag-value	The value of a tag assigned to the resource. This filter is independent of the tag-key filter.	String
tag:key	Filters the response based on a specific tag/value combination.	String

Get-EC2Image

Filter	Description	Type
architecture	The image architecture. Valid values: i386 | x86_64.	String
block-device-mapping. delete-on-termination	Whether the Amazon EBS volume is deleted on instance termination.	Boolean
block-device-mapping. device-name	The device name (for example, /dev/sdh) for the Amazon EBS volume.	String
block-device-mapping. snapshot-id	The ID of the snapshot used for the Amazon EBS volume.	String
block-device-mapping. volume-size	The volume size of the Amazon EBS volume, in GiB.	Integer
block-device-mapping. volume-type	The volume type of the Amazon EBS volume. Valid values: standard | io1.	String
description	The description of the image (provided during image creation).	String
image-id	The ID of the image.	String
image-type	The image type. Valid values: machine | kernel | ramdisk.	String
is-public	Whether the image is public.	Boolean
kernel-id	The kernel ID.	String
manifest-location	The location of the image manifest.	String
name	The name of the AMI (provided during image creation).	String
owner-alias	The AWS account alias (for example, amazon).	String

(continued)

Filter	Description	Type
owner-id	The AWS account ID of the image owner.	String
platform	The platform. To only list Windows-based AMIs, use windows. Valid value: windows.	String
product-code	The product code.	String
product-code.type	The type of the product code. Valid values: devpay | marketplace.	String
ramdisk-id	The RAM disk ID.	String
root-device-name	The name of the root device volume (for example, /dev/sda1).	String
root-device-type	The type of the root device volume. Valid values: ebs | instance-store.	String
state	The state of the image. Valid values: available | pending | failed.	String
state-reason-code	The reason code for the state change.	String
state-reason-message	The message for the state change.	String
tag-key	The key of a tag assigned to the resource. This filter is independent of the tag-value filter. For example, if you use both the filter "tag-key=Purpose" and the filter "tag-value=X", you get any resources assigned both the tag key Purpose (regardless of what the tag's value is), and the tag value X (regardless of what the tag's key is). If you want to list only resources where Purpose is X, see the tag:key filter.	String
tag-value	The value of a tag assigned to the resource. This filter is independent of the tag-key filter.	String
tag:key	Filters the response based on a specific tag/value combination.	String
virtualization-type	The virtualization type. Valid values: paravirtual | hvm.	String
hypervisor	The hypervisor type. Valid values: ovm | xen.	String

Get-EC2Instance

Filter	Description	Type
architecture	The instance architecture. Valid values: i386 | x86_64.	String
availability-zone	The availability zone of the instance.	String
block-device-mapping.attach-time	The attach time for an Amazon EBS volume mapped to the instance (for example, 2010-09-15T17:15:20.000Z).	DateTime
block-device-mapping.delete-on-termination	Indicates whether the Amazon EBS volume is deleted on instance termination.	Boolean
block-device-mapping.device-name	The device name (for example, /dev/sdh) for the Amazon EBS volume.	String

(continued)

Filter	Description	Type
block-device-mapping.status	The status for the Amazon EBS volume. Valid values: attaching | attached | detaching | detached.	String
block-device-mapping.volume-id	The volume ID of the Amazon EBS volume.	String
client-token	The idempotency token you provided when you launched the instance.	String
dns-name	The public DNS name of the instance.	String
group-id	The ID of the security group for the instance. If the instance is in EC2-Classic or a default VPC, you can use group-name instead.	String
group-name	The name of the security group for the instance. If the instance is in a nondefault VPC, you must use group-id instead.	String
image-id	The ID of the image used to launch the instance.	String
instance-id	The ID of the instance.	String
instance-lifecycle	Indicates whether this is a Spot Instance. Valid value: spot.	String
instance-state-code	The state of the instance. The high byte is an opaque internal value and should be ignored. The low byte is set based on the state represented. Valid values: 0 (pending) | 16 (running) | 32 (shutting-down) | 48 (terminated) | 64 (stopping) | 80 (stopped).	Integer (16-bit unsigned integer)
instance-state-name	The state of the instance. Valid values: pending | running | shutting-down | terminated | stopping | stopped.	String
instance-type	The type of instance (for example, m1.small).	String
instance.group-id	The ID of the security group for the instance. If the instance is in EC2-Classic or a default VPC, you can use instance.group-name instead.	String
instance.group-name	The name of the security group for the instance. If the instance is in a nondefault VPC, you must use instance.group-id instead.	String
ip-address	The public IP address of the instance.	String
kernel-id	The kernel ID.	String
key-name	The name of the key pair used when the instance was launched.	String
launch-index	When launching multiple instances, this is the index for the instance in the launch group (for example, 0, 1, 2, and so on).	String
launch-time	The time when the instance was launched (for example, 2010-08-07T11:54:42.000Z).	DateTime

(continued)

Filter	Description	Type
monitoring-state	Indicates whether monitoring is enabled for the instance. Valid values: disabled | enabled.	String
owner-id	The AWS account ID of the instance owner.	String
placement-group-name	The name of the placement group for the instance.	String
platform	The platform. Use windows if you have Windows-based instances; otherwise, leave blank. Valid value: windows.	String
private-dns-name	The private DNS name of the instance.	String
private-ip-address	The private IP address of the instance.	String
product-code	The product code associated with the AMI used to launch the instance.	String
product-code.type	The type of product code. Valid values: devpay | marketplace.	String
ramdisk-id	The RAM disk ID.	String
reason	The reason for the current state of the instance (for example, shows "User Initiated [date]" when you stop or terminate the instance). Similar to the state-reason-code filter.	String
requester-id	The ID of the entity that launched the instance on your behalf (for example, AWS Management Console, Auto Scaling, and so on)	String
reservation-id	The ID of the instance's reservation. A reservation ID is created any time you launch an instance. A reservation ID has a one-to-one relationship with an instance launch request, but can be associated with more than one instance if you launch multiple instances using the same launch request. For example, if you launch one instance, you'll get one reservation ID. If you launch 10 instances using the same launch request, you'll also get one reservation ID.	String
root-device-name	The name of the root device for the instance (for example, /dev/sda1).	String
root-device-type	The type of root device that the instance uses. Valid values: ebs | instance-store.	String
source-dest-check	Indicates whether the instance performs source/destination checking. A value of true means that checking is enabled, and false means checking is disabled. The value must be false for the instance to perform network address translation (NAT) in your VPC.	Boolean
spot-instance-request-id	The ID of the Spot Instance request.	String
state-reason-code	The reason code for the state change.	String
state-reason-message	A message that describes the state change.	String
subnet-id	The ID of the subnet for the instance.	String

(continued)

Filter	Description	Type
tag-key	The key of a tag assigned to the resource. This filter is independent of the tag-value filter. For example, if you use both the filter "tag-key=Purpose" and the filter "tag-value=X", you get any resources assigned both the tag key Purpose (regardless of what the tag's value is), and the tag value X (regardless of what the tag's key is). If you want to list only resources where Purpose is X, see the tag:key filter.	String
tag-value	The value of a tag assigned to the resource. This filter is independent of the tag-key filter.	String
tag:key	Filters the response based on a specific tag/value combination.	String
virtualization-type	The virtualization type of the instance. Valid values: paravirtual | hvm.	String
vpc-id	The ID of the VPC that the instance is running in.	String
hypervisor	The hypervisor type of the instance. Valid values: ovm | xen.	String
network-interface.description	The description of the network interface.	String
network-interface.subnet-id	The ID of the subnet for the network interface.	String
network-interface.vpc-id	The ID of the VPC for the network interface.	String
network-interface.network-interface.id	The ID of the network interface.	String
network-interface.owner-id	The ID of the owner of the network interface.	String
network-interface.availability-zone	The availability zone for the network interface.	String
network-interface.requester-id	The requester ID for the network interface.	String
network-interface.requester-managed	Indicates whether the network interface is being managed by AWS.	Boolean
network-interface.status	The status of the network interface. Valid values: available | in-use.	String
network-interface.mac-address	The MAC address of the network interface. Valid values: available | in-use.	String
network-interface-private-dns-name	The private DNS name of the network interface.	String
network-interface.source-destination-check	Whether the network interface performs source/destination checking. A value of true means checking is enabled, and false means checking is disabled. The value must be false for the network interface to perform network address translation (NAT) in your VPC.	Boolean
network-interface.group-id	The ID of a security group associated with the network interface.	String

(continued)

Filter	Description	Type
network-interface.group-name	The name of a security group associated with the network interface.	String
network-interface.attachment.attachment-id	The ID of the interface attachment.	String
network-interface.attachment.instance-id	The ID of the instance to which the network interface is attached.	String
network-interface.attachment.instance-owner-id	The owner ID of the instance to which the network interface is attached.	String
network-interface.addresses.private-ip-address	The private IP address associated with the network interface.	String
network-interface.attachment.device-index	The device index to which the network interface is attached.	Integer
network-interface.attachment.status	The status of the attachment. Valid values: attaching | attached | detaching | detached.	String
network-interface.attachment.attach-time	The time that the network interface was attached to an instance.	Date
network-interface.attachment.delete-on-termination	Specifies whether the attachment is deleted when an instance is terminated.	Boolean
network-interface.addresses.primary	Specifies whether the IP address of the network interface is the primary private IP address.	Boolean
network-interface.addresses.association.public-ip	The ID of the association of an Elastic IP address with a network interface.	String
network-interface.addresses.association.ip-owner-id	The owner ID of the private IP address associated with the network interface.	String
association.public-ip	The address of the Elastic IP address bound to the network interface.	String
association.ip-owner-id	The owner of the Elastic IP address associated with the network interface.	String
association.allocation-id	The allocation ID returned when you allocated the Elastic IP address for your network interface.	String
association.association-id	The association ID returned when the network interface was associated with an IP address.	String

Get-EC2InstanceStatus

Filter	Description	Type
availability-zone	The availability zone of the instance.	String
event.code	The code identifying the type of event. Valid values: instance-reboot | system-reboot | system-maintenance | instance-retirement | instance-stop.	String
event.description	A description of the event.	String
event.not-after	The latest end time for the scheduled event.	DateTime
event.not-before	The earliest start time for the scheduled event.	DateTime
instance-state-name	The state of the instance. Valid values: pending | running | shutting-down | terminated | stopping | stopped.	String
instance-state-code	A code representing the state of the instance. The high byte is an opaque internal value and should be ignored. The low byte is set based on the state represented. Valid values: 0 (pending) | 16 (running) | 32 (shutting-down) | 48 (terminated) | 64 (stopping) | 80 (stopped).	Integer (16-bit unsigned integer)
system-status.status	The system status of the instance. Valid values: ok | impaired | initializing | insufficient-data | not-applicable.	String
system-status.reachability	Filters on system status where the name is reachability. Valid values: passed | failed | initializing | insufficient-data.	String
instance-status.status	The status of the instance. Valid values: ok | impaired | initializing | insufficient-data | not-applicable.	String
instance-status.reachability	Filters on instance status where the name is reachability. Valid values: passed | failed | initializing | insufficient-data.	String

Get-EC2InternetGateway

Filter	Description	Type
attachment.state	The current state of the attachment between the gateway and the VPC. Returned only if a VPC is attached. Valid value: available.	String
attachment.vpc-id	The ID of an attached VPC.	String
internet-gateway-id	The ID of the Internet gateway.	String
tag-key	The key of a tag assigned to the resource. This filter is independent of the tag-value filter. For example, if you use both the filter "tag-key=Purpose" and the filter "tag-value=X", you get any resources assigned both the tag key Purpose (regardless of what the tag's value is), and the tag value X (regardless of what the tag's key is). If you want to list only resources where Purpose is X, see the tag:key filter.	String

(continued)

Filter	Description	Type
tag-value	The value of a tag assigned to the resource. This filter is independent of the tag-key filter.	String
tag:key	Filters the response based on a specific tag/value combination.	String

Get-EC2KeyPair

Filter	Description	Type
fingerprint	The fingerprint of the key pair.	String
key-name	The name of the key pair.	String

Get-EC2NetworkAcl

Filter	Description	Type
association.association-id	The ID of an association ID for the ACL.	String
association.network-acl-id	The ID of the network ACL involved in the association.	String
association.subnet-id	The ID of the subnet involved in the association.	String
default	Indicates whether the ACL is the default network ACL for the VPC.	Boolean
entry.cidr	The CIDR range specified in the entry.	String
entry.egress	Indicates whether the entry applies to egress traffic.	Boolean
entry.icmp.code	The ICMP code specified in the entry, if any.	Integer
entry.icmp.type	The ICMP type specified in the entry, if any.	Integer
entry.port-range.from	The start of the port range specified in the entry.	Integer
entry.port-range.to	The end of the port range specified in the entry.	Integer
entry.protocol	The protocol specified in the entry. Valid values: tcp | udp | icmp or a protocol number.	String
entry.rule-action	Allows or denies the matching traffic. Valid values: allow | deny.	String
entry.rule-number	The number of an entry (in other words, rule) in the ACL's set of entries.	Integer
network-acl-id	The ID of the network ACL.	String
tag-key	The key of a tag assigned to the resource. This filter is independent of the tag-value filter. For example, if you use both the filter "tag-key=Purpose" and the filter "tag-value=X", you get any resources assigned both the tag key Purpose (regardless of what the tag's value is), and the tag value X (regardless of what the tag's key is). If you want to list only resources where Purpose is X, see the tag:key filter.	String

(continued)

Filter	Description	Type
tag-value	The value of a tag assigned to the resource. This filter is independent of the tag-key filter.	String
tag:key	Filters the response based on a specific tag/value combination.	String
vpc-id	The ID of the VPC for the network ACL.	String

Get-EC2NetworkInterface

Filter	Description	Type
addresses.private-ip-address	The private IP addresses associated with the network interface.	String
addresses.primary	Whether the private IP address is the primary IP address associated with the network interface.	Boolean
addresses.association.public-ip	The association ID returned when the network interface was associated with the Elastic IP address.	String
addresses.association.owner-id	The owner ID of the addresses associated with the network interface.	String
association.association-id	The association ID returned when the network interface was associated with an IP address.	String
association.allocation-id	The allocation ID returned when you allocated the Elastic IP address for your network interface.	String
association.ip-owner-id	The owner of the Elastic IP address associated with the network interface.	String
association.public-ip	The address of the Elastic IP address bound to the network interface.	String
attachment.attachment-id	The ID of the interface attachment.	String
attachment.instance-id	The ID of the instance to which the network interface is attached.	String
attachment.instance-owner-id	The owner ID of the instance to which the network interface is attached.	String
attachment.device-index	The device index to which the network interface is attached.	Integer
attachment.status	The status of the attachment. Valid values: attaching | attached | detaching | detached.	String
attachment.attach.time	The time that the network interface was attached to an instance.	DateTime
attachment.delete-on-termination	Indicates whether the attachment is deleted when an instance is terminated.	Boolean
availability-zone	The availability zone of the network interface.	String
description	The description of the network interface.	String
group-id	The ID of a security group associated with the network interface.	String

(*continued*)

Filter	Description	Type
group-name	The name of a security group associated with the network interface.	String
mac-address	The MAC address of the network interface.	String
network-interface-id	The ID of the network interface.	String
owner-id	The AWS account ID of the network interface owner.	String
private-ip-address	The private IP address or addresses of the network interface.	String
private-dns-name	The private DNS name of the network interface.	String
requester-id	The ID of the entity that launched the instance on your behalf (for example, AWS Management Console, Auto Scaling, and so on).	String
requester-managed	Indicates whether the network interface is being managed by an AWS service (for example, AWS Management Console, Auto Scaling, and so on).	Boolean
source-dest-check	Indicates whether the network interface performs source/destination checking. A value of true means checking is enabled, and false means checking is disabled. The value must be false for the network interface to perform Network Address Translation (NAT) in your VPC.	Boolean
status	The status of the network interface. If the network interface is not attached to an instance, the status shows available; if a network interface is attached to an instance the status shows in-use. Valid values: available | in-use.	String
subnet-id	The ID of the subnet for the network interface.	String
tag-key	The key of a tag assigned to the resource. This filter is independent of the tag-value filter. For example, if you use both the filter "tag-key=Purpose" and the filter "tag-value=X," you get any resources assigned both the tag key Purpose (regardless of what the tag's value is), and the tag value X (regardless of what the tag's key is). If you want to list only resources where Purpose is X, see the tag:key filter.	String
tag-value	The value of a tag assigned to the resource. This filter is independent of the tag-key filter.	String
tag:key	Filters the response based on a specific tag/value combination.	String
vpc-id	The ID of the VPC for the network interface.	String

Get-EC2PlacementGroup

Filter	Description	Type
group-name	The name of the placement group.	String
state	The state of the placement group. Valid values: pending | available | deleting | deleted.	String
strategy	The strategy of the placement group. Valid value: cluster.	String

Get-EC2Region

Filter	Description	Type
endpoint	The endpoint of the region (for example, ec2.us-east-1.amazonaws.com).	String
region-name	The name of the region.	String

Get-EC2ReservedInstance

Filter	Description	Type
availability-zone	The availability zone where the Reserved Instance can be used.	String
duration	The duration of the Reserved Instance (one year or three years), in seconds. Valid values: 31536000 | 94608000.	Long
end	The time when the Reserved Instance expires.	DateTime
fixed-price	The purchase price of the Reserved Instance (for example, 9800.0).	Double
instance-type	The instance type on which the Reserved Instance can be used.	String
product-description	The product description of the Reserved Instance. Valid values: Linux/UNIX | Linux/UNIX (Amazon VPC) | Windows | Windows (Amazon VPC).	String
reserved-instances-id	The ID of the Reserved Instance.	String
start	The time at which the Reserved Instance purchase request was placed (for example, 2010-08-07T11:54:42.000Z).	DateTime
state	The state of the Reserved Instance. Valid values: pending-payment | active | payment-failed | retired.	String
tag-key	The key of a tag assigned to the resource. This filter is independent of the tag-value filter. For example, if you use both the filter "tag-key=Purpose" and the filter "tag-value=X," you get any resources assigned both the tag key Purpose (regardless of what the tag's value is), and the tag value X (regardless of what the tag's key is). If you want to list only resources where Purpose is X, see the tag:key filter.	String

(continued)

235

Filter	Description	Type
tag-value	The value of a tag assigned to the resource. This filter is independent of the tag-key filter.	String
tag:key	Filters the response based on a specific tag/value combination.	String

Get-EC2ReservedInstancesListing

Filter	Description	Type
status	Status of the Reserved Instance listing. Valid values: pending | active | cancelled | closed.	String
status-message	Reason for the status.	String
reserved-instances-listing-id	The ID of the Reserved Instances listing.	String
reserved-instances-id	The ID of the Reserved Instances.	String

Get-EC2ReservedInstancesOffering

Filter	Description	Type
availability-zone	The availability zone where the Reserved Instance can be used.	String
duration	The duration of the Reserved Instance (for example, one year or three years), in seconds. Valid values: 31536000 | 94608000.	Long
fixed-price	The purchase price of the Reserved Instance (for example, 9800.0).	Double
instance-type	The instance type on which the Reserved Instance can be used.	String
marketplace	Set to true to show only Reserved Instance Marketplace offerings. When this filter is not used, which is the default behavior, all offerings from AWS and Reserved Instance Marketplace are listed.	Boolean
product-description	The description of the Reserved Instance. Valid values: Linux/UNIX | Linux/UNIX (Amazon VPC) | Windows | Windows (Amazon VPC).	String
reserved-instances-offering-id	The Reserved Instances offering ID.	String
usage-price	The usage price of the Reserved Instance, per hour (for example, 0.84).	Double

Get-EC2RouteTable

Filter	Description	Type
`association.route-table-association-id`	The ID of an association ID for the route table.	String
`association.route-table-id`	The ID of the route table involved in the association.	String
`association.subnet-id`	The ID of the subnet involved in the association.	String
`association.main`	Indicates whether the route table is the main route table for the VPC.	Boolean
`route-table-id`	The ID of the route table.	String
`route.destination-cidr-block`	The CIDR range specified in a route in the table.	String
`route.gateway-id`	The ID of a gateway specified in a route in the table.	String
`route.instance-id`	The ID of an instance specified in a route in the table.	String
`route.origin`	Describes how the route was created. Valid values: `CreateRouteTable` | `CreateRoute` | `EnableVgwRoutePropagation`. `CreateRouteTable` indicates that the route was automatically created when the route table was created. `CreateRoute` indicates that the route was manually added to the route table. `EnableVgwRoutePropagation` indicates that the route was propagated by route propagation.	String
`route.state`	The state of a route in the route table. The blackhole state indicates that the route's target isn't available (for example, the specified gateway isn't attached to the VPC, the specified NAT instance has been terminated, and so on). Valid values: `active` | `blackhole`.	String
`tag-key`	The key of a tag assigned to the resource. This filter is independent of the `tag-value` filter. For example, if you use both the filter "tag-key=Purpose" and the filter "tag-value=X", you get any resources assigned both the tag key Purpose (regardless of what the tag's value is), and the tag value X (regardless of what the tag's key is). If you want to list only resources where Purpose is X, see the `tag:key` filter.	String
`tag-value`	The value of a tag assigned to the resource. This filter is independent of the `tag-key` filter.	String
`tag:key`	Filters the response based on a specific tag/value combination.	String
`vpc-id`	The ID of the VPC for the route table.	String

Get-EC2SecurityGroup

Filter	Description	Type
description	The description of the security group.	String
group-id	The ID of the security group.	String
group-name	The name of the security group.	String
ip-permission.cidr	The CIDR range that has been granted the permission.	String
ip-permission.from-port	The start of port range for the TCP and UDP protocols, or an ICMP type number.	String
ip-permission.group-name	The name of security group that has been granted the permission.	String
ip-permission.protocol	The IP protocol for the permission. Valid values: tcp | udp | icmp or a protocol number.	String
ip-permission.to-port	The end of port range for the TCP and UDP protocols, or an ICMP code.	String
ip-permission.user-id	The ID of an AWS account that has been granted the permission.	String
owner-id	The AWS account ID of the owner of the security group.	String
tag-key	The key of a tag assigned to the security group.	String
tag-value	The value of a tag assigned to the security group.	String
vpc-id	Only returns the security groups that belong to the specified EC2-VPC ID.	String

Get-EC2Snapshot

Filter	Description	Type
description	A description of the snapshot.	String
owner-alias	The AWS account alias (for example, amazon) that owns the snapshot.	String
owner-id	The ID of the AWS account that owns the snapshot.	String
progress	The progress of the snapshot, as a percentage (for example, 80%).	String
snapshot-id	The snapshot ID.	String
start-time	The time stamp when the snapshot was initiated.	DateTime
status	The status of the snapshot. Valid values: **pending | completed | error**.	String
tag-key	The key of a tag assigned to the resource. This filter is independent of the tag-value filter. For example, if you use both the filter "tag-key=Purpose" and the filter "tag-value=X," you get any resources assigned both the tag key Purpose (regardless of what the tag's value is), and the tag value X (regardless of what the tag's key is). If you want to list only resources where Purpose is X, see the tag:key filter.	String

(*continued*)

Filter	Description	Type
tag-value	The value of a tag assigned to the resource. This filter is independent of the tag-key filter.	String
tag:key	Filters the response based on a specific tag/value combination.	String
volume-id	The ID of the volume the snapshot is for.	String
volume-size	The size of the volume, in GiB (for example, 20).	String

Get-EC2SpotInstanceRequest

Filter	Description	Type
availability-zone-group	The availability zone group. If you specify the same availability zone group for all Spot Instance requests, all Spot Instances are launched in the same availability zone.	String
create-time	The time stamp when the Spot Instance request was created.	String
fault-code	The fault code related to the request.	String
fault-message	The fault message related to the request.	String
instance-id	The ID of the instance that fulfilled the request.	String
launch-group	The Spot Instance launch group. Launch groups are Spot Instances that launch together and terminate together.	String
launch.block-device-mapping.delete-on-termination	Whether the Amazon EBS volume is deleted on instance termination.	Boolean
launch.block-device-mapping.device-name	The device name (for example, /dev/sdh) for the Amazon EBS volume.	String
launch.block-device-mapping.snapshot-id	The ID of the snapshot used for the Amazon EBS volume.	String
launch.block-device-mapping.volume-size	The volume size of the Amazon EBS volume, in GiB.	String
launch.block-device-mapping.volume-type	The volume type of the Amazon EBS volume. Valid values: standard	io1.	String
launch.group-id	The security group for the instance.	String
launch.image-id	The ID of the AMI.	String
launch.instance-type	The type of instance (for example, m1.small).	String
launch.kernel-id	The kernel ID.	String
launch.key-name	The name of the key pair the instance launched with.	String
launch.monitoring-enabled	Whether monitoring is enabled for the Spot Instance.	Boolean
launch.ramdisk-id	The RAM disk ID.	String

(continued)

239

Filter	Description	Type
launch.network-interface. network-interface-id	The ID of the network interface.	String
launch.network-interface. device-index	The index of the device for the network interface attachment on the instance.	Integer
launch.network-interface. subnet-id	The ID of the subnet for the instance.	String
launch.network-interface. description	A description of the network interface.	String
launch.network-interface. private-ip-address	The primary private IP address of the network interface.	String
launch.network-interface. delete-on-termination	Indicates whether the network interface is deleted when the instance is terminated.	Boolean
launch.network-interface. group-id	The ID of the security group associated with the network interface.	String
launch.network-interface. group-name	The name of the security group associated with the network interface.	String
launch.network-interface. addresses.primary	Indicates whether the IP address is the primary private IP address.	String
product-description	The product description associated with the instance. Valid values: Linux/UNIX | Windows.	String
spot-instance-request-id	The Spot Instance request ID.	String
spot-price	The maximum hourly price for any Spot Instance launched to fulfill the request.	String
state	The state of the Spot Instance request. Spot bid status information can help you track your Amazon EC2 Spot Instance requests. Valid values: open | active | closed | cancelled | failed.	String
status-code	The short code describing the most recent evaluation of your Spot Instance request.	String
status-message	The message explaining the status of the Spot Instance request.	String
tag-key	The key of a tag assigned to the resource. This filter is independent of the tag-value filter. For example, if you use both the filter "tag-key=Purpose" and the filter "tag-value=X," you get any resources assigned both the tag key Purpose (regardless of what the tag's value is), and the tag value X (regardless of what the tag's key is). If you want to list only resources where Purpose is X, see the tag:key filter.	String
tag-value	The value of a tag assigned to the resource. This filter is independent of the tag-key filter.	String
tag:key	Filters the response based on a specific tag/value combination.	String

(continued)

Filter	Description	Type
type	The type of Spot Instance request. Valid values: one-time | persistent.	String
launched-availability-zone	The availability zone in which the bid is launched.	String
valid-from	The start date of the request.	DateTime
valid-until	The end date of the request.	DateTime

Get-EC2SpotPriceHistory

Filter	Description	Type
instance-type	The type of instance (for example, m1.small).	String
product-description	The product description for the Spot Price. Valid values: Linux/UNIX | SUSE Linux | Windows | Linux/UNIX (Amazon VPC) | SUSE Linux (Amazon VPC) | Windows (Amazon VPC).	String
spot-price	The Spot Price. The value must match exactly (or use wildcards; greater than or less than comparison is not supported).	String
timestamp	The timestamp of the Spot Price history (for example, 2010-08-16T05:06:11.000Z). You can use wildcards (* and ?). Greater than or less than comparison is not supported.	DateTime
availability-zone	The availability zone for which prices should be returned.	String

Get-EC2Subnet

Filter	Description	Type
availability-zone	The availability zone for the subnet.	String
available-ip-address-count	The number of IP addresses in the subnet that are available.	String
cidr	The CIDR block of the subnet. The CIDR block you specify must exactly match the subnet's CIDR block for information to be returned for the subnet. Constraints: Must contain the slash followed by one or two digits (for example, /28).	String
defaultForAz	Indicates whether this is the default subnet for the availability zone.	Boolean
state	The state of the subnet. Valid values: pending | available.	String
subnet-id	The ID of the subnet.	String

(continued)

Filter	Description	Type
tag-key	The key of a tag assigned to the resource. This filter is independent of the tag-value filter. For example, if you use both the filter "tag-key=Purpose" and the filter "tag-value=X," you get any resources assigned both the tag key Purpose (regardless of what the tag's value is), and the tag value X (regardless of what the tag's key is). If you want to list only resources where Purpose is X, see the tag:key filter.	String
tag-value	The value of a tag assigned to the resource. This filter is independent of the tag-key filter.	String
tag:key	Filters the response based on a specific tag/value combination.	String
vpc-id	The ID of the VPC for the subnet.	String

Get-EC2Tag

Filter	Description	Type
key	The tag key.	String
resource-id	The resource ID.	String
resource-type	The resource type. Valid values: customer-gateway | dhcp-options | image | instance | internet-gateway | network-acl | network-interface | reserved-instances | route-table | security-group | snapshot | spot-instances-request | subnet | volume | vpc | vpn-connection | vpn-gateway.	String
value	The tag value.	String

Get-EC2Volume

Filter	Description	Type
attachment.attach-time	The time stamp when the attachment initiated.	DateTime
attachment.delete-on-termination	Whether the volume is deleted on instance termination.	Boolean
attachment.device	The device name that is exposed to the instance (for example, /dev/sda1).	String
attachment.instance-id	The ID of the instance the volume is attached to.	String
attachment.status	The attachment state. Valid values: attaching | attached | detaching | detached.	String
availability-zone	The availability zone in which the volume was created.	String
create-time	The time stamp when the volume was created.	DateTime
size	The size of the volume, in GiB (for example, 20).	String

(continued)

Filter	Description	Type
snapshot-id	The snapshot from which the volume was created.	String
status	The status of the volume. Valid values: creating | available | in-use | deleting | deleted | error.	String
tag-key	The key of a tag assigned to the resource. This filter is independent of the tag-value filter. For example, if you use both the filter "tag-key=Purpose" and the filter "tag-value=X," you get any resources assigned both the tag key Purpose (regardless of what the tag's value is), and the tag value X (regardless of what the tag's key is). If you want to list only resources where Purpose is X, see the tag:key filter.	String
tag-value	The value of a tag assigned to the resource. This filter is independent of the tag-key filter.	String
tag:key	Filters the response based on a specific tag/value combination.	String
volume-id	The volume ID.	String
volume-type	The Amazon EBS volume type. If the volume is an io1 volume, the response includes the IOPS as well. Valid values: standard | io1.	String

Get-EC2VolumeStatus

Filter	Description	Type
availability-zone	The availability zone of the instance.	String
volume-status.status	The status of the volume. Valid values: ok | impaired | warning | insufficient-data.	String
volume-status.details-name	The cause for the volume-status.status. Valid values: io-enabled | io-performance.	String
volume-status.details-status	The status of the volume-status.details-name. Valid values for io-enabled: passed | failed. Valid values for io-performance: normal | degraded | severely-degraded | stalled.	String
event.description	A description of the event.	String
event.not-after	The latest end time for the event.	DateTime
event.not-before	The earliest start time for the event.	DateTime
event.event-id	The event ID.	String
event.event-type	The event type. Valid values for io-enabled: potential-data-inconsistency. Valid values for io-performance: io-performance:degraded | io-performance:severely-degraded | io-performance:stalled.	String
action.code	The action code for the event for example, enable-volume-io.	String
action.event-id	The event ID associated with the action.	String
action.description	A description of the action.	String

Get-EC2Vpc

Filter	Description	Type
cidr	The CIDR block of the VPC. The CIDR block you specify must exactly match the VPC's CIDR block for information to be returned for the VPC. Constraints: must contain the slash followed by one or two digits (for example, /28)	String
dhcp-options-id	The ID of a set of DHCP options.	String
isDefault	Indicates whether the VPC is the default VPC.	Boolean
state	The state of the VPC. Valid values: pending	available.	String
tag-key	The key of a tag assigned to the resource. This filter is independent of the tag-value filter. For example, if you use both the filter "tag-key=Purpose" and the filter "tag-value=X," you get any resources assigned both the tag key Purpose (regardless of what the tag's value is), and the tag value X (regardless of what the tag's key is). If you want to list only resources where Purpose is X, see the tag:key filter.	String
tag-value	The value of a tag assigned to the resource. This filter is independent of the tag-key filter.	String
tag:key	Filters the response based on a specific tag/value combination.	String
vpc-id	The ID of the VPC.	String

Get-EC2VpnConnection

Filter	Description	Type
customer-gateway-configuration	The configuration information for the customer gateway.	String
customer-gateway-id	The ID of a customer gateway associated with the VPN connection.	String
state	The state of the VPN connection. Valid values: pending	available	deleting	deleted.	String
option.static-routes-only	Indicates whether the connection has static routes only. Used for devices that do not support Border Gateway Protocol (BGP).	Boolean
route.destination-cidr-block	The destination CIDR block. This corresponds to the subnet used in a customer data center.	String
bgp-asn	The BGP Autonomous System Number (ASN) associated with a BGP device.	Integer
tag-key	The key of a tag assigned to the resource. This filter is independent of the tag-value filter. For example, if you use both the filter "tag-key=Purpose" and the filter "tag-value=X," you get any resources assigned both the tag key Purpose (regardless of what the tag's value is), and the tag value X (regardless of what the tag's key is). If you want to list only resources where Purpose is X, see the tag:key filter.	String

(*continued*)

Filter	Description	Type
tag-value	The value of a tag assigned to the resource. This filter is independent of the tag-key filter.	String
tag:key	Filters the response based on a specific tag/value combination.	String
type	The type of VPN connection. Currently the only supported type is ipsec.1. Valid value: ipsec.1.	String
vpn-connection-id	The ID of the VPN connection.	String
vpn-gateway-id	The ID of a virtual private gateway associated with the VPN connection.	String

Get-EC2VpnGateway

Filter	Description	Type
attachment.state	The current state of the attachment between the gateway and the VPC. Valid values: attaching | attached | detaching | detached.	String
attachment.vpc-id	The ID of an attached VPC.	String
availability-zone	The availability zone for the virtual private gateway.	String
state	The state of the virtual private gateway. Valid values: pending | available | deleting | deleted.	String
tag-key	The key of a tag assigned to the resource. This filter is independent of the tag-value filter. For example, if you use both the filter "tag-key=Purpose" and the filter "tag-value=X," you get any resources assigned both the tag key Purpose (regardless of what the tag's value is), and the tag value X (regardless of what the tag's key is). If you want to list only resources where Purpose is X, see the tag:key filter.	String
tag-value	The value of a tag assigned to the resource. This filter is independent of the tag-key filter.	String
tag:key	Filters the response based on a specific tag/value combination.	String
type	The type of virtual private gateway. Currently the only supported type is ipsec.1. Valid value: ipsec.1.	String
vpn-gateway-id	The ID of the virtual private gateway.	String

List of API Methods by Command

This appendix includes a list of all the PowerShell commands and the corresponding web service methods. You may have noticed that there is very little documentation available for the AWS PowerShell libraries. When you find the PowerShell help files inadequate, you can search for help on the web service method, which is usually much more complete. In addition, the web service method name is used to allow or deny access in IAM policies.

Note This appendix has been adapted from documentation available on the AWS web site as of October 31, 2013. For the most current version of the AWS documentation, please visit `http://aws.amazon.com/documentation/`.

AWS Support

PowerShell Command	API Method
Resolve-ASACase	ResolveCase
New-ASACase	CreateCase
Get-ASACases	DescribeCases
Get-ASACommunications	DescribeCommunications
Add-ASACommunicationToCase	AddCommunicationToCase
Get-ASAdjustmentType	DescribeAdjustmentTypes
Get-ASAServices	DescribeServices
Get-ASASeverityLevels	DescribeSeverityLevels
Request-ASATrustedAdvisorCheckRefresh	RefreshTrustedAdvisorCheck
Get-ASATrustedAdvisorCheckRefreshStatuses	DescribeTrustedAdvisorCheckRefreshStatuses
Get-ASATrustedAdvisorCheckResult	DescribeTrustedAdvisorCheckResult
Get-ASATrustedAdvisorChecks	DescribeTrustedAdvisorChecks
Get-ASATrustedAdvisorCheckSummaries	DescribeTrustedAdvisorCheckSummaries

Auto Scaling

PowerShell Command	API Method
Update-ASAutoScalingGroup	UpdateAutoScalingGroup
Get-ASAutoScalingGroup	DescribeAutoScalingGroups
Remove-ASAutoScalingGroup	DeleteAutoScalingGroup
New-ASAutoScalingGroup	CreateAutoScalingGroup
Get-ASAutoScalingInstance	DescribeAutoScalingInstances
Get-ASAutoScalingNotificationType	DescribeAutoScalingNotificationTypes
Set-ASDesiredCapacity	SetDesiredCapacity
Set-ASInstanceHealth	SetInstanceHealth
Stop-ASInstanceInAutoScalingGroup	TerminateInstanceInAutoScalingGroup
Remove-ASLaunchConfiguration	DeleteLaunchConfiguration
Get-ASLaunchConfiguration	DescribeLaunchConfigurations
New-ASLaunchConfiguration	CreateLaunchConfiguration
Get-ASMetricCollectionType	DescribeMetricCollectionTypes
Enable-ASMetricsCollection	EnableMetricsCollection
Disable-ASMetricsCollection	DisableMetricsCollection
Get-ASNotificationConfiguration	DescribeNotificationConfigurations
Remove-ASNotificationConfiguration	DeleteNotificationConfiguration
Write-ASNotificationConfiguration	PutNotificationConfiguration
Start-ASPolicy	ExecutePolicy
Remove-ASPolicy	DeletePolicy
Get-ASPolicy	DescribePolicies
Suspend-ASProcess	SuspendProcesses
Resume-ASProcess	ResumeProcesses
Get-ASScalingActivity	DescribeScalingActivities
Write-ASScalingPolicy	PutScalingPolicy
Get-ASScalingProcessType	DescribeScalingProcessTypes
Remove-ASScheduledAction	DeleteScheduledAction
Get-ASScheduledAction	DescribeScheduledActions
Write-ASScheduledUpdateGroupAction	PutScheduledUpdateGroupAction
Set-ASTag	CreateOrUpdateTags
Get-ASTag	DescribeTags
Remove-ASTag	DeleteTags
Get-ASTerminationPolicyType	DescribeTerminationPolicyTypes

CloudFront

PowerShell Command	API Method
Get-CFCloudFrontOriginAccessIdentities	ListCloudFrontOriginAccessIdentities
Get-CFCloudFrontOriginAccessIdentity	GetCloudFrontOriginAccessIdentity
Update-CFCloudFrontOriginAccessIdentity	UpdateCloudFrontOriginAccessIdentity
New-CFCloudFrontOriginAccessIdentity	CreateCloudFrontOriginAccessIdentity
Remove-CFCloudFrontOriginAccessIdentity	DeleteCloudFrontOriginAccessIdentity
Get-CFCloudFrontOriginAccessIdentityConfig	GetCloudFrontOriginAccessIdentityConfig
Get-CFDistribution	GetDistribution
Update-CFDistribution	UpdateDistribution
Remove-CFDistribution	DeleteDistribution
New-CFDistribution	CreateDistribution
Get-CFDistributionConfig	GetDistributionConfig
Get-CFDistributions	ListDistributions
Get-CFInvalidation	GetInvalidation
New-CFInvalidation	CreateInvalidation
Get-CFInvalidations	ListInvalidations
New-CFNStack	CreateStack
Remove-CFNStack	DeleteStack
Update-CFNStack	UpdateStack
Get-CFNStack	DescribeStacks
Get-CFNStackEvent	DescribeStackEvents
Get-CFNStackResource	DescribeStackResource
Get-CFNStackResources	DescribeStackResources
Get-CFNStackResourceSummary	ListStackResources
Get-CFNStackSummary	ListStacks
Test-CFNTemplate	ValidateTemplate
Get-CFNTemplate	GetTemplate
Measure-CFNTemplateCost	EstimateTemplateCost
Get-CFStreamingDistribution	GetStreamingDistribution
Remove-CFStreamingDistribution	DeleteStreamingDistribution
New-CFStreamingDistribution	CreateStreamingDistribution
Update-CFStreamingDistribution	UpdateStreamingDistribution
Get-CFStreamingDistributionConfig	GetStreamingDistributionConfig
Get-CFStreamingDistributions	ListStreamingDistributions

CloudSearch

PowerShell Command	API Method
Update-CSDefaultSearchField	UpdateDefaultSearchField
Get-CSDefaultSearchField	DescribeDefaultSearchField
Get-CSDomain	DescribeDomains
New-CSDomain	CreateDomain
Remove-CSDomain	DeleteDomain
Start-CSIndex	IndexDocuments
Remove-CSIndexField	DeleteIndexField
Set-CSIndexField	DefineIndexField
Get-CSIndexField	DescribeIndexFields
Get-CSRankExpression	DescribeRankExpressions
Remove-CSRankExpression	DeleteRankExpression
Set-CSRankExpression	DefineRankExpression
Update-CSServiceAccessPolicy	UpdateServiceAccessPolicies
Get-CSServiceAccessPolicy	DescribeServiceAccessPolicies
Get-CSStemmingOption	DescribeStemmingOptions
Update-CSStemmingOption	UpdateStemmingOptions
Update-CSStopwordOption	UpdateStopwordOptions
Get-CSStopwordOption	DescribeStopwordOptions
Get-CSSynonymOption	DescribeSynonymOptions
Update-CSSynonymOption	UpdateSynonymOptions

CloudWatch

PowerShell Command	API Method
Get-CWAlarm	DescribeAlarms
Remove-CWAlarm	DeleteAlarms
Enable-CWAlarmAction	EnableAlarmActions
Disable-CWAlarmAction	DisableAlarmActions
Get-CWAlarmForMetric	DescribeAlarmsForMetric
Get-CWAlarmHistory	DescribeAlarmHistory
Set-CWAlarmState	SetAlarmState
Write-CWMetricAlarm	PutMetricAlarm
Write-CWMetricData	PutMetricData
Get-CWMetrics	ListMetrics
Get-CWMetricStatistics	GetMetricStatistics

Direct Connect

PowerShell Command	API Method
Get-DCConnection	DescribeConnections
Remove-DCConnection	DeleteConnection
New-DCConnection	CreateConnection
Get-DCConnectionDetail	DescribeConnectionDetail
Get-DCOffering	DescribeOfferings
Get-DCOfferingDetail	DescribeOfferingDetail
New-DCPrivateVirtualInterface	CreatePrivateVirtualInterface
New-DCPublicVirtualInterface	CreatePublicVirtualInterface
Get-DCVirtualGateway	DescribeVirtualGateways
Get-DCVirtualInterface	DescribeVirtualInterfaces
Remove-DCVirtualInterface	DeleteVirtualInterface

Data Pipeline

PowerShell Command	API Method
Invoke-DPExpression	EvaluateExpression
Get-DPObject	DescribeObjects
Find-DPObject	QueryObjects
New-DPPipeline	CreatePipeline
Remove-DPPipeline	DeletePipeline
Get-DPPipeline	ListPipelines
Enable-DPPipeline	ActivatePipeline
Get-DPPipelineDefinition	GetPipelineDefinition
Write-DPPipelineDefinition	PutPipelineDefinition
Test-DPPipelineDefinition	ValidatePipelineDefinition
Get-DPPipelineDescription	DescribePipelines
Set-DPStatus	SetStatus
Get-DPTask	PollForTask
Update-DPTaskProgress	ReportTaskProgress
Update-DPTaskRunnerHeartbeat	ReportTaskRunnerHeartbeat
Set-DPTaskStatus	SetTaskStatus

Elastic Beanstalk

PowerShell Command	API Method
Remove-EBApplication	DeleteApplication
Get-EBApplication	DescribeApplications
Update-EBApplication	UpdateApplication
New-EBApplication	CreateApplication
New-EBApplicationVersion	CreateApplicationVersion
Update-EBApplicationVersion	UpdateApplicationVersion
Remove-EBApplicationVersion	DeleteApplicationVersion
Get-EBApplicationVersion	DescribeApplicationVersions
Restart-EBAppServer	RestartAppServer
Get-EBAvailableSolutionStack	ListAvailableSolutionStacks
Get-EBConfigurationOption	DescribeConfigurationOptions
Get-EBConfigurationSetting	DescribeConfigurationSettings
Test-EBConfigurationSetting	ValidateConfigurationSettings
Remove-EBConfigurationTemplate	DeleteConfigurationTemplate
New-EBConfigurationTemplate	CreateConfigurationTemplate
Update-EBConfigurationTemplate	UpdateConfigurationTemplate
Get-EBDNSAvailability	CheckDNSAvailability
Stop-EBEnvironment	TerminateEnvironment
Get-EBEnvironment	DescribeEnvironments
Update-EBEnvironment	UpdateEnvironment
New-EBEnvironment	CreateEnvironment
Set-EBEnvironmentCNAME	SwapEnvironmentCNAMEs
Remove-EBEnvironmentConfiguration	DeleteEnvironmentConfiguration
Request-EBEnvironmentInfo	RequestEnvironmentInfo
Get-EBEnvironmentInfo	RetrieveEnvironmentInfo
Start-EBEnvironmentRebuild	RebuildEnvironment
Get-EBEnvironmentResource	DescribeEnvironmentResources
Get-EBEvent	DescribeEvents
New-EBStorageLocation	CreateStorageLocation

Elastic Compute Cloud (EC2)

PowerShell Command	API Method
Get-EC2AccountAttributes	DescribeAccountAttributes
Get-EC2Address	DescribeAddresses
Remove-EC2Address	ReleaseAddress
Unregister-EC2Address	DisassociateAddress
Register-EC2Address	AssociateAddress
New-EC2Address	AllocateAddress
Get-EC2AvailabilityZone	DescribeAvailabilityZones
Get-EC2BundleTask	DescribeBundleTasks
Stop-EC2BundleTask	CancelBundleTask
Get-EC2ConsoleOutput	GetConsoleOutput
Stop-EC2ConversionTask	CancelConversionTask
Get-EC2ConversionTask	DescribeConversionTasks
Get-EC2CustomerGateway	DescribeCustomerGateways
New-EC2CustomerGateway	CreateCustomerGateway
Remove-EC2CustomerGateway	DeleteCustomerGateway
Remove-EC2DhcpOption	DeleteDhcpOptions
Register-EC2DhcpOption	AssociateDhcpOptions
Get-EC2DhcpOption	DescribeDhcpOptions
New-EC2DhcpOption	CreateDhcpOptions
Copy-EC2Image	CopyImage
New-EC2Image	CreateImage
Register-EC2Image	RegisterImage
Unregister-EC2Image	DeregisterImage
Get-EC2Image	DescribeImages
Edit-EC2ImageAttribute	ModifyImageAttribute
Reset-EC2ImageAttribute	ResetImageAttribute
Get-EC2ImageAttribute	DescribeImageAttribute
Get-EC2ImageByName	NA
New-EC2Instance	RunInstances
Stop-EC2Instance	StopInstances
Restart-EC2Instance	RebootInstances
Import-EC2Instance	ImportInstance

(continued)

PowerShell Command	API Method
Start-EC2Instance	StartInstances
Get-EC2Instance	DescribeInstances
Get-EC2InstanceAttribute	DescribeInstanceAttribute
Reset-EC2InstanceAttribute	ResetInstanceAttribute
Edit-EC2InstanceAttribute	ModifyInstanceAttribute
New-EC2InstanceBundle	BundleInstance
Stop-EC2InstanceMonitoring	UnmonitorInstances
Start-EC2InstanceMonitoring	MonitorInstances
Send-EC2InstanceStatus	ReportInstanceStatus
Get-EC2InstanceStatus	DescribeInstanceStatus
Dismount-EC2InternetGateway	DetachInternetGateway
Get-EC2InternetGateway	DescribeInternetGateways
Add-EC2InternetGateway	AttachInternetGateway
Remove-EC2InternetGateway	DeleteInternetGateway
New-EC2InternetGateway	CreateInternetGateway
New-EC2KeyPair	CreateKeyPair
Import-EC2KeyPair	ImportKeyPair
Get-EC2KeyPair	DescribeKeyPairs
Remove-EC2KeyPair	DeleteKeyPair
Get-EC2License	DescribeLicenses
Disable-EC2License	DeactivateLicense
Enable-EC2License	ActivateLicense
Get-EC2NetworkAcl	DescribeNetworkAcls
New-EC2NetworkAcl	CreateNetworkAcl
Remove-EC2NetworkAcl	DeleteNetworkAcl
Set-EC2NetworkAclAssociation	ReplaceNetworkAclAssociation
Set-EC2NetworkAclEntry	ReplaceNetworkAclEntry
New-EC2NetworkAclEntry	CreateNetworkAclEntry
Remove-EC2NetworkAclEntry	DeleteNetworkAclEntry
Add-EC2NetworkInterface	AttachNetworkInterface
Remove-EC2NetworkInterface	DeleteNetworkInterface
New-EC2NetworkInterface	CreateNetworkInterface
Get-EC2NetworkInterface	DescribeNetworkInterfaces

(continued)

PowerShell Command	API Method
Dismount-EC2NetworkInterface	DetachNetworkInterface
Get-EC2NetworkInterfaceAttribute	DescribeNetworkInterfaceAttribute
Reset-EC2NetworkInterfaceAttribute	ResetNetworkInterfaceAttribute
Edit-EC2NetworkInterfaceAttribute	ModifyNetworkInterfaceAttribute
Get-EC2PasswordData	GetPasswordData
New-EC2PlacementGroup	CreatePlacementGroup
Remove-EC2PlacementGroup	DeletePlacementGroup
Get-EC2PlacementGroup	DescribePlacementGroups
Register-EC2PrivateIpAddress	AssignPrivateIpAddresses
Unregister-EC2PrivateIpAddress	UnassignPrivateIpAddresses
Confirm-EC2ProductInstance	ConfirmProductInstance
Get-EC2Region	DescribeRegions
New-EC2ReservedInstance	PurchaseReservedInstancesOffering
Get-EC2ReservedInstance	DescribeReservedInstances
Get-EC2ReservedInstancesListing	DescribeReservedInstancesListings
New-EC2ReservedInstancesListing	CreateReservedInstancesListing
Stop-EC2ReservedInstancesListing	CancelReservedInstancesListing
Get-EC2ReservedInstancesOffering	DescribeReservedInstancesOfferings
Set-EC2Route	ReplaceRoute
Remove-EC2Route	DeleteRoute
New-EC2Route	CreateRoute
Get-EC2RouteTable	DescribeRouteTables
New-EC2RouteTable	CreateRouteTable
Remove-EC2RouteTable	DeleteRouteTable
Register-EC2RouteTable	AssociateRouteTable
Unregister-EC2RouteTable	DisassociateRouteTable
Set-EC2RouteTableAssociation	ReplaceRouteTableAssociation
New-EC2SecurityGroup	CreateSecurityGroup
Get-EC2SecurityGroup	DescribeSecurityGroups
Remove-EC2SecurityGroup	DeleteSecurityGroup
Grant-EC2SecurityGroupEgress	AuthorizeSecurityGroupEgress
Revoke-EC2SecurityGroupEgress	RevokeSecurityGroupEgress
Revoke-EC2SecurityGroupIngress	RevokeSecurityGroupIngress

(continued)

PowerShell Command	API Method
Grant-EC2SecurityGroupIngress	AuthorizeSecurityGroupIngress
Remove-EC2Snapshot	DeleteSnapshot
Get-EC2Snapshot	DescribeSnapshots
New-EC2Snapshot	CreateSnapshot
Copy-EC2Snapshot	CopySnapshot
Edit-EC2SnapshotAttribute	ModifySnapshotAttribute
Get-EC2SnapshotAttribute	DescribeSnapshotAttribute
Reset-EC2SnapshotAttribute	ResetSnapshotAttribute
Get-EC2SpotDatafeedSubscription	DescribeSpotDatafeedSubscription
Remove-EC2SpotDatafeedSubscription	DeleteSpotDatafeedSubscription
New-EC2SpotDatafeedSubscription	CreateSpotDatafeedSubscription
Request-EC2SpotInstance	RequestSpotInstances
Get-EC2SpotInstanceRequest	DescribeSpotInstanceRequests
Stop-EC2SpotInstanceRequest	CancelSpotInstanceRequests
Get-EC2SpotPriceHistory	DescribeSpotPriceHistory
New-EC2Subnet	CreateSubnet
Get-EC2Subnet	DescribeSubnets
Remove-EC2Subnet	DeleteSubnet
Remove-EC2Tag	DeleteTags
Get-EC2Tag	DescribeTags
New-EC2Tag	CreateTags
Disable-EC2VGWRoutePropagation	DisableVGWRoutePropagation
Enable-EC2VGWRoutePropagation	EnableVGWRoutePropagation
Get-EC2Volume	DescribeVolumes
Remove-EC2Volume	DeleteVolume
Import-EC2Volume	ImportVolume
Dismount-EC2Volume	DetachVolume
Add-EC2Volume	AttachVolume
New-EC2Volume	CreateVolume
Edit-EC2VolumeAttribute	ModifyVolumeAttribute
Get-EC2VolumeAttribute	DescribeVolumeAttribute
Enable-EC2VolumeIO	EnableVolumeIO
Get-EC2VolumeStatus	DescribeVolumeStatus

(continued)

PowerShell Command	API Method
Remove-EC2Vpc	DeleteVpc
Get-EC2Vpc	DescribeVpcs
New-EC2Vpc	CreateVpc
Get-EC2VpcAttribute	DescribeVpcAttribute
Edit-EC2VpcAttribute	ModifyVpcAttribute
New-EC2VpnConnection	CreateVpnConnection
Get-EC2VpnConnection	DescribeVpnConnections
Remove-EC2VpnConnection	DeleteVpnConnection
Remove-EC2VpnConnectionRoute	DeleteVpnConnectionRoute
New-EC2VpnConnectionRoute	CreateVpnConnectionRoute
Get-EC2VpnGateway	DescribeVpnGateways
New-EC2VpnGateway	CreateVpnGateway
Dismount-EC2VpnGateway	DetachVpnGateway
Remove-EC2VpnGateway	DeleteVpnGateway
Add-EC2VpnGateway	AttachVpnGateway

ElastiCache

PowerShell Command	API Method
Restart-ECCacheCluster	RebootCacheCluster
Edit-ECCacheCluster	ModifyCacheCluster
Remove-ECCacheCluster	DeleteCacheCluster
New-ECCacheCluster	CreateCacheCluster
Get-ECCacheCluster	DescribeCacheClusters
Get-ECCacheEngineVersions	DescribeCacheEngineVersions
Get-ECCacheParameter	DescribeCacheParameters
Edit-ECCacheParameterGroup	ModifyCacheParameterGroup
Get-ECCacheParameterGroup	DescribeCacheParameterGroups
New-ECCacheParameterGroup	CreateCacheParameterGroup
Reset-ECCacheParameterGroup	ResetCacheParameterGroup
Remove-ECCacheParameterGroup	DeleteCacheParameterGroup
Get-ECCacheSecurityGroup	DescribeCacheSecurityGroups
Remove-ECCacheSecurityGroup	DeleteCacheSecurityGroup

(continued)

PowerShell Command	API Method
New-ECCacheSecurityGroup	CreateCacheSecurityGroup
Revoke-ECCacheSecurityGroupIngress	RevokeCacheSecurityGroupIngress
Approve-ECCacheSecurityGroupIngress	AuthorizeCacheSecurityGroupIngress
New-ECCacheSubnetGroup	CreateCacheSubnetGroup
Edit-ECCacheSubnetGroup	ModifyCacheSubnetGroup
Remove-ECCacheSubnetGroup	DeleteCacheSubnetGroup
Get-ECCacheSubnetGroups	DescribeCacheSubnetGroups
Get-ECEngineDefaultParameter	DescribeEngineDefaultParameters
Get-ECEvent	DescribeEvents
Get-ECReservedCacheNode	DescribeReservedCacheNodes
Request-ECReservedCacheNodesOffering	PurchaseReservedCacheNodesOffering
Get-ECReservedCacheNodesOffering	DescribeReservedCacheNodesOfferings

Elastic Load Balancing (ELB)

PowerShell Command	API Method
New-ELBAppCookieStickinessPolicy	CreateAppCookieStickinessPolicy
Disable-ELBAvailabilityZoneForLoadBalancer	DisableAvailabilityZonesForLoadBalancer
Enable-ELBAvailabilityZoneForLoadBalancer	EnableAvailabilityZonesForLoadBalancer
Set-ELBHealthCheck	ConfigureHealthCheck
Remove-ELBInstanceFromLoadBalancer	DeregisterInstancesFromLoadBalancer
Get-ELBInstanceHealth	DescribeInstanceHealth
Register-ELBInstanceWithLoadBalancer	RegisterInstancesWithLoadBalancer
New-ELBLBCookieStickinessPolicy	CreateLBCookieStickinessPolicy
New-ELBLoadBalancer	CreateLoadBalancer
Get-ELBLoadBalancer	DescribeLoadBalancers
Remove-ELBLoadBalancer	DeleteLoadBalancer
Dismount-ELBLoadBalancerFromSubnet	DetachLoadBalancerFromSubnets
Remove-ELBLoadBalancerListener	DeleteLoadBalancerListeners
New-ELBLoadBalancerListener	CreateLoadBalancerListeners
Set-ELBLoadBalancerListenerSSLCertificate	SetLoadBalancerListenerSSLCertificate
Get-ELBLoadBalancerPolicy	DescribeLoadBalancerPolicies
Remove-ELBLoadBalancerPolicy	DeleteLoadBalancerPolicy

(continued)

PowerShell Command	API Method
New-ELBLoadBalancerPolicy	CreateLoadBalancerPolicy
Set-ELBLoadBalancerPolicyForBackendServer	SetLoadBalancerPoliciesForBackendServer
Set-ELBLoadBalancerPolicyOfListener	SetLoadBalancerPoliciesOfListener
Get-ELBLoadBalancerPolicyType	DescribeLoadBalancerPolicyTypes
Add-ELBLoadBalancerToSubnet	AttachLoadBalancerToSubnets
Join-ELBSecurityGroupToLoadBalancer	ApplySecurityGroupsToLoadBalancer

Elastic Map Reduce (EMR)

PowerShell Command	API Method
Add-EMRInstanceGroup	AddInstanceGroups
Edit-EMRInstanceGroup	ModifyInstanceGroups
Start-EMRJobFlow	RunJobFlow
Stop-EMRJobFlow	TerminateJobFlows
Get-EMRJobFlow	DescribeJobFlows
Add-EMRJobFlowStep	AddJobFlowSteps
Set-EMRTerminationProtection	SetTerminationProtection
Set-EMRVisibleToAllUsers	SetVisibleToAllUsers

Elastic Transcoder

PowerShell Command	API Method
Read-ETSJob	ReadJob
Stop-ETSJob	CancelJob
New-ETSJob	CreateJob
Get-ETSJobsByPipeline	ListJobsByPipeline
Get-ETSJobsByStatus	ListJobsByStatus
Update-ETSPipeline	UpdatePipeline
Read-ETSPipeline	ReadPipeline
Remove-ETSPipeline	DeletePipeline
New-ETSPipeline	CreatePipeline
Get-ETSPipeline	ListPipelines
Update-ETSPipelineNotifications	UpdatePipelineNotifications

(continued)

PowerShell Command	API Method
Update-ETSPipelineStatus	UpdatePipelineStatus
Get-ETSPreset	ListPresets
Remove-ETSPreset	DeletePreset
Read-ETSPreset	ReadPreset
New-ETSPreset	CreatePreset
Test-ETSRole	TestRole

Identity and Access Management (IAM)

PowerShell Command	API Method
New-IAMAccessKey	CreateAccessKey
Update-IAMAccessKey	UpdateAccessKey
Get-IAMAccessKey	ListAccessKeys
Remove-IAMAccessKey	DeleteAccessKey
New-IAMAccountAlias	CreateAccountAlias
Get-IAMAccountAlias	ListAccountAliases
Remove-IAMAccountAlias	DeleteAccountAlias
Remove-IAMAccountPasswordPolicy	DeleteAccountPasswordPolicy
Update-IAMAccountPasswordPolicy	UpdateAccountPasswordPolicy
Get-IAMAccountPasswordPolicy	GetAccountPasswordPolicy
Get-IAMAccountSummary	GetAccountSummary
Update-IAMAssumeRolePolicy	UpdateAssumeRolePolicy
New-IAMGroup	CreateGroup
Remove-IAMGroup	DeleteGroup
Update-IAMGroup	UpdateGroup
Get-IAMGroup	GetGroup
Get-IAMGroupForUser	ListGroupsForUser
Get-IAMGroupPolicies	ListGroupPolicies
Write-IAMGroupPolicy	PutGroupPolicy
Get-IAMGroupPolicy	GetGroupPolicy
Remove-IAMGroupPolicy	DeleteGroupPolicy
Get-IAMGroups	ListGroups
Get-IAMInstanceProfile	GetInstanceProfile

(continued)

PowerShell Command	API Method
New-IAMInstanceProfile	CreateInstanceProfile
Remove-IAMInstanceProfile	DeleteInstanceProfile
Get-IAMInstanceProfileForRole	ListInstanceProfilesForRole
Get-IAMInstanceProfiles	ListInstanceProfiles
Update-IAMLoginProfile	UpdateLoginProfile
Remove-IAMLoginProfile	DeleteLoginProfile
New-IAMLoginProfile	CreateLoginProfile
Get-IAMLoginProfile	GetLoginProfile
Disable-IAMMFADevice	DeactivateMFADevice
Get-IAMMFADevice	ListMFADevices
Enable-IAMMFADevice	EnableMFADevice
Sync-IAMMFADevice	ResyncMFADevice
Edit-IAMPassword	ChangePassword
Remove-IAMRole	DeleteRole
Get-IAMRole	GetRole
New-IAMRole	CreateRole
Remove-IAMRoleFromInstanceProfile	RemoveRoleFromInstanceProfile
Get-IAMRolePolicies	ListRolePolicies
Get-IAMRolePolicy	GetRolePolicy
Write-IAMRolePolicy	PutRolePolicy
Remove-IAMRolePolicy	DeleteRolePolicy
Get-IAMRoles	ListRoles
Add-IAMRoleToInstanceProfile	AddRoleToInstanceProfile
Update-IAMServerCertificate	UpdateServerCertificate
Remove-IAMServerCertificate	DeleteServerCertificate
Get-IAMServerCertificate	GetServerCertificate
Publish-IAMServerCertificate	UploadServerCertificate
Get-IAMServerCertificates	ListServerCertificates
Get-IAMSigningCertificate	ListSigningCertificates
Update-IAMSigningCertificate	UpdateSigningCertificate
Publish-IAMSigningCertificate	UploadSigningCertificate
Remove-IAMSigningCertificate	DeleteSigningCertificate
Update-IAMUser	UpdateUser

(continued)

PowerShell Command	API Method
Remove-IAMUser	DeleteUser
Get-IAMUser	GetUser
New-IAMUser	CreateUser
Remove-IAMUserFromGroup	RemoveUserFromGroup
Get-IAMUserPolicies	ListUserPolicies
Write-IAMUserPolicy	PutUserPolicy
Remove-IAMUserPolicy	DeleteUserPolicy
Get-IAMUserPolicy	GetUserPolicy
Get-IAMUsers	ListUsers
Add-IAMUserToGroup	AddUserToGroup
New-IAMVirtualMFADevice	CreateVirtualMFADevice
Get-IAMVirtualMFADevice	ListVirtualMFADevices
Remove-IAMVirtualMFADevice	DeleteVirtualMFADevice

Import/Export

PowerShell Command	API Method
Get-IEJob	ListJobs
Update-IEJob	UpdateJob
New-IEJob	CreateJob
Stop-IEJob	CancelJob
Get-IEStatus	GetStatus

OpsWorks

PowerShell Command	API Method
Remove-OPSApp	DeleteApp
Update-OPSApp	UpdateApp
New-OPSApp	CreateApp
Get-OPSApps	DescribeApps
Get-OPSCommands	DescribeCommands
New-OPSDeployment	CreateDeployment
Get-OPSDeployments	DescribeDeployments
Get-OPSElasticIps	DescribeElasticIps
Dismount-OPSElasticLoadBalancer	DetachElasticLoadBalancer

(continued)

PowerShell Command	API Method
Add-OPSElasticLoadBalancer	AttachElasticLoadBalancer
Get-OPSElasticLoadBalancers	DescribeElasticLoadBalancers
Get-OPSHostnameSuggestion	GetHostnameSuggestion
Remove-OPSInstance	DeleteInstance
Restart-OPSInstance	RebootInstance
New-OPSInstance	CreateInstance
Start-OPSInstance	StartInstance
Update-OPSInstance	UpdateInstance
Stop-OPSInstance	StopInstance
Get-OPSInstances	DescribeInstances
New-OPSLayer	CreateLayer
Remove-OPSLayer	DeleteLayer
Update-OPSLayer	UpdateLayer
Get-OPSLayers	DescribeLayers
Set-OPSLoadBasedAutoScaling	SetLoadBasedAutoScaling
Get-OPSLoadBasedAutoScaling	DescribeLoadBasedAutoScaling
Set-OPSPermission	SetPermission
Get-OPSPermissions	DescribePermissions
Get-OPSRaidArrays	DescribeRaidArrays
Get-OPSServiceErrors	DescribeServiceErrors
Stop-OPSStack	StopStack
Start-OPSStack	StartStack
Remove-OPSStack	DeleteStack
Update-OPSStack	UpdateStack
New-OPSStack	CreateStack
Copy-OPSStack	CloneStack
Get-OPSStacks	DescribeStacks
Get-OPSTimeBasedAutoScaling	DescribeTimeBasedAutoScaling
Set-OPSTimeBasedAutoScaling	SetTimeBasedAutoScaling
Update-OPSUserProfile	UpdateUserProfile
Remove-OPSUserProfile	DeleteUserProfile
New-OPSUserProfile	CreateUserProfile
Get-OPSUserProfiles	DescribeUserProfiles
Get-OPSVolumes	DescribeVolumes

Route 53

PowerShell Command	API Method
Get-R53Change	GetChange
Remove-R53HealthCheck	DeleteHealthCheck
New-R53HealthCheck	CreateHealthCheck
Get-R53HealthCheck	GetHealthCheck
Get-R53HealthChecks	ListHealthChecks
Get-R53HostedZone	GetHostedZone
New-R53HostedZone	CreateHostedZone
Remove-R53HostedZone	DeleteHostedZone
Get-R53HostedZones	ListHostedZones
Get-R53ResourceRecordSet	ListResourceRecordSets
Edit-R53ResourceRecordSet	ChangeResourceRecordSets

Relational Database Service (RDS)

PowerShell Command	API Method
Get-RDSDBEngineVersion	DescribeDBEngineVersions
Restart-RDSDBInstance	RebootDBInstance
Get-RDSDBInstance	DescribeDBInstances
New-RDSDBInstance	CreateDBInstance
Remove-RDSDBInstance	DeleteDBInstance
Edit-RDSDBInstance	ModifyDBInstance
Restore-RDSDBInstanceFromDBSnapshot	RestoreDBInstanceFromDBSnapshot
New-RDSDBInstanceReadReplica	CreateDBInstanceReadReplica
Restore-RDSDBInstanceToPointInTime	RestoreDBInstanceToPointInTime
Get-RDSDBParameter	DescribeDBParameters
Remove-RDSDBParameterGroup	DeleteDBParameterGroup
Edit-RDSDBParameterGroup	ModifyDBParameterGroup
Reset-RDSDBParameterGroup	ResetDBParameterGroup
New-RDSDBParameterGroup	CreateDBParameterGroup
Get-RDSDBParameterGroup	DescribeDBParameterGroups
Remove-RDSDBSecurityGroup	DeleteDBSecurityGroup

(continued)

PowerShell Command	API Method
Get-RDSDBSecurityGroup	DescribeDBSecurityGroups
New-RDSDBSecurityGroup	CreateDBSecurityGroup
Enable-RDSDBSecurityGroupIngress	AuthorizeDBSecurityGroupIngress
Revoke-RDSDBSecurityGroupIngress	RevokeDBSecurityGroupIngress
Get-RDSDBSnapshot	DescribeDBSnapshots
Copy-RDSDBSnapshot	CopyDBSnapshot
New-RDSDBSnapshot	CreateDBSnapshot
Remove-RDSDBSnapshot	DeleteDBSnapshot
Remove-RDSDBSubnetGroup	DeleteDBSubnetGroup
New-RDSDBSubnetGroup	CreateDBSubnetGroup
Get-RDSDBSubnetGroup	DescribeDBSubnetGroups
Edit-RDSDBSubnetGroup	ModifyDBSubnetGroup
Get-RDSEngineDefaultParameter	DescribeEngineDefaultParameters
Get-RDSEvent	DescribeEvents
Get-RDSEventCategories	DescribeEventCategories
New-RDSEventSubscription	CreateEventSubscription
Remove-RDSEventSubscription	DeleteEventSubscription
Edit-RDSEventSubscription	ModifyEventSubscription
Get-RDSEventSubscriptions	DescribeEventSubscriptions
New-RDSOptionGroup	CreateOptionGroup
Get-RDSOptionGroup	DescribeOptionGroups
Edit-RDSOptionGroup	ModifyOptionGroup
Remove-RDSOptionGroup	DeleteOptionGroup
Get-RDSOptionGroupOption	DescribeOptionGroupOptions
Get-RDSOrderableDBInstanceOption	DescribeOrderableDBInstanceOptions
Convert-RDSReadReplicaToStandalone	PromoteReadReplica
Get-RDSReservedDBInstance	DescribeReservedDBInstances
Get-RDSReservedDBInstancesOffering	PurchaseReservedDBInstancesOffering
Get-RDSReservedDBInstancesOfferings	DescribeReservedDBInstancesOfferings
Remove-RDSSourceIdentifierFromSubscription	RemoveSourceIdentifierFromSubscription
Add-RDSSourceIdentifierToSubscription	AddSourceIdentifierToSubscription
Get-RDSTagForResource	ListTagsForResource
Remove-RDSTagFromResource	RemoveTagsFromResource
Add-RDSTagsToResource	AddTagsToResource

Redshift

PowerShell Command	API Method
Remove-RSCluster	DeleteCluster
Restart-RSCluster	RebootCluster
New-RSCluster	CreateCluster
Edit-RSCluster	ModifyCluster
Edit-RSClusterParameterGroup	ModifyClusterParameterGroup
Reset-RSClusterParameterGroup	ResetClusterParameterGroup
New-RSClusterParameterGroup	CreateClusterParameterGroup
Remove-RSClusterParameterGroup	DeleteClusterParameterGroup
Get-RSClusterParameterGroups	DescribeClusterParameterGroups
Get-RSClusterParameters	DescribeClusterParameters
Get-RSClusters	DescribeClusters
Remove-RSClusterSecurityGroup	DeleteClusterSecurityGroup
New-RSClusterSecurityGroup	CreateClusterSecurityGroup
Revoke-RSClusterSecurityGroupIngress	RevokeClusterSecurityGroupIngress
Approve-RSClusterSecurityGroupIngress	AuthorizeClusterSecurityGroupIngress
Get-RSClusterSecurityGroups	DescribeClusterSecurityGroups
Remove-RSClusterSnapshot	DeleteClusterSnapshot
Copy-RSClusterSnapshot	CopyClusterSnapshot
New-RSClusterSnapshot	CreateClusterSnapshot
Get-RSClusterSnapshots	DescribeClusterSnapshots
New-RSClusterSubnetGroup	CreateClusterSubnetGroup
Edit-RSClusterSubnetGroup	ModifyClusterSubnetGroup
Remove-RSClusterSubnetGroup	DeleteClusterSubnetGroup
Get-RSClusterSubnetGroups	DescribeClusterSubnetGroups
Get-RSClusterVersions	DescribeClusterVersions
Get-RSDefaultClusterParameters	DescribeDefaultClusterParameters
Get-RSEvents	DescribeEvents
Restore-RSFromClusterSnapshot	RestoreFromClusterSnapshot
Get-RSOrderableClusterOptions	DescribeOrderableClusterOptions
Request-RSReservedNodeOffering	PurchaseReservedNodeOffering
Get-RSReservedNodeOfferings	DescribeReservedNodeOfferings
Get-RSReservedNodes	DescribeReservedNodes
Get-RSResize	DescribeResize
Revoke-RSSnapshotAccess	RevokeSnapshotAccess
Approve-RSSnapshotAccess	AuthorizeSnapshotAccess

Simple Storage Service (S3)

PowerShell Command	API Method
Set-S3ACL	SetACL
Get-S3ACL	GetACL
Get-S3Bucket	ListBucket
Remove-S3Bucket	DeleteBucket
New-S3Bucket	CreateBucket
Test-S3Bucket	NA
Get-S3BucketLocation	GetBucketLocation
Disable-S3BucketLogging	DisableBucketLogging
Enable-S3BucketLogging	EnableBucketLogging
Get-S3BucketLogging	GetBucketLogging
Remove-S3BucketPolicy	DeleteBucketPolicy
Write-S3BucketPolicy	PutBucketPolicy
Get-S3BucketPolicy	GetBucketPolicy
Get-S3BucketTagging	GetBucketTagging
Remove-S3BucketTagging	DeleteBucketTagging
Write-S3BucketTagging	PutBucketTagging
Set-S3BucketVersioning	SetBucketVersioning
Get-S3BucketVersioning	GetBucketVersioning
Write-S3BucketWebsite	PutBucketWebsite
Get-S3BucketWebsite	GetBucketWebsite
Remove-S3BucketWebsite	DeleteBucketWebsite
Get-S3CORSConfiguration	GetCORSConfiguration
Remove-S3CORSConfiguration	DeleteCORSConfiguration
Write-S3CORSConfiguration	PutCORSConfiguration
Remove-S3LifecycleConfiguration	DeleteLifecycleConfiguration
Write-S3LifecycleConfiguration	PutLifecycleConfiguration
Get-S3LifecycleConfiguration	GetLifecycleConfiguration
Set-S3NotificationConfiguration	SetNotificationConfiguration
Get-S3NotificationConfiguration	GetNotificationConfiguration
Read-S3Object	GetBucket
Copy-S3Object	NA

(continued)

PowerShell Command	API Method
Get-S3Object	ListBucket
Write-S3Object	Put-Object
Remove-S3Object	Delete-Object
Restore-S3Object	RestoreObject
Get-S3ObjectMetadata	GetObjectMetadata
Get-S3PreSignedURL	GetPreSignedURL
Get-S3Version	ListVersions

Simple Email Service (SES)

PowerShell Command	API Method
Confirm-SESDomainDkim	VerifyDomainDkim
Confirm-SESDomainIdentity	VerifyDomainIdentity
Send-SESEmail	SendEmail
Confirm-SESEmailAddress	VerifyEmailAddress
Confirm-SESEmailIdentity	VerifyEmailIdentity
Remove-SESIdentity	DeleteIdentity
Get-SESIdentity	ListIdentities
Get-SESIdentityDkimAttribute	GetIdentityDkimAttributes
Set-SESIdentityDkimEnabled	SetIdentityDkimEnabled
Set-SESIdentityFeedbackForwardingEnabled	SetIdentityFeedbackForwardingEnabled
Get-SESIdentityNotificationAttribute	GetIdentityNotificationAttributes
Set-SESIdentityNotificationTopic	SetIdentityNotificationTopic
Get-SESIdentityVerificationAttribute	GetIdentityVerificationAttributes
Send-SESRawEmail	SendRawEmail
Get-SESSendQuota	GetSendQuota
Get-SESSendStatistics	GetSendStatistics
Remove-SESVerifiedEmailAddress	DeleteVerifiedEmailAddress
Get-SESVerifiedEmailAddress	ListVerifiedEmailAddresses

Storage Gateway (SG)

PowerShell Command	API Method
Update-SGBandwidthRateLimit	UpdateBandwidthRateLimit
Remove-SGBandwidthRateLimit	DeleteBandwidthRateLimit
Get-SGBandwidthRateLimit	DescribeBandwidthRateLimit
Add-SGCache	AddCache
Get-SGCache	DescribeCache
Get-SGCachediSCSIVolume	DescribeCachediSCSIVolumes
New-SGCachediSCSIVolume	CreateCachediSCSIVolume
Get-SGChapCredentials	DescribeChapCredentials
Update-SGChapCredentials	UpdateChapCredentials
Remove-SGChapCredentials	DeleteChapCredentials
Remove-SGGateway	DeleteGateway
Enable-SGGateway	ActivateGateway
Stop-SGGateway	ShutdownGateway
Start-SGGateway	StartGateway
Get-SGGateway	ListGateways
Get-SGGatewayInformation	DescribeGatewayInformation
Update-SGGatewayInformation	UpdateGatewayInformation
Update-SGGatewaySoftwareNow	UpdateGatewaySoftwareNow
Get-SGLocalDisk	ListLocalDisks
Update-SGMaintenanceStartTime	UpdateMaintenanceStartTime
Get-SGMaintenanceStartTime	DescribeMaintenanceStartTime
New-SGSnapshot	CreateSnapshot
New-SGSnapshotFromVolumeRecoveryPoint	CreateSnapshotFromVolumeRecoveryPoint
Remove-SGSnapshotSchedule	DeleteSnapshotSchedule
Update-SGSnapshotSchedule	UpdateSnapshotSchedule
Get-SGSnapshotSchedule	DescribeSnapshotSchedule
New-SGStorediSCSIVolume	CreateStorediSCSIVolume
Get-SGStorediSCSIVolume	DescribeStorediSCSIVolumes
Add-SGUploadBuffer	AddUploadBuffer
Get-SGUploadBuffer	DescribeUploadBuffer
Remove-SGVolume	DeleteVolume
Get-SGVolume	ListVolumes
Get-SGVolumeRecoveryPoint	ListVolumeRecoveryPoints
Add-SGWorkingStorage	AddWorkingStorage
Get-SGWorkingStorage	DescribeWorkingStorage

Simple Notification Service (SNS)

PowerShell Command	API Method
Remove-SNSEndpoint	DeleteEndpoint
Set-SNSEndpointAttributes	SetEndpointAttributes
Get-SNSEndpointAttributes	GetEndpointAttributes
Get-SNSEndpointsByPlatformApplication	ListEndpointsByPlatformApplication
Publish-SNSMessage	Publish
Disconnect-SNSNotification	Unsubscribe
Connect-SNSNotification	Subscribe
Add-SNSPermission	AddPermission
Remove-SNSPermission	RemovePermission
New-SNSPlatformApplication	CreatePlatformApplication
Remove-SNSPlatformApplication	DeletePlatformApplication
Get-SNSPlatformApplicationAttributes	GetPlatformApplicationAttributes
Set-SNSPlatformApplicationAttributes	SetPlatformApplicationAttributes
Get-SNSPlatformApplications	ListPlatformApplications
New-SNSPlatformEndpoint	CreatePlatformEndpoint
Get-SNSSubscription	ListSubscriptions
Confirm-SNSSubscription	ConfirmSubscription
Get-SNSSubscriptionAttribute	GetSubscriptionAttributes
Set-SNSSubscriptionAttribute	SetSubscriptionAttributes
Get-SNSSubscriptionByTopic	ListSubscriptionsByTopic
Get-SNSTopic	ListTopics
New-SNSTopic	CreateTopic
Remove-SNSTopic	DeleteTopic
Get-SNSTopicAttribute	GetTopicAttributes
Set-SNSTopicAttribute	SetTopicAttributes

Simple Queue Service (SQS)

PowerShell Command	API Method
Remove-SQSMessage	DeleteMessage
Receive-SQSMessage	ReceiveMessage
Send-SQSMessage	SendMessage
Send-SQSMessageBatch	SendMessageBatch
Remove-SQSMessageBatch	DeleteMessageBatch
Edit-SQSMessageVisibility	ChangeMessageVisibility
Edit-SQSMessageVisibilityBatch	ChangeMessageVisibilityBatch
Remove-SQSPermission	RemovePermission
Add-SQSPermission	AddPermission
Remove-SQSQueue	DeleteQueue
Get-SQSQueue	ListQueues
New-SQSQueue	CreateQueue
Get-SQSQueueAttribute	GetQueueAttributes
Set-SQSQueueAttribute	SetQueueAttributes
Get-SQSQueueUrl	GetQueueUrl
Convert-STSAuthorizationMessage	DecodeAuthorizationMessage

Secure Token Service (STS)

PowerShell Command	API Method
Get-STSFederationToken	GetFederationToken
Use-STSRole	AssumeRole
Get-STSSessionToken	GetSessionToken
Use-STSWebIdentityRole	AssumeRoleWithWebIdentity

■ ■ ■

CloudWatch Metrics and Dimensions

This appendix includes a list of CloudWatch metrics and dimensions for the services we discussed in this book. You can use these to create alarms to warn you when something is wrong. This list is adapted from the *Cloud Watch Developer Guide* available from http://docs.aws.amazon.com/AmazonCloudWatch/latest/DeveloperGuide.

■ **Note**   This appendix has been adapted from documentation available on the AWS web site as of October 31, 2013. For the most current version of the AWS documentation, please visit http://aws.amazon.com/documentation/.

Auto Scaling

Namespace: AWS/AutoScaling

Metric	Description
GroupMinSize	The minimum size of the Auto Scaling group.
GroupMaxSize	The maximum size of the Auto Scaling group.
GroupDesiredCapacity	The number of instances that the Auto Scaling group attempts to maintain.
GroupInServiceInstances	The number of instances that are running as part of the Auto Scaling group. This metric does not include instances that are pending or terminating.
GroupPendingInstances	The number of instances that are pending. A pending instance is not yet in service. This metric does not include instances that are in service or terminating.
GroupTerminatingInstances	The number of instances that are in the process of terminating. This metric does not include instances that are in service or pending.
GroupTotalInstances	The total number of instances in the Auto Scaling group. This metric identifies the number of instances that are in service, pending, and terminating.

The only dimension that Auto Scaling sends to CloudWatch is the name of the Auto Scaling group. This means that all available statistics are filtered by Auto Scaling group name.

Billing

Namespace: AWS/Billing

Metric	Description
EstimatedCharges	The estimated charges for your AWS usage. This can either be estimated charges for one service or a roll-up of estimated charges for all services.

Dimension	Description
ServiceName	The name of the AWS service. This dimension is omitted for the total of estimated charges across all services.
LinkedAccount	The linked account number. This is used for consolidated billing only. This dimension is omitted for the total of all accounts.
Currency	The monetary currency to bill the account. This dimension is required. Unit: USD

Elastic Block Storage

Namespace: AWS/EBS

Metric	Description
VolumeReadBytes	The total number of bytes transferred in the period. Data is only reported to Amazon CloudWatch when the volume is active. If the volume is idle, no data is reported to Amazon CloudWatch. Units: Bytes
VolumeWriteBytes	The total number of bytes transferred in the period. Data is only reported to Amazon CloudWatch when the volume is active. If the volume is idle, no data is reported to Amazon CloudWatch. Units: Bytes
VolumeReadOps	The total number of operations in the period. Units: Count
VolumeWriteOps	The total number of operations in the period. Units: Count
VolumeTotalReadTime	The total number of seconds spent by all operations that completed in the period. If multiple requests are submitted at the same time, this total could be greater than the length of the period. For example, say the period is 5 minutes (300 seconds); if 700 operations completed during that period, and each operation took 1 second, the value would be 700 seconds. Units: Seconds
VolumeTotalWriteTime	The total number of seconds spent by all operations that completed in the period. If multiple requests are submitted at the same time, this total could be greater than the length of the period. For example, say the period is 5 minutes (300 seconds); if 700 operations completed during that period, and each operation took 1 second, the value would be 700 seconds. Units: Seconds
VolumeIdleTime	The total number of seconds in the period when no read or write operations were submitted. Units: Seconds
VolumeQueueLength	The number of read and write operation requests waiting to be completed in the period. Units: Count

(continued)

Metric	Description
VolumeThroughputPercentage	Used with Provisioned IOPS volumes only. The percentage of I/O operations per second (IOPS) delivered out of the IOPS provisioned for an EBS volume. Provisioned IOPS volumes deliver within 10 percent of the Provisioned IOPS performance 99.9 percent of the time over a given year. Units: Percent
VolumeConsumedReadWriteOps	Used with Provisioned IOPS volumes only. The total amount of read and write operations consumed in the period. Units: Count

The only dimension that Amazon EBS sends to CloudWatch is the Volume ID. This means that all available statistics are filtered by Volume ID.

Elastic Compute Cloud

Namespace: AWS/EC2

Metric	Description
CPUUtilization	The percentage of allocated EC2 compute units that are currently in use on the instance. This metric identifies the processing power required to run an application upon a selected instance. Units: Percent
DiskReadOps	Completed read operations from all ephemeral disks available to the instance (if your instance uses Amazon EBS, see EBS Metrics). This metric identifies the rate at which an application reads a disk. This can be used to determine the speed in which an application reads data from a hard disk. Units: Count
DiskWriteOps	Completed write operations to all ephemeral disks available to the instance (if your instance uses Amazon EBS, see EBS Metrics). This metric identifies the rate at which an application writes to a hard disk. This can be used to determine the speed in which an application saves data to a hard disk. Units: Count
DiskReadBytes	Bytes read from all ephemeral disks available to the instance (if your instance uses Amazon EBS, see EBS Metrics). This metric is used to determine the volume of the data the application reads from the hard disk of the instance. This can be used to determine the speed of the application. Units: Bytes
DiskWriteBytes	Bytes written to all ephemeral disks available to the instance (if your instance uses Amazon EBS, EBS Metrics). This metric is used to determine the volume of the data the application writes onto the hard disk of the instance. This can be used to determine the speed of the application. Units: Bytes
NetworkIn	The number of bytes received on all network interfaces by the instance. This metric identifies the volume of incoming network traffic to an application on a single instance. Units: Bytes
NetworkOut	The number of bytes sent out on all network interfaces by the instance. This metric identifies the volume of outgoing network traffic to an application on a single instance. Units: Bytes
StatusCheckFailed	A combination of StatusCheckFailed_Instance and StatusCheckFailed_System that reports if either of the status checks has failed. Values for this metric are either 0 (zero) or 1 (one). A zero indicates that the status check passed. A one indicates a status check failure. Units: Count

(continued)

Metric	Description
StatusCheckFailed_Instance	Reports whether the instance has passed the EC2 instance status check in the last 5 minutes. Values for this metric are either 0 (zero) or 1 (one.) A zero indicates that the status check passed. A one indicates a status check failure. Units: Count
StatusCheckFailed_System	Reports whether the instance has passed the EC2 system status check in the last 5 minutes. Values for this metric are either 0 (zero) or 1 (one.) A zero indicates that the status check passed. A one indicates a status check failure. Units: Count

Dimension	Description
AutoScalingGroupName	This dimension filters the data you request for all instances in a specified capacity group. An AutoScalingGroup is a collection of instances you define if you're using the Auto Scaling service. This dimension is available only for EC2 metrics when the instances are in such an AutoScalingGroup. Available for instances with Detailed or Basic Monitoring enabled.
ImageId	This dimension filters the data you request for all instances running this EC2 Amazon Machine Image (AMI). Available for instances with Detailed Monitoring enabled.
InstanceId	This dimension filters the data you request for the identified instance only. This helps you pinpoint an exact instance from which to monitor data. Available for instances with Detailed Monitoring enabled.
InstanceType	This dimension filters the data you request for all instances running with this specified instance type. This helps you categorize your data by the type of instance running. For example, you might compare data from an m1.small instance and an m1.large instance to determine which has the better business value for your application. Available for instances with Detailed Monitoring enabled.

Elastic Load Balancer

Namespace: AWS/ELB

Metric	Description
HealthyHostCount	The count of the number of healthy instances in each availability zone. Hosts are declared healthy if they meet the threshold for the number of consecutive health checks that are successful. Hosts that have failed more health checks than the value of the unhealthy threshold are considered unhealthy. Preferred statistic: Average
UnhealthyHostCount	The count of the number of unhealthy instances in each availability zone. Hosts that have failed more health checks than the value of the unhealthy threshold are considered unhealthy. Instances may become unhealthy due to connectivity issues, health checks returning non-200 responses (in the case of HTTP or HTTPS health checks), or timeouts when performing the health check. Preferred statistic: Average

(continued)

Metric	Description
RequestCount	The count of the number of completed requests that were received and routed to the back-end instances. Preferred statistic: Sum
Latency	Measures the time elapsed in seconds after the request leaves the load balancer until the response is received. Preferred statistic: Average
HTTPCode_ELB_4XX	The count of the number of HTTP 4XX client error codes generated by the load balancer when the listener is configured to use HTTP or HTTPS protocols. Client errors are generated when a request is malformed or is incomplete. Preferred statistic: Sum
HTTPCode_ELB_5XX	The count of the number of HTTP 5XX server error codes generated by the load balancer when the listener is configured to use HTTP or HTTPS protocols. This metric does not include any responses generated by back-end instances. The metric is reported if there are no back-end instances that are healthy or registered to the load balancer, or if the request rate exceeds the capacity of the instances or the load balancers. Preferred statistic: Sum
HTTPCode_Backend_2XX	The count of the number of HTTP response codes generated by back-end instances. This metric does not include any response codes generated by the load balancer. Preferred statistic: Sum
HTTPCode_Backend_3XX	The count of the number of HTTP response codes generated by back-end instances. This metric does not include any response codes generated by the load balancer. Preferred statistic: Sum
HTTPCode_Backend_4XX	The count of the number of HTTP response codes generated by back-end instances. This metric does not include any response codes generated by the load balancer. Preferred statistic: Sum
HTTPCode_Backend_5XX	The count of the number of HTTP response codes generated by back-end instances. This metric does not include any response codes generated by the load balancer. Preferred statistic: Sum
BackendConnectionErrors	The count of the number of connections that were not successfully established between the load balancer and the registered instances. Because the load balancer will retry when there are connection errors, this count can exceed the request rate. Preferred statistic: Sum
SurgeQueueLength	A count of the total number of requests that are pending submission to a registered instance. Preferred statistic: Max
SpilloverCount	A count of the total number of requests that were rejected due to the queue being full. Preferred statistic: Sum

Dimension	Description
LoadBalancerName	Limits the metric data to Amazon EC2 instances that are connected to the specified load balancer.
AvailabilityZone	Limits the metric data to load balancers in the specified Availability Zone.

Relational Database Service

Namespace: AWS/RDS

Metric	Description
BinLogDiskUsage	The amount of disk space occupied by binary logs on the master. Units: Bytes
CPUUtilization	The percentage of CPU utilization. Units: Percent
DatabaseConnections	The number of database connections in use. Units: Count
DiskQueueDepth	The number of outstanding IOs (read/write requests) waiting to access the disk. Units: Count
FreeableMemory	The amount of available random access memory. Units: Bytes
FreeStorageSpace	The amount of available storage space. Units: Bytes
ReplicaLag	The amount of time a Read Replica DB Instance lags behind the source DB Instance. Units: Seconds
SwapUsage	The amount of swap space used on the DB Instance. Units: Bytes
ReadIOPS	The average number of disk I/O operations per second. Units: Count/Second
WriteIOPS	The average number of disk I/O operations per second. Units: Count/Second
ReadLatency	The average amount of time taken per disk I/O operation. Units: Seconds
WriteLatency	The average amount of time taken per disk I/O operation. Units: Seconds
ReadThroughput	The average number of bytes read from disk per second. Units: Bytes/Second
WriteThroughput	The average number of bytes written to disk per second. Units: Bytes/Second

Dimension	Description
DBInstanceIdentifier	This dimension filters the data you request for a specific database instance.
DatabaseClass	This dimension filters the data you request for all instances in a database class. For example, you can aggregate metrics for all instances that belong to the database class db.m1.small.
EngineName	This dimension filters the data you request for the identified engine name only. For example, you can aggregate metrics for all instances that have the engine name mysql.

APPENDIX F

███

SQL Server RDS Parameters

This appendix includes a list of RDS parameters for SQL Server. Parameters are used to control the behavior of SQL Server. You can modify a parameter using the Edit-RDSDBParameterGroup command as described in Chapter 9.

█ **Note** This appendix has been adapted from documentation available on the AWS web site as of October 31, 2013. For the most current version of the AWS documentation, please visit http://aws.amazon.com/documentation/.

Name	Apply Type*	Data Type	Description
1204	dynamic	boolean	Returns the resources and types of locks participating in a deadlock and also the current command affected.
1211	dynamic	boolean	Disables lock escalation based on memory pressure, or based on number of locks. The SQL Server Database Engine will not escalate row or page locks to table locks.
1222	dynamic	boolean	Returns the resources and types of locks that are participating in a deadlock and also the current command affected, in an XML format that does not comply with any XSD schema.
1224	dynamic	boolean	Disables lock escalation based on the number of locks. However, memory pressure can still activate lock escalation.
2528	dynamic	boolean	Disables parallel checking of objects by DBCC CHECKDB, DBCC CHECKFILEGROUP, and DBCC CHECKTABLE.
3205	dynamic	boolean	Disable hardware compression for tape drivers.
3226	dynamic	boolean	Suppress log entries for backup operations.
3625	dynamic	boolean	Limits the amount of information returned in error messages.
4199	dynamic	boolean	Controls multiple query optimizer changes previously made under multiple trace flags.

(continued)

Name	Apply Type*	Data Type	Description
4616	dynamic	boolean	Makes server-level metadata visible to application roles.
6527	dynamic	boolean	Disables generation of a memory dump on the first occurrence of an out-of-memory exception in CLR integration.
7806	dynamic	boolean	Enables a dedicated administrator connection (DAC) on SQL Server Express.
access check cache bucket count	dynamic	integer	Number of buckets used by the internal access check result cache.
access check cache quota	dynamic	integer	Number of entries used by the internal access check result cache.
ad hoc distributed queries	dynamic	boolean	Enable ad hoc distributed queries using OPENROWSET and OPENDATASOURCE.
affinity i/o mask	static	integer	Bind disk I/O to specified subset of CPUs.
affinity mask	dynamic	integer	Dynamically control CPU affinity.
agent xps	dynamic	boolean	Enable the SQL Server Agent extended stored procedures on this server.
allow updates	dynamic	boolean	Setting has no effect.
awe enabled	static	boolean	Enable Address Windowing Extensions (AWE) to provide access to physical memory in excess of the limits set on configured virtual memory.
backup compression default	dynamic	boolean	Default on whether to use compression during backups.
blocked process threshold (s)	dynamic	integer	Threshold, in seconds, at which blocked process reports are generated.
c2 audit mode	static	boolean	Enable C2 auditing.
clr enabled	dynamic	boolean	Whether assemblies can be run by SQL Server.
common criteria compliance enabled	static	boolean	Enable elements required for Common Criteria compliance.
contained database authentication	dynamic	boolean	Enable contained databases authentication to create or attach contained databases to Database Engine without authenticating a login at the Database Engine level.
cost threshold for parallelism	dynamic	integer	Threshold at which Microsoft SQL Server creates and runs parallel plans for queries.
cross db ownership chaining	dynamic	boolean	Configure cross-database ownership chaining for an instance of Microsoft SQL Server.
cursor threshold	dynamic	integer	Number of rows in the cursor set at which cursor keysets are generated asynchronously.

(continued)

Name	Apply Type*	Data Type	Description
database mail xps	dynamic	boolean	Enable Database Mail on the server.
default full-text language	dynamic	integer	Default language value for full-text indexed columns.
default language	dynamic	integer	Default language for all newly created logins.
default trace enabled	dynamic	boolean	Enable or disable the default trace log files.
disallow results from triggers	dynamic	boolean	Whether triggers can return result sets.
ekm provider enabled	static	boolean	Enable Extensible Key Management device support in SQL Server.
filestream access level	dynamic	integer	Change the FILESTREAM access level for this instance of SQL Server.
fill factor (%)	static	integer	Server-wide default fill-factor value.
ft crawl bandwidth (max)	dynamic	integer	Maximum size to which the pool of large memory buffers can grow for full-text searching.
ft crawl bandwidth (min)	dynamic	integer	Minimum size to which the pool of large memory buffers can grow for full-text searching.
ft notify bandwidth (max)	dynamic	integer	Maximum size to which the pool of small memory buffers can grow for full-text searching.
ft notify bandwidth (min)	dynamic	integer	Minimum size to which the pool of small memory buffers can grow for full-text searching.
index create memory (kb)	dynamic	integer	Maximum amount of memory initially allocated for creating indexes.
in-doubt xact resolution	dynamic	integer	Control default outcome of transactions that the Microsoft Distributed Transaction Coordinator (MS DTC) is unable to resolve.
lightweight pooling	static	boolean	Whether to switch to fiber mode scheduling.
locks	static	integer	Maximum number of available locks.
max degree of parallelism	dynamic	integer	Number of processors to use in a parallel plan execution.
max full-text crawl range	dynamic	integer	Number of partitions that Microsoft SQL Server should use during a full index crawl.
max server memory (mb)	dynamic	integer	Maximum amount of memory in megabytes in the buffer pool used by an instance of Microsoft SQL Server.
max text repl size (b)	dynamic	integer	Maximum size in bytes of text, ntext, varchar(max), nvarchar(max), varbinary(max), xml, and image data that can be added to a replicated column or captured in a single INSERT, UPDATE, WRITETEXT, or UPDATETEXT statement.

(continued)

Name	Apply Type*	Data Type	Description
max worker threads	static	integer	Number of worker threads available to Microsoft SQL Server processes.
media retention	dynamic	integer	System-wide default length of time to retain each backup set.
min memory per query (kb)	dynamic	integer	Minimum amount of memory in kilobytes that are allocated for the execution of a query.
min server memory (mb)	dynamic	integer	Minimum amount of memory in megabytes in the buffer pool used by an instance of Microsoft SQL Server.
nested triggers	dynamic	boolean	Control whether an AFTER trigger can cascade.
network packet size (b)	dynamic	integer	Packet size (in bytes) used across the entire network.
ole automation procedures	dynamic	boolean	Whether OLE Automation objects can be instantiated within Transact-SQL batches.
open objects	static	integer	Setting has no effect.
optimize for ad hoc workloads	dynamic	boolean	Improve efficiency of the plan cache for workloads that contain many single use ad hoc batches.
ph timeout (s)	dynamic	integer	Time, in seconds, that the full-text protocol handler should wait to connect to a database before timing out.
precompute rank	dynamic	boolean	Not implemented in SQL Server 2008.
priority boost	static	boolean	Whether Microsoft SQL Server should run at a higher Windows Server scheduling priority than other processes on the same computer.
query governor cost limit	dynamic	integer	Upper limit on the time period in which query can run.
query wait (s)	dynamic	integer	Time in seconds that a query waits for resources before timing out.
recovery interval (min)	dynamic	integer	Maximum number of minutes per database that Microsoft SQL Server needs to recover databases.
remote access	static	boolean	Control the execution of stored procedure from local or remote servers on which instances of Microsoft SQL Server are running.
remote admin connections	dynamic	boolean	Enable client applications on remote computers to use the dedicated administrator connection (DAC).
remote login timeout (s)	dynamic	integer	Number of seconds to wait before returning from a failed attempt to log in to a remote server.
remote proc trans	dynamic	boolean	Protect the actions of a server-to-server procedure through a Microsoft Distributed Transaction Coordinator (MS DTC) transaction.

(continued)

Name	Apply Type*	Data Type	Description
remote query timeout (s)	dynamic	integer	How long, in seconds, a remote operation can take before Microsoft SQL Server times out.
replication xps	dynamic	boolean	Internal use only.
scan for startup procs	static	boolean	Scan for automatic execution of stored procedures at Microsoft SQL Server startup time.
server trigger recursion	dynamic	boolean	Whether to allow server-level triggers to fire recursively.
set working set size	static	boolean	Setting has no effect.
show advanced options	dynamic	boolean	Display the sp_configure system stored procedure advanced options.
smo and dmo xps	dynamic	boolean	Enable SQL Server Management Object (SMO) and SQL Distributed Management Object (SQL-DMO) extended stored procedures on this server.
sql mail xps	dynamic	boolean	Enable SQL Mail on this server.
transform noise words	dynamic	boolean	Suppress an error message if noise words cause a Boolean operation on a full-text query to return zero rows.
two digit year cutoff	dynamic	integer	Cutoff year for interpreting two-digit years as four-digit years.
user connections	static	integer	Maximum number of simultaneous user connections. Please note that the service may use up to 40 connections for system maintenance.
user options	dynamic	integer	Specify global default query processing options for all users.
xp_cmdshell	dynamic	boolean	Enable whether the xp_cmdshell extended stored procedure can be executed on the system.

* If the method specified is "immediate" and the parameter apply type is "dynamic," the change will take place without restarting the DB Instances. If the method specified is "pending-reboot" or the parameter apply type is "static," you will have to reboot the DB Instances using the rds-reboot-db-instance command.

Index

Get the eBook for only $10!

Now you can take the weightless companion with you anywhere, anytime. Your purchase of this book entitles you to 3 electronic versions for only $10.

This Apress title will prove so indispensible that you'll want to carry it with you everywhere, which is why we are offering the eBook in 3 formats for only $10 if you have already purchased the print book.

Convenient and fully searchable, the PDF version enables you to easily find and copy code—or perform examples by quickly toggling between instructions and applications. The MOBI format is ideal for your Kindle, while the ePUB can be utilized on a variety of mobile devices.

Go to www.apress.com/promo/tendollars to purchase your companion eBook.